Strategic Politicians, Institutions, and Foreign Policy

University of California

IGCC

Institute on Global Conflict and Cooperation

Strategic Politicians, Institutions, and Foreign Policy

Edited by
RANDOLPH M. SIVERSON

Ann Arbor
THE UNIVERSITY OF MICHIGAN PRESS

Copyright © by the University of Michigan 1998
All rights reserved
Published in the United States of America by
The University of Michigan Press
Manufactured in the United States of America
♾ Printed on acid-free paper

2001   2000   1999   1998   4   3   2   1

A CIP catalog record for this book is available from the British Library.

Library of Congress Cataloging-in-Publication Data applied for
ISBN 0-472-10842-5

In memory of Andrew Martin Siverson
August 5, 1969–November 16, 1994

Acknowledgments

The appearance of this book was made possible only through the help of a number of people in a variety of roles. The essays grew out of a conference held in the spring of 1995 at the University of California, Davis, that was made possible through the financial assistance of the University of California's Institute on Global Conflict and Cooperation, whose director, Susan Shirk, has been constantly encouraging and supportive despite my many lapses. For this I owe her my deepest thanks. A grant from the National Science Foundation (SBER–9409225) made it possible to hire Steve Nicholson, who has served as an altogether admirable research assistant and, alas, occasional conscience about tasks left undone.

My most profound debt, however, is a deeply personal one to my wife, Suzanne. On the morning of November 16, 1994, our son Andrew died in an automobile accident as he was coming to take me to the airport. His world ended and ours was shattered. More than one day since then it has been difficult for me to focus on what needs to be done. Without Suzanne I could not have done it. Our daughters, Erica and Courtney, have been another source of strength, despite their own loss. Others, too, have helped. In particular, I owe my deepest thanks to Arlene and Bruce Bueno de Mesquita and Mary and Robert Jackman for being friends better than any I ever hoped to have. Finally, I want to acknowledge my debt to Raymond Wolfinger and Richard Brody for their continued tolerance of my usually half-baked ideas. They began as my teachers (though they may deny it), but I now count them as friends.

Contents

Introduction

Randolph M. Siverson

A venerable axiom of political analysis is that officeholders desire to continue to hold office and behave accordingly. This simple assumption has furnished the theoretical underpinnings for a considerable amount of political analysis, as in, for example, the huge body of work inspired by Downs's *An Economic Theory of Democracy* (1957). However, the impact of this idea on the study of international politics has been decidedly less than in other areas of political analysis. Perhaps the possible significance of this assumption has been overlooked because so much of international politics appeared to be explained by structural realist theories under which the central theoretical assumption is that political leaders act to maximize the power of the state. Those who hold the primacy of this view can point to at least two strong reasons for adhering to it. First, there is no denying that it has furnished an apparently firm foundation for a considerable amount of theoretical and empirical research over the last two decades. Second, alternative approaches, particularly those anchored within the state, have lacked either a firm theoretical foundation or, to put it gently, have been unparsimonious to an extreme degree.

For theories based upon the realist assumption of state power maximization the problem is that in recent years there has been increasing empirical evidence that is inconsistent with hypotheses implied by the theory, or, perhaps more precisely, evidence began appearing showing that what happened within the state had important implications for the choices of policymakers, even when structural factors were held constant. The most notable part of this evidence is data showing that democracies do not fight each other in wars (Doyle 1986; Bremer 1992; Maoz and Abdolali 1989). Other data show that democracies have allied more than they should have in comparison with a baseline probability model, a pattern that should not obtain if the internal political institutions of a state are not relevant to policy choices (Siverson and Emmons 1991). Other evidence reveals that regime changes inside a state lead to changes in security and foreign policy, even when the distribution of power is held constant (Siverson and Starr 1994). More recently, a theory has been put forward under which leaders will be more inclined to enter conflict over different kinds of issues (i.e., policy, territory, and regime type), depending upon the institutional arrangements that maintain them in office (Siverson and Bueno de Mesquita 1996). Based upon an analysis of more than 1,100 international conflicts between 1815 and 1965, the empirical results sustain the hypotheses. Such evidence might not have been viewed as particularly damaging to realist theories except that statements by realist theorists have explicitly denied the possibility that internal factors have anything to do with determining patterns of war, security choices, or the issues of conflict (Waltz 1979, 7–8).

In search of an alternative model that would incorporate factors within the state, a recent line of research has begun to emerge from the assumption that political leaders shape their foreign policy choices with a view toward maintaining themselves in office, the same assumption that has shaped so much other political analysis (Bueno de Mesquita and Siverson 1995a, 1995b). A noteworthy feature of this work is that it does not discard completely the realist idea that leaders act to maximize the power of the state, but rather it integrates it through the broader notion that leaders act to maximize their own political position since increasing power relative to others within the international system is likely to lead to greater policy success at home. Success is sought simply because it will lead to more time in power, whereas policy failure can provide the tools for opponents to remove a leader from power.[1] As put by Bueno de Mesquita and Siverson (1995a, 853):

> [T]he leader, whether President, Prime Minister, or President for Life, who adopts policies that reduce the security of the state does so at the risk of affording his or her political opponents the opportunity of weakening the leader's grasp on power. Put differently, a leader's search for the security of the state intertwines with the search for policies that will maintain the leader in power against domestic opposition. The desire to remain in power hence provides the linchpin between the threats and uncertainties of the international system and the inevitable imperatives of fending off domestic opposition.

The essays that comprise this volume have in common the view that the foreign policies of states are heavily influenced by the strategic behavior of politicians who wish to retain office, the political institutions of the state within which they are located, and, in some instances, a combination of the two. While some of the essays try to bridge the so-called levels of analysis problem and include within their framework the effects of the international environment, collectively the main thrust of the essays is that powerful explanations for state behavior may be identified that do not rely on differences in the distribution of power in an anarchic system.

The book is presented in two parts. The first set of essays deals with issues of political economy, both within the state and between states. The second set of essays is concerned with issues of international conflict. In this introduction I want to deal with them not in terms of their individual contributions to those substantive areas but rather as they variously cast light on foreign policy choices through the effects of the desire of political leaders to survive in office and/or the political institutions of the state. Let me turn first to the desire to survive.

Survival

To one degree or another the essays in this volume are explicit in their reliance on the idea that leaders have an almost lexical preference for staying in power. In the second sentence of his essay, Smith asserts: "A leader's success internationally affects her survival at home." Why is this so? Simply because leaders are assumed, not surprisingly, to prefer staying in office to being turned out. Smith shows how a leader's belief about the prospect for retaining office under varying circumstances shapes the kinds of policies that are chosen and the leader's willingness to make commitments about various choices. While the argument on behalf of this behavior is complex (and is given formally in the essay's appendix), the overall theoretical consequence is the hypothesis that "leaders choose those policies that help them survive."

Siverson and Bueno de Mesquita hold a view that is similar to Smith's. To them, the desire of political leaders to survive in office provides a powerful linchpin between theories of foreign policy and structuralist theories that rely upon assumptions about the maximization of state power. Leaders choose to maximize power because by doing so they maximize the chances of foreign policy success, the standard by which they are judged. Put differently, leaders maximize power in order to safeguard the interests of those who maintain them in power.

Gilligan and Hunt are also explicit on this point. In their view, realism is wrong because states do not "make policies, people do, and these people may have objectives different from the welfare of the state as a whole." Thus, rather than attempting to build a model of security policy, the critical element is not the survival of the state from foreign attack but rather "the political survival of the politicians that make security policy." (Of course, there may well be a congruence of state interests and the survival of leaders; it is even tempting to use the interest of the leaders as the interest of the state, but Bueno de Mesquita and Siverson show how these may depart from each other, since under some circumstances leaders may move away from the position of the median voter, whose position is the national interest.)

But not all the essays dismiss the security dilemma and the importance of the external environment. To Gaubatz, the security dilemma is inescapable and leaders choose their policies on the basis of the degree of uncertainty about whether they will either deter or provoke an opposing state. The connecting link to internal politics and the desire of leaders to survive is the electoral process, under which voters, understood broadly to include all those who are political participants, choose between a government and a domestic opposition in light of their preferences with regard to policies and the apparent differential effects of their respective policies in the international arena. Through this conjunction of the domestic and international models, Gaubatz describes the ways in which assumptions about the domestic political environment—and particularly about the nature of political competition and selection—affect the incentives that strategic politicians face in trying to formulate and implement policies toward other states. At the same time, he offers insights into the domestic political arena and suggests the conditions under which politicians will be willing to sacrifice domestic political gains for the exigencies of international political demands.

Like Gaubatz, electoral incentives are critical to McGillivray's model. Working within the issue area of international economic agreements, McGillivray assumes that governments, and by extension their leaders, desire reelection, and when voters care about international agreements the government will behave strategically to improve both the content and the credibility of an agreement. Further, even when governments are not in a strong bargaining position in a negotiation with another state, they can use the advantages of incumbency to inform voters about what they and the opposition would do in future policy negotiations. The desire to retain office shapes choices and strategies.

Iida presents an intriguing variant of leader survival when he suggests that leaders may behave strategically to maintain leaders in other states. Seeing strategic policy behavior as the outcome of choices that are at once (1) forward looking in terms of improving an actor's welfare, (2) involve the manipulation of information, and (3) take into account the possible consequences of one's own actions for the choices of others leads to several interesting conclusions about how policymakers will behave. What is most important, however, is that Iida also includes within his description of strategic behavior the recognition that the choices an actor makes may affect the survival of actors in other states and, to the extent that policies between states are linked, thus their own survival. In Iida's research the focus is on a possible link between economic policy in Japan and the United States, but the recognition that one leader's policies may have an effect on the welfare of another state's leaders, and thus for the leader himself or herself, is not limited to the economic domain. For example, according to the account of Robert Kennedy (1969, 124), during the Cuban missile crisis, President John Kennedy was acutely aware of the importance of not pursuing policies that would humiliate Khrushchev. Although this argument is framed in terms of not pushing Khrushchev into a corner, it could not have escaped President Kennedy that such a humiliation could result in the fall of Khrushchev and his replacement with an even more bellicose leader (67).[2]

Institutions

The institutional context within which leaders make choices also has an effect on policy, since it has some influence on how leaders hold and wield power. The most common distinction made in the political institutions of states, of course, is that between democracy and autocracy, recognizing that there are a number of political systems, often called anocracies (Maoz and Abdolali 1989), that do not fall neatly into either category. Although the importance of this distinction is often couched in terms of the phenomena of the "democratic peace," as some of the essays in this volume will show the distinction has other implications that can inform our understanding of how the policy choices of political leaders are affected by their institutional context as well as by the nature of the international system. Let me now turn to these essays.

Morgan and Palmer incorporate into their model the effects of both the international system and domestic political institutions. As they put it: "Leaders of some states may have greater leeway in altering their foreign policies in response to environmental change than do other leaders." Using two domestic variables, namely, the method of leadership selection and the basis of how foreign policy decisions are made, they construct a model that accounts for patterns of dispute initiation and reciprocation. Their test of the model across a number of states over a long period renders results that are highly encouraging with respect to the potency of domestic political institutions.

Similarly, Ishida models defense spending by a state not just in terms of the international environment it faces, the typical model used in unitary actor models of arms races, but also by including within his model a budget constraint driven by welfare spending. Of particular interest in his two-level model is the income distribution of the state. It is the distribution of this income that the two competing parties use as an issue in seeking to gain office. The model assumes that the government spends its revenues from income taxes on two distinct goals: the provision of national defense, a public good, and the redistribution of income among citizens. At the international level, the defense spending of one state has a security-reducing negative externality effect on its adversary. On the domestic level, the tradeoffs within a budget induce different income groups to have different preferences over the level of defense spending. Within this framework, Ishida identifies and analyzes Nash equilibrium levels of defense spending in which neither a state nor its adversary has either a domestic or an international incentive to deviate from its choice of military expenditure. As a result, the voting decisions of their constituents, the campaign strategies of the parties, and the defense-spending decisions of the government are endogenously explained. Ishida also produces some interesting hypotheses; for example, the more unequal the distribution of income is, the lower will be the level of spending on national defense.

In her essay, Martin examines the strategic logic of the president's use of executive agreements and treaties in the United States. Because these two different forms of agreement constitute alternative domestic institutions for achieving international agreement, understanding the logic behind the circumstances in which they are used sheds light on the broader problem of how domestic institutions influence states' ability to conclude international agreements. The literature on executive agreements reflects the perspective of the "imperial presidency" in which informal agreements that do not require formal ratification are seen as ways in which presidents can evade Senate constraints on the ability to make agreements with other states. Martin challenges this interpretation, arguing instead that Congress as a whole has at its disposal numerous mechanisms for influencing and shaping executive agreements. Because of this capacity, executive agreements that are intended solely to circumvent a hostile Congress are likely to lack credibility in the eyes of other states. As an alternative, Martin argues that the very considerations of credibility that must inhere in any agreement explain the patterns in the use of executive agreements and treaties. Thus, a state's institutions can influence the credibility of commitments. Substantial empirical evidence is offered that supports the credibility hypothesis. Theoretically, like Morgan and Palmer as well as Ishida, Martin's research emphasizes the interaction of a strategic leader's institutional context and the international environment.

Also attentive to the interaction of a state's domestic institutions and the international environment is the essay by Schultz and Weingast. Their work addresses an apparent paradox. The lack of institutional constraints in authoritarian states seems to furnish them with the capacity to act quickly, while liberal states, with their concern for due process and deliberation, are often portrayed as hindered and relatively slow to react. Yet, as Schultz and Weingast point out, liberal states not only win wars (Lake 1992), but they have also "triumphed in every extended, multidecade rivalry with an authoritarian state for world power." Why is this so? Schultz and Weingast argue that liberal states show this strength not because of their deliberative nature but rather because they have access to credit on far better terms than authoritarian states do. The latter have less advantageous access to capital because with their proclivities to default on debt they are bad risks in the eyes of lenders. In other words, their authoritarian power within the state insulates them from political punishment in the event of default. In liberal states the leaders are at risk; if they do not honor their obligations they, unlike their authoritarian counterparts, face political retribution from creditors. This possibility actually makes it easier for the sovereigns in liberal states, where the mechanisms of punishment are present, to raise the funds necessary to fight and even, as Schultz and Weingast argue, to obtain the funding at lower levels of interest than would otherwise be the case. If liberal institutions have this effect, then they will also increase the opportunities for both leaders and regimes to survive politically.

Survival, Institutions, and Choice

One of the key implications of the views just summarized is that, if the policies chosen by leaders are selected because leaders believe they will enhance their positions and thus lengthen their time in office, then the conflicts we see in history do not represent a random sample of all possible conflicts but rather are a biased sample of wars that were selected by state leaders because they had the expectation of a favorable outcome that would improve their positions. In the words of Fearon (forthcoming, 3–4): "The historical cases we use to evaluate theories—be they cases of military threats, foreign policy success, war, revolution, democracy, or whatever—typically become 'cases' by virtue of prior choices made by individuals." Fearon's work has provided a strong theoretical foundation for an understanding of the relationship between selection effects and deterrence. What I wish to argue briefly is that there are some closely related questions in international conflict that presently appear as puzzles but become more comprehensible in light of the notion of a selection effect.

Two significant issues in international conflict are the nature of the democratic peace and the expansion of war. Despite considerable research, each continues to have its puzzling aspects. With respect to the democratic peace, it is unclear what maintains it, while for war expansion, it has been unclear why more wars do not expand. Yet, if we reason that leaders are intent on staying in office and that failed policies, such as defeat in an international conflict, are costly and damaging to the leader, then it is possible to cast some new light on these questions. I turn to the former first.

How can we account for the "democratic peace"? Two possible explanations have been presented: (1) democratic political culture and (2) institutionalized constraints. The first of these, ably summarized by Russett (1993) and Maoz and Russett (1993), emphasizes that democracies share broad sets of common values, norms, and practices and expect each other to deal with problems and conflicts in accord with these norms. From this cooperative reciprocity is the evolutionary norm of behavior. In conflicts with nondemocratic states, however, democracies behave much more in accord with the dictates of realism, since they do not have the same expectations about how these states will behave. The shared values and expectations, and the respect for the "rule of law," thus serve to explain the absence of war between democracies, while the absence of such shared values and expectations also explains why democracies participate actively in wars against nondemocratic states.

The institutional constraints argument asserts that the diffuse nature of shared political participation in democracies constrains leaders. As put by Layne (1994, 9): "States with executives answerable to a selection body, with institutionalized political competition, and with decision making responsibility spread among multiple institutions or individuals, should be more highly constrained and hence less likely to go to war."

The second main version of the institutionalized constraints argument is that the participatory nature of the states' political institutions constrain leaders because the populations that must bear the costs of war may be unwilling to do so if the costs are high or the policy fails. Morgan and Campbell (1991, 189) state that "the key feature of democracy is government by the people and that the people, who must bear the costs of war, are usually unwilling to fight. . ." At the same time, sooner or later democratic political institutions provide those who disapprove of a policy with the opportunity to hold their leaders accountable. If the population is unwilling to fight because of the loss of life and treasure, then costly or unsuccessful wars may hasten a political reckoning or increase the chances of leadership change. Because political leaders recognize the possibility of ex post punishment in the loss of office, ex ante they select policies they believe will be successful and hence will lengthen their tenure.

However, as argued by Layne, if either of these versions of the constraints argument is correct then we should expect to find that democracies in general are less war prone than are other types of political systems. This is not so. Early research by Small and Singer (1976) demonstrated that democratic states were as likely to be involved in war as other states were, and, moreover, they were about as likely to initiate a war. The results of Maoz and Abdolali (1989) are broadly consistent with this.

These analyses, however, treat a war as a war; that is, war is a nominal category in which all of them are the same regardless of cost. But plainly some wars are prospectively less lethal than others and thus carry fewer prospective political risks. Consequently, if democratic political leaders are constrained by the possible costs of war, I would expect them to initiate selectively those wars that would have more favorable outcomes and have *fewer* prospective costs than those initiated by nondemocratic states. I would also expect democratic initiators to have *lower* costs on average than democratic targets, which have less choice about war involvement than the initiators do. Lake (1992) has shown that democracies have an overwhelming pattern of winning in war (and in this volume Schultz and Weingast give us insight into why this is the case). But what about the costs of war? An analysis of democratic war participation since 1815 sustains this expectation that democratic leaders will choose their conflicts carefully (Siverson 1996). When they are the initiator, democracies have lower costs, measured in terms of casualties, than when they are the target, and, in addition, they also have fewer casualties than nondemocratic initiators do.

Bueno de Mesquita and Siverson's essay in this collection gives us further insight into the strategic behavior of leaders with respect to war initiation. While the hold of democratic leaders on power is subject to the review of others, nondemocratic leaders who hold power by other than constitutional means are, in effect, subject to continuous review by their constituents. As time passes, their hold on power increases, either because their skill increases or because they use the power of the state in one form or another to strengthen their position. Because of this their participation in war is, on average, late in their tenure relative to that of democratic leaders. Moreover, because they see their position as strong, they are more inclined to takes risks than democratic leaders are, and consequently they lose more than the leaders of democratic states do.

A second topic in the study of international war is its expansion in size as more states join (for a survey, see Vasquez 1993). There is a considerable amount of research on this question (Siverson and King 1979; Altfeld and Bueno de Mesquita 1979; Most and Starr 1980; Siverson and Starr 1991), but the inescapable fact is that most wars do not become enlarged between the original two participants. Why is this so? Recent research argues that this may be due to the selection effect (Gartner and Siverson 1996). More precisely, the argument is that leaders who, for whatever reason, are contemplating a conflict with another state that could become a war attempt to calculate the likely outcome. In this calculation they estimate the probability that they could defeat their adversary in a bilateral war and, contingent on that calculation, make estimates of the likelihood that the adversary will obtain help in the form of wartime coalition partners. The potential initiator also may estimate whether or not it requires coalition partners of its own. Absent favorable calculations, war is not undertaken. Put simply, the fundamental idea is that wars do not expand because initiators in the aggregate make accurate estimates about their ability to prevail under the relevant circumstances. The empirical expectation that follows from this is that (1) initiators will tend to win wars unless (2) third parties enter the war on the side of the target. Data analysis on war since 1815 sustains both of these expectations (Gartner and Siverson 1996).

The essays that follow are directed toward understanding the manner in which institutions and the desire of leaders to survive shape foreign policy behavior. There is, of course, much to be done in moving this research area forward, but as this brief account of the consequences of selection effects shows there may be considerable value in doing so.

NOTES

1. Note that in his classic *The Theory of Political Coalitions,* Riker (1962, 22) defines politically rational actors as those who strive to win. Beyond overcoming the

shortcomings of the idea of power maximization as the focus of rational actors, Riker does not explain why winning is important. From the perspective advanced here it is that without winning leaders will not be able to gain office and, once in office, will not be able to retain it. For them, winning is critically important. Beyond politics, others seem well aware of the importance of winning versus losing. For example, recall the comment generally attributed to the well-known football philosopher Red Sanders: "Winning isn't everything, it's the only thing."

2. Kennedy's awareness of this might have been sharpened by the fact that the decision to cancel the joint U.S.–U.K. Skybolt missile program had the unintended consequence of almost bringing down the Macmillan government (Neustadt 1970).

REFERENCES

Altfeld, Michael, and Bruce Bueno de Mesquita. 1979. Choosing Sides in War. *International Studies Quarterly* 23:87–112.
Bremer, Stuart A. 1992. Dangerous Dyads: Conditions Affecting the Likelihood of Interstate War, 1816–1965. *Journal of Conflict Resolution* 36:309–41.
Bueno de Mesquita, Bruce, and Randolph M. Siverson. 1995a. War and the Survival of Political Leaders. *American Political Science Review* 89:841–55.
Bueno de Mesquita, Bruce, and Randolph M. Siverson. 1995b. Nasty or Nice. Paper presented at the annual meeting of the American Political Science Association, Chicago, August 31–September 3.
Downs, Anthony. 1957. *An Economic Theory of Democracy.* New York: HarperCollins.
Doyle, Michael W. 1986. Liberalism and World Politics. *American Political Science Review* 80:1151–70.
Fearon, James. Forthcoming. Selection Effects and Deterrence. In *Deterrence Debates: Problems of Definition, Specification, and Estimation,* edited by Kenneth Oye. Ann Arbor: University of Michigan Press.
Gartner, Scott Sigmund, and Randolph M. Siverson. 1996. War Expansion and War Outcome. *Journal of Conflict Resolution* 40:4–15.
Kennedy, Robert F. 1969. *Thirteen Days.* New York: Norton.
Lake, David A. 1992. Powerful Pacifists: Democratic States and War. *American Political Science Review* 86:24–37.
Layne, Christopher. 1994. Kant or Cant: The Myth of the Democratic Peace. *International Security* 19:5–49.
Maoz, Zeev, and Nasrin Abdolali. 1989. Regime Types and International Conflict, 1816–1976. *Journal of Conflict Resolution* 33:3–36.
Maoz, Zeev, and Bruce Russett. 1993. Normative and Structural Causes of Democratic Peace, 1946–1986. *American Political Science Review* 87:624–38.
Morgan, T. Clifton, and Sally Howard Campbell. 1991. Domestic Structure, Decisional Constraints, and War. *Journal of Conflict Resolution* 35:187–211.
Most, Benjamin, and Harvey Starr. 1980. Diffusion, Reinforcement, Geo-Politics, and the Spread of War. *American Political Science Review* 74:932–46.
Neustadt, Richard E. 1970. *Alliance Politics.* New York: Columbia University Press.

Riker, William R. 1962. *The Theory of Political Coalitions.* New Haven: Yale University Press.

Russett, Bruce M. 1993. *Grasping the Democratic Peace.* Princeton: Princeton University Press.

Siverson, Randolph M. 1996. Democracies and War Participation: In Defense of the Institutional Constraints Argument. *European Journal of International Relations* 1:481–89.

Siverson, Randolph M., and Bruce Bueno de Mesquita. 1996. Inside-Out: A Theory of Domestic Political Institutions and the Issues of International Conflict. Paper presented at the annual meeting of the American Political Science Association, San Francisco, August 29–September 1.

Siverson, Randolph M., and Juliann Emmons. 1991. Birds of a Feather: Democratic Political Systems and Alliance Choices in the Twentieth Century. *Journal of Conflict Resolution* 35:285–306.

Siverson, Randolph M., and Joel King. 1979. Alliances and the Expansion of War. In *To Augur Well,* edited by J. D. Singer and Michael Wallace. Beverly Hills, CA: Sage.

Siverson, Randolph M., and Harvey Starr. 1991. *The Diffusion of War: A Study of Opportunity and Willingness.* Ann Arbor: University of Michigan Press.

Siverson, Randolph M., and Harvey Starr. 1994. Regime Change and the Restructuring of Alliances. *American Journal of Political Science* 38:145–61.

Small, Melvin, and J. David Singer. 1976. The War Proneness of Democratic Regimes. *Jerusalem Journal of International Relations* 1:49–69.

Vasquez, John A. 1993. *The War Puzzle.* Cambridge: Cambridge University Press.

Waltz, Kenneth. 1979. *Theory of International Politics.* Reading, MA: Addison-Wesley.

International Political Economy

Limited Governments, Powerful States

Kenneth A. Schultz and Barry R. Weingast

1. Introduction

States with limited government present a paradox for international relations. In contrast to authoritarian states, states with limited government have obvious disadvantages (e.g., Lippmann 1955; Friedrich 1938; Morgenthau 1973). The authoritarian states' relative lack of political constraints seems to endow them with the capacity to act quickly and decisively, while liberal states can be slow to react and uncertain in their ability to adhere to announced policies. A common illustration is England's perceived failure in the 1930s to prepare for conflict, while Hitler's Germany built up its capabilities (Taylor 1961).

And, yet, recent work suggests that liberal states tend to win the wars they fight (Lake 1992). Moreover, since the late sixteenth century, liberal states have triumphed in every extended, multidecade rivalry with an authoritarian state for world power (Schultz and Weingast 1996): the Dutch successfully fought Habsburg Spain, the most powerful state in Europe, from the late sixteenth through the early seventeenth centuries; England won a series of wars over France in the eighteenth century and, after the defeat of Napoleon, emerged as the dominant state in Europe; the Anglo-French-American alliance successfully triumphed over Germany, from the late nineteenth century through World War II; and, in the latter half of the twentieth century, the United States and its allies triumphed over the Soviet Union in the Cold War. How do we explain this pattern of events? What are the sources of the advantage enjoyed by liberal states over their authoritarian counterparts?

The principal argument of this essay is that states with limited governments have a heretofore unrecognized advantage that more than compensates for their perceived liabilities in extended rivalries (Schultz and Weingast 1996). Liberal institutions constrain the discretion of the state by providing low-cost mechanisms by which citizens can monitor and punish government officials. This means that, in contrast to authoritarian states, liberal states have a greater ability to make credible commitments: the state is less likely to renege on its obligations when it is subject to sanctions for doing so.

The ability to make credible commitments conveys two critical advantages. First, it endows liberal states with the ability to provide the political foundations for secure property rights and long-term economic growth (De Long and Shleifer 1993; North 1990; North and Thomas 1973; Olson 1982; Root 1994; Weingast 1995). Ceteris paribus, limits on potential political exactions promote economic growth, providing a larger and healthier economy and increasing the total resources that can be tapped in prolonged rivalries.

Second, liberal states' greater capacity to commit implies far greater access to credit. Institutions that permit creditors to punish the state in the event of default make loan agreements credible and thus improve the attractiveness of investments in public debt. As the "sinews of power" (Brewer 1989), access to deficit financing in times of perceived need allows liberal states to access resources far beyond their capacity to generate tax revenue (Schultz and Weingast 1996).

Although previous international relations scholars emphasized the liabilities of liberal states, they failed to recognize these states' compensating advantages. Put simply, limited government provides a powerful asset not available to authoritarian regimes: an ability to honor its promises and hence to grant credible commitments. That, in turn, provides significant advantages in long-term international rivalry.

To learn more about the unrecognized advantage of liberal states, this essay focuses on the second advantage accorded to liberal states—the ability to finance deficits via debt during periods of heightened conflict. The advantage of debt in extended conflict is that it allows states to raise far more resources than they could through taxation alone. If two states have roughly the same resources via taxes, then the state with the greater borrowing capacity can outspend its rival, affording it a competitive advantage.

The logic of the enhanced borrowing capacity of liberal states follows from the economic theory of sovereign debt (e.g., Atkeson 1991; Bulow and Rogoff 1989; Eaton, Gersovitz, and Stiglitz 1986). The core finding of this literature is that a sovereign's willingness to honor a loan agreement depends on whether or not creditors can impose sanctions in the event of default. If no such sanctions exist, then the sovereign cannot credibly commit to repay his debts, and lenders will be reluctant to extend any loans. If, on the other hand, significant punishments can be imposed in the case of default, then the sovereign's commitment to repay is credible. This framework yields an important comparative statics result: any increase in the penalty lenders can impose on the sovereign should also increase the sovereign's access to credit.

This comparative statics result provides for the role of political institutions, since these institutions create the means by which lenders can punish the sovereign. Unorganized creditors can only engage in partial credit boycotts, which, in the presence of multiple lenders, are not particularly costly to the sovereign. Institutions that can coordinate creditors' responses to impose a complete credit boycott have considerably more effect (Weingast 1997). Liberal institutions, however, provide for greater limits on sovereign behavior by allowing the lending community to depose the sovereign in the event of default. States possessing such institutions therefore have far greater access to credit than states with less effective punishment regimes do.

To illustrate these claims, we study the financial aspects of two early rivalries between liberal and authoritarian states: the Dutch revolt against Spain in the sixteenth and seventeenth centuries and the rivalry between England and France in the eighteenth century. The evidence reveals the substantial financial advantages held by liberal states.[1] Ceteris paribus, greater financial capabilities allowed these states to finance larger and longer wars. In both cases, deficit finance provided an important margin in victory.

This essay proceeds as follows. Section 2 presents a model of the sovereign debt problem and discusses the role of political institutions in solving it. Section 3 applies the theory to the rivalry between Spain and the Dutch Republic. Section 4 examines the Anglo-French rivalry. Our conclusions follow in section 5.

2. Political Institutions and Sovereign Debt

The central dilemma of sovereign debt concerns how loan agreements are enforced (e.g., Atkeson 1991; Bulow and Rogoff 1989; Conklin 1995; Eaton, Gersovitz, and Stiglitz 1986; Rasmusen 1992). Private loan agreements in developed economies are enforced by the courts and backed by the sanction of the state. When a private borrower obtains a loan to purchase a house, the latter typically serves as collateral so that if the buyer defaults on the loan the lender may seize the house. In contrast, when the borrower is a sovereign power, this type of arrangement is generally unavailable. If prospective creditors lack any means of imposing punishment in the case of default, then the sovereign's loan agreements are not credible and creditors will be wary of extending loans that the sovereign cannot be forced to repay. The credibility of the sovereign's contracts—and thus his access to credit—depends on the creation of some mechanism for punishing the sovereign in the event of default.

A Model of Sovereign Debt

To illustrate the sovereign debt problem and the role of institutions in mitigating it, we present a simple model of the debtor-creditor relationship. The model has two actors: a sovereign and a lender. We assume for now that the sovereign has some exogenously generated need to borrow a sum of money. This loan is consumed in the first period and must either be repaid or defaulted on in the second. If the sovereign chooses to repay the loan, he must raise taxes to do so. Because there is a political cost to raising these taxes, the sovereign must decide whether to incur the costs of higher taxes or suffer whatever sanction the lender can impose for default, if any.

The lender selects the interest rate that it will charge for such a loan. Though we treat the lender in this model as a unitary agent, it in fact represents a competitive market consisting of multiple lenders, and the interest rate is determined by this market. We assume that lenders have an alternative investment for their capital that has some fixed, risk-free rate of return. Because the market for loans is competitive, the expected return on loans to the sovereign must equal this risk-free rate. We also assume that the lenders can impose a penalty, P, on the sovereign for a failure to repay the loan. The exact nature and credibility of this penalty will be discussed later.

The sovereign's finances, and hence his ability to repay the loan, depends on a number of factors, including the state of the nation's economy and the outcome of international wars. We represent uncertainty over these outcomes by assuming that nature determines the state of the world, s, after the loan is extended but before the sovereign decides whether or not to repay. There are two possible states of the world: good and bad ($s \in \{G,B\}$). Nature's choice affects the political costs of raising taxes, which are greater in bad times than in good. This stylized interaction is intended to capture the uncertainty involved in lending to sovereigns engaged in international military competition.

The political costs of raising taxes are a function of the amount being raised and the state of the world, s. Denote the costs associated with taxes of magnitude T as $c(T;s)$, with $s \in \{B,G\}$. We set $c(0;s) = 0$ and assume that both total costs and marginal costs increase with T. Moreover, since raising taxes is harder in bad times than in good times, $c(T;B) > c(T;G)$.[2]

The sequence of the game is as follows. The lenders have the first move and must determine the interest rate, i, they will charge for a loan of size D. We leave open the possibility that lenders will refuse to extend the loan at any interest rate and assume that they have an alternative, risk-free investment that yields a return of r. Nature moves next, determining the state of the world; the state is bad with probability q and good with probability $1 - q$. Both actors observe nature's choice. The sovereign then chooses either to raise taxes and repay the loan or to default (and not alter taxes). If the sovereign defaults, lenders can impose the punishment of P. Figure 1 depicts this interaction.

The appendix provides a formal statement and solution of this model. The following discussion summarizes the basic results.

The core finding of the model is that the sovereign's decision on whether to repay the loan depends on the magnitude of the punishment.[3] And, since the payoff to the lenders hinges on whether or not they will be repaid, the interest rate they charge also depends on the magnitude of the punishment. In particu-

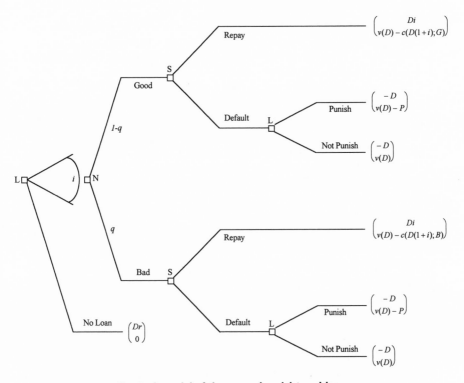

Fig. 1. A model of the sovereign debt problem

lar, there are three kinds of sovereign behavior, depending upon the value of P, each associated with a different interest rate, i.

CASE 1: Large Punishments $(P \geq c(D(1 + i);B))$

For sufficiently large punishments—P large relative to the costs of raising taxes—the sovereign will repay the loan regardless of the state of the world. Because the sovereign always repays, the loan is risk free. Thus, the lender charges the prevailing risk-free interest rate, r.

CASE 2: Middle-Sized Punishments $(c(D(1 + i);B) > P \geq c(D(1 + i);G))$

For medium-sized punishments—those larger than the costs of taxes in good times but lower than the costs of taxes in bad times—the sovereign will repay the loan in good times but default in bad times. Because the sovereign defaults in bad times, the lenders will lose their money with some positive probability, q. In equilibrium, the interest rate must adjust to compensate lenders for this risk. The market clears at an interest rate of $i^* > r$.[4] The sovereign must thus pay a risk premium when there is a prospect that he will default.

CASE 3: Low Punishments $(P < c(D(1 + i);G))$

For relatively low punishments—those less than the cost of raising taxes to repay the loan even in good times—the sovereign always defaults and is thus a poor credit risk. Given this behavior, lenders will lose money at *any interest rate*, so they are better off investing their capital elsewhere. This case therefore exhibits *credit rationing:* despite the sovereign's demand for funds, there is no interest rate that will induce lenders to extend a loan. This holds because the sovereign's promise to honor the loan agreement is not credible.[5]

The core result of the analysis is illustrated in figure 2. As the punishment the lenders can impose increases, the interest rate that they charge decreases stepwise. The intuition behind this finding is straightforward: the harder it is to sanction the sovereign for default, the riskier are loans to the sovereign. Consequently, lenders demand a risk premium when lending to a sovereign that cannot be readily punished.

Predictions of the Model

The model yields a rich set of predictions.[6] The first comparative statics result concerns a seeming paradox. In terms of his ability to borrow money, the sovereign benefits from an increase in the punishment that lenders can impose on him for defaulting. *The greater that penalty is, the greater is his access to loans.* For a sovereign who is credit constrained (case 3), an increase in the punishment available to lenders potentially puts him in case 2 or 1, thus providing access to loans. The reason this holds is that the boundaries between the cases depend on the relative magnitude of P and D. Significant increases in P have the potential to move the sovereign from one case to another, thus potentially increasing his credit.

A second comparative statics result concerns the size of the loan sought by the sovereign. The above results assumed that the sovereign's demand for funds, D, was fixed. In reality, when states are engaged in prolonged international competition, they seek greater and greater funds in an effort to outspend their rivals. Because the definitions of the three cases depend on the relationship between P and D, *increases in D potentially make loans to the sovereign more risky.* Thus, in a competitive environment driving states to larger and larger military expenditures, sovereigns will reach the limits of their debt.

The formulas defining the cases also imply that, for a given r, q, and P, there are explicit debt ceilings defining the maximum debt the sovereign can borrow at interest rate r and at interest rate i^*. These debt ceilings are an in-

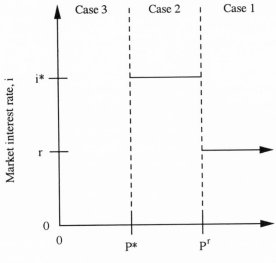

Magnitude of the Punishment, P

Fig. 2. The interest rate as a function of the punishment

creasing function of *P,* so *the maximum the sovereign can borrow at a given interest rate increases with the punishment that can be imposed upon him.*

A final comparative statics result deals with the political costs associated with raising a given amount of taxes. *As the cost of paying off a given amount of debt decreases, the punishment needed to enforce that debt also decreases.* Declining costs of raising revenue also imply an increase in the debt ceilings.

Punishments and Political Institutions

Up to this point, we have left the problem of penalties on the sovereign abstract. The foregoing model raises two issues about these punishments: their magnitude and their credibility. Clearly, these are related issues, since the effectiveness of a punishment depends in part on how likely it is to be imposed. The nature of a state's domestic political institutions can affect both factors.

There are two separate credibility problems identified by the literature on sovereign debt. The first arises because there is a community of lenders, and a default by the sovereign against one does not automatically imply that all other lenders will apply costly sanctions. Indeed, Weingast (1997) demonstrates in the context of a repeated game that the sovereign can provide sufficient incentives to induce other members of the lending community to defect from the sanctions. Solving the lending community's coordination problem is one factor in improving the credibility of sanctions against a sovereign.

But coordination among lenders is not the only credibility problem. The reason is that sanctions are costly for lenders to impose. Bulow and Rogoff (1989), for example, show that when the sanctions are in the form of a trade embargo, lenders cannot credibly impose the maximum feasible penalty because an embargo hurts them as well. The sovereign can generally forestall punishment by offering to renegotiate the loan, leaving lenders better off than if they were to impose the sanctions. This second credibility problem induces a search for forms of punishment that hurt the sovereign while limiting the harm imposed on the lenders.

These results suggest a partial ranking of punishments. The maximum penalty that can be credibly imposed on the sovereign when lenders have solved neither problem is $P(0)$. When lenders have solved their coordination problem but not the second problem of minimizing harm to themselves, the maximum penalty they can impose on the sovereign is $P(1) > P(0)$. When they have solved both problems, the maximum penalty they can impose on the sovereign is $P(2) > P(1)$.

The ability of lenders to overcome these credibility problems depends in large part on their institutional capacity. Unorganized lenders with no means of coordinating their behavior have little credible punishment. At best, those lenders who have been harmed by a default can unilaterally withhold future loans, but in a market with multiple lenders this threat carries little weight. The marginal value to the sovereign of any one lender is low (Weingast 1997).

Lenders can impose a higher level of punishment if they possess institutions that can coordinate a full, community boycott of future loans. Such institutions must have some means of ensuring that lenders do not defect from the boycott. In general, this requires that lenders have the ability to monitor and sanction each other to ensure compliance (Greif, Milgrom, and Weingast 1994). Institutional mechanisms of this sort are evident in the Genoese-led banking cartels that the Spanish Crown relied on for short-term loans, in the corporate lending bodies formed by the French Crown during the ancien régime, and in the Bank of England.

Although such coordinating mechanisms enhance the magnitude and credibility of the lenders' punishment, they do not overcome the second credibility problem. Because a full credit boycott harms the lenders as well as the sovereign, the sovereign can generally induce lenders to renegotiate the terms of the original loan instead of imposing the boycott (Bulow and Rogoff 1989). The prospect of getting some of the original loan back is often sufficient to forestall a permanent cutoff of funds.

Liberal political institutions provide a more effective punishment for enforcing sovereign loans because they make available a punishment of high magnitude and credibility: removal from office. Like the other authors in this volume, we assume that state leaders are primarily interested in staying in power. Although a credit boycott can make it difficult for the sovereign to carry out his desired policies, the threat of removal jeopardizes the sovereign's core interest.

Though all sovereigns face a threat of removal, liberal institutions provide a low-cost mechanism for doing so. In contrast to the uncertainty of coups and revolutions, liberal institutions provide regular means for removing sovereigns, governments, and elected officials who violate fundamental political rules. Moreover, liberal institutions concentrate the costs of the punishment on the sovereign, rather than on the lenders, thereby helping lenders overcome the second credibility problem.

Introduction of Cases

To probe the empirical plausibility of the theory presented in this section, we analyze two military rivalries pitting a liberal against a nonliberal state: the rivalry between the Dutch Republic and Spain in the sixteenth and seventeenth centuries and the rivalry between England and France in the eighteenth century. Both cases involved prolonged competition and frequent warfare, requiring states to mobilize enormous resources over a long period of time. Moreover, they coincide temporally with the "military revolution" that greatly increased the importance of state borrowing to finance wars (Parker 1988, 1990). With the transition from feudal to professional armies, the fiscal burden of warfare exceeded the level that could be financed through taxation or forced loans.[7] Consequently, these rivalries permit us to explore the long-term effect of domestic political institutions on a state's ability to sustain international competition.

These cases are also particularly interesting because in both instances the liberal state appeared at the outset to be the weaker rival. According to traditional indicators of power—such as population, territory, and size of the economy—both the Dutch Republic and Great Britain were at a marked disadvantage when the rivalries began. Nevertheless, in each case, the liberal states emerged victorious. The Dutch won their independence from Spain and went on to become the dominant European power during the seventeenth century. Great Britain defeated France in a series of wars and emerged as a leading power for much of the eighteenth and nineteenth centuries. The nonliberal states, on the other hand, came out of these rivalries economically and politically exhausted. Spain lost much of its empire and would never again be considered a great power. France lost its New World colonies and plunged into revolution.

We recognize that the outcomes of century-long rivalries such as these hinge on no single factor. A large number of variables influences who wins and loses in war. Our goal in looking at extended rivalries rather than single events is to uncover a long-term pattern: even if access to credit was not decisive in any one war, its effects may be discerned over a century of conflict.

This analysis suggests that political institutions play a key role in this respect, but we cannot exclude alternative explanations for the observed outcomes. Moreover, since much of our theory is built on the analysis of comparative statics, proper testing requires cases in which other relevant variables are held constant. We cannot claim that such controls exist in our case studies. Thus, we offer these cases more as illustrations of our theory than as proof.

3. The Dutch Revolt against Spain

In 1568, when several towns in the Netherlands rose in armed revolt against Spanish rule, the rebellious regions had a population of only 75,000; by the turn of the century, the seven provinces that formed the Dutch Republic had around one million people. The Spanish monarchy, by contrast, controlled a population of around 16 million and could draw on resources from a vast empire. And yet, when the Eighty Years' War ended in 1648, the Dutch Republic emerged as the predominant European state, while Spain lost its status as a major power. In all, the Dutch spent 88 of the 132 years between the beginning of the revolt and the eighteenth century engaged in wars (see table 1). Of these, it lost only one, the Anglo-Dutch war of 1652–54.

In this section, we study the institutional and financial factors helping the Dutch succeed in their unlikely triumph against Spain. At the outset, it must be conceded that many factors contributed to Dutch military success. Spain, while powerful, had a range of other military commitments. At the same time that it sought to suppress the Dutch Revolt, it was expanding its empire in the New World, repelling Turk advances in the Mediterranean, and fighting occasional wars against France and England. Geography—including the distance between

TABLE 1.   Major Wars of the Dutch Republic, 1568–1700

War	Dates	Years
Eighty Years' War	1568–1609	41
	1621–48	27
First Anglo-Dutch War	1652–54	2
Second Anglo-Dutch War	1665–67	2
War of Devolution	1668	1
Franco-Dutch War	1672–78	6
Nine Years' War	1688–97	9
Total		88

Spain and the Netherlands and the unusual features of the Low Countries themselves—worked in favor of the rebellious provinces.

Nonetheless, we argue that institutions limiting the discretion of the Dutch government were necessary for the Republic's success. The Dutch Revolt established a system of representative government that underpinned strong public finances. Because lenders' interests were represented in government, investment in public debt was both safe and popular. As a result, the Dutch had access to seemingly inexhaustible sums of money at low interest rates. This permitted the Republic to exercise military power out of proportion to its small size and population. Spain and the other monarchies, by contrast, suffered from high interest rates and credit rationing endemic to such systems. Institutions of limited government thus gave the Dutch Republic an advantage in international competition against these states.

Political Institutions and Sovereign Debt in Spain and the Dutch Republic

The Dutch Republic

The system of public finance employed by the Dutch Republic emerged half a century before the revolt against Spain, largely at the urging of the Netherlands' Habsburg rulers. In 1515, the ministers of Charles V convinced the estates of several provinces to assume responsibility for the collection and repayment of long-term debt. The estates were assemblies consisting of representatives of each province's wealth holders and merchants. Thus, the Habsburgs sought to shift responsibility for public borrowing from the central government in Brussels to the local level.

The impetus for this reform came from the growing deficits caused by Spain's recurrent wars against France and the inadequate methods the government had to finance those deficits. Until that point, the primary source of credit for the Brussels government consisted of short-term loans from bankers in Antwerp. The interest rates on these loans were quite high; though rates below 10 percent are reported on a few occasions, they were generally in the 12 to 16 percent range and often topped 20 percent (Homer 1977, 114–15). The reason that credit was so costly follows from our discussion in section 2: as Tracy (1985, 41) reports, "lenders had no confidence in the personal bond of Charles V or in any of his princely kin." Margaret of Austria, the Habsburg regent in the Spanish Netherlands from 1506 to 1530, called these loans a "'cancer' on the body politic" and thus resorted to the Antwerp exchange as little as possible (41–42).

Reorganizing state borrowing from the central to the provincial level was seen as a way out of this sovereign debt problem. Provincial estates began to sell long-term debt instruments called *renten* and pledged the collective responsibility of the entire province as security. By law, this meant that if a province failed to keep up with interest payments on the *renten* it sold, the injured parties could recover damages by confiscating the wealth of any burgher from that province whom they encountered (Tracy 1985, 58). These reforms thus transferred control over debt repayment from an unaccountable sovereign to representatives of the very people who would suffer in the event of default: wealth holders and merchants.[8] In terms of the model laid out in section 2, the punishment regime available to debt holders shifted from $P(0)$ to $P(2)$.

This reform had a dramatic effect on public finance. While the central government was paying double-digit interest rates on its loans, the same government, relying on the borrowing power of the provincial estates, could now raise money at a rate of only 6.25 percent (Tracy 1985, 60–62). Not surprisingly, the sale of *renten* became the preferred way for the government of the Netherlands to finance its deficits. Thus, the reforms of 1515 bear out the comparative static result of section 2: an increase in the punishment that debt holders can inflict increases the borrower's access to credit.

Further reforms reinforced this change. Starting in 1542, the central government gave provincial estates the right to establish and collect new taxes on land, wealth, and commerce in order to secure *renten* sales (Tracy 1985, chap. 3). Up to this point, provinces repaid these loans through the ordinary taxes levied on behalf of the Brussels government. This practice, however, began to drain the revenues going to the Crown. Thus, the provinces were allowed to raise their own taxes—at whatever rates and on whatever items they chose—in order to pay the interest and principal on outstanding *renten.* Decisions over taxes, as well as the duty of collecting them and disbursing the revenues, fell under the jurisdiction of the provincial estates and their administrative bodies. This reform further improved the creditworthiness of the estates. The very people who had an interest in seeing the *renten* repaid now had the power to raise the funds to ensure that repayments could be made.

A natural outgrowth of this system was that *renten* purchases were popular among town magistrates and members of the "regent class" that controlled the provincial estates (Tracy 1985, chap. 5). Investments in public debt were particularly attractive to such people because they were in a position to approve the taxes and make the payments that would ensure the return on those investments. Indeed, the strength of Dutch credit can be traced to the fact that the people most able to lend money had control over the mechanisms of public finance; as Parker notes, "the chief investors ran the government" (1974, 572; see also Tracy 1985, 216–17; 't Hart 1993, 178). Over time, as the estates gained a reputation for paying their debts, the base of people willing to buy *renten* greatly increased and even included citizens in the lower middle class (Tracy 1985, chap. 4; 't Hart 1993, 220). The provinces had a remarkable ability to sell debt domestically, to a broad range of citizens, without resort to coercion ('t Hart 1993, 179).

Upon its secession from Spain, the new Dutch Republic inherited these arrangements largely intact. The new state was built on a federal structure, with an Estates-General at the union level, provincial estates at the next level, and town councils at the lowest level. Bodies at each level had the ability to raise debt, but it is interesting to note that governmental units low in the federal hierarchy had more access to credit than those above them did. The union government had little ability to borrow on its own and generally had to have its loans guaranteed by the provincial estate of Holland. Similarly, local receivers in the towns and cities generally collected more than their counterparts at the provincial level ('t Hart 1993, 165–68, 220). Consistent with our argument, wealth holders were more likely to extend loans to governmental units that were close and easy to police.

Spain

Institutional arrangements in Spain were markedly different. Spain is generally described as an absolutist state, though it is important not to overstate the Crown's power. Like most absolute monarchs, the Spanish Crown faced important constraints, especially with respect to debt and taxes.

Significant enforcement mechanisms underpinned both short- and long-term loans to the Spanish Crown (Conklin 1995). The primary source of short-term capital was a Genoese-led banking cartel. In addition to providing short-term loans, called *asientos,* the cartel provided a number of exchange and transfer services, including the transport of money from the Mediterranean to the Low Countries. Indeed, *asientos* were crucial to financing Spain's military campaigns since the money raised was sent directly to areas where troops were fighting in the local coin of the region (Conklin 1995, 2). Loans from the Genoese were backed by the threat of a cutoff of these services. Such a cutoff occurred following the bankruptcy of 1575, and for more than two years the Crown could not get sufficient funds to its troops fighting in the Netherlands. The ability of the cartel to impose such a boycott suggests it had the institutional capacity to overcome the problem of coordinating multiple lenders. In terms of the model described previously, the punishment regime available to them can be characterized as $P(1)$.

Despite this, the Crown's creditors did not have to resort to the kind of representative institutions that empowered wealth holders in the Dutch Republic. A revealing episode during the financial crisis of 1575 clearly illustrates the relative impotence of Spain's creditors. Genoese bankers pleaded with Philip II not to repudiate his obligations to them. Unmoved, Philip went ahead with his plans to declare bankruptcy and noted that "the decree was passed without listening to them" (Lovett 1980, 910). Philip's freedom to ignore his creditors contrasts markedly with the limitations placed on Dutch decision makers.

The Crown's long-term debt was issued in the form of annuities, called *ju-*

ros, the primary holders of which were important subjects in Castile. Conklin maintains that the implicit punishment underlying the *juros* arose from the "political standing" of their holders: "The Crown found it better to honor that debt than to alienate the politically powerful holders of the instruments and possibly jeopardize its reign" (1995, 3). Indeed, while the Crown frequently reneged on *asientos,* it made a concerted effort to honor the *juros.* This suggests that the enforcement mechanism underpinning these long-term instruments was more effective than that underlying the *asientos,* at least temporarily. Nevertheless, despite their political importance, the Castilian notables lacked institutionalized means for removing the Crown. Indeed, as we will see, even the *juro* was an unsafe investment by the 1630s.

Financial Consequences

Spanish political institutions placed some constraints on the discretion of the Crown but not to the extent of those in the Dutch Republic. The consequences of this difference follow logically from the theory presented previously: relative to the Dutch, Spain faced greater limits on its credit, including higher interest rates.

Spain's financial history during this period demonstrates that the commitment technology underlying its loans was not sufficient to fund the wide-ranging demands on its treasury. Bankruptcies were a regular occurrence, with major ones taking place roughly every 20 years: 1557, 1575, 1596, 1607, 1627, 1647, 1686, and 1700. The crises were triggered when the Genoese bankers refused to extend further loans. Such a cutoff is consistent with the theory of sovereign debt: creditors impose a debt ceiling at the maximum level of debt that can be enforced. The Genoese generally cut the Crown off when arrears reached the level of one year's royal revenue (Conklin 1995, 27). On each occasion, the Crown responded by restructuring its debt. Short-term, high-interest loans were converted into long-term, low-interest *juros,* in some cases with a write-down on principal as well. The conversions entailed substantial losses for the Crown's creditors, and indeed many weaker creditors were ruined or refused to extend new loans (Conklin 1995; Thompson 1994, 160–62).

The Crown's ability to convert its debts in this way shows that the Genoese could not overcome the second credibility problem discussed in section 2. Because a financial boycott harmed the creditors as well as the Crown, it could easily be defused by offers to renegotiate the original loan.

As predicted by our model, the danger of periodic bankruptcies led to higher interest rates on Spain's debt. The Genoese demanded a return of 8 to 20 percent on *asientos* even though the opportunity cost of the funds lent was only 1.2 to 4 percent (Conklin 1995, 4). The difference in part reflects a risk premium, since creditors had to demand an interest rate "high enough to recoup, in advance, the loss which was known to be inevitable" (Lovett 1982, 2). Thus, even with the frequent bankruptcies, the Genoese enjoyed a high overall rate of return (Conklin 1995, 5).

Nevertheless, the long and costly war against the Dutch made this pattern of high interest rates and recurrent bankruptcies unsustainable. High borrowing costs created a large burden of debt service, which, together with military expenditures, forced the Crown to borrow still more. This cycle could be sustained only as long as the Spanish economy was growing and precious metal kept flowing in. When growth slowed in the early seventeenth century, the financial crises became more acute.

By the 1630s, even *juros* had become unreliable investments. Interest payments were made in copper, if at all (Homer 1977, 130). At that point, "the *juro* and suspension decrees simply became arbitrary exactions" (Thompson 1994, 164). Interest rates rose in reflection of the increased risk of lending to the Crown. Though data are not available for most of the seventeenth century, there is evidence of a short-term loan in 1673 at a rate of 40 percent and interest rates of 16 to 20 percent on *juros* during the 1680s (Homer 1977, 130; Thompson 1994, 164). By the end of the century, a bankrupt Spain was forced to withdraw from the center stage of European politics.

The Dutch Republic, on the other hand, underwent a financial revolution following its split from Spain. Over the next century, the Dutch became renowned and envied for their ability to raise large sums of money quickly and at low interest rates. The success of Dutch finance can be seen in figure 3, which plots the interest rates on Holland's government bonds and the size of the province's debt over the seventeenth century.[9] Despite the fact that the provincial debt increased 40-fold from 1620 to 1676, interest rates declined from 8.3 to 3 percent at the end of the century. The two increases in rates correspond to the French invasion in 1672 and the Nine Years' War (1688–97). However, the war with Spain (1621–48), two wars against England (1652–54, 1665–67), and a war against France (1668) witnessed no similar increases (Homer 1977, 128).

The decline in interest rates reflects both the institutional mechanisms discussed previously, which led to a high level of trust in government securities, and the Republic's strong economic growth in this century. "With prosperous trade, there was usually more capital seeking investment than there were safe borrowers" (Homer 1977, 125). Government debt became an attractive investment precisely because it was the safest investment to be found.[10]

This appetite for Dutch securities gave the Republic a major advantage in wartime. Whereas most European countries funded wars through high-interest, short-term loans, the Dutch could rely on low-interest, long-term bonds. In 1664, as the second Anglo-Dutch War was approaching, a loan issue of one million florins at 3 percent was fully subscribed in just two days. Two years into the war, the leader of the Estates-General, Johan de Witt, predicted that he could

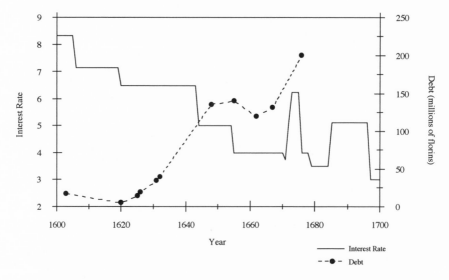

Fig. 3. Interests rates and provincial debt in Holland, 1600–1700. (Data from Barbour 1950, 82–83; Tacy 1985, 209; Homer 1977, 128; and 't Hart 1993, 164–65. Interest rates in war years [1672–73, 1688–97] are averages of figures provided by Homer.)

raise 20 million more at 4 percent with no problem (Barbour 1950, 81–82). By comparison, emergency loans to the English Crown during that period had interest rates ranging from 8 to 30 percent; short-term loans to the French Crown carried rates of at least 15 percent and could go as high as 50 to 60 percent; and, as we have already seen, a short-term loan to the Spanish Crown in this period bore a rate of 40 percent (Homer 1977, 126–30).

Military Consequences of Financial Strength

The Dutch Republic's superior access to credit had direct consequences on the battlefield and in large part explains its military success over Spain and other rivals. The ability to raise large amounts of money in wartime permitted the Dutch to exercise military power out of proportion to their limited natural resources and small population.

First, the Dutch were able to field large armies despite a relatively small population. The Republic's military manpower routinely exceeded that of other states when measured as a percentage of population. In the 1630s, for example, the Dutch population of roughly 1.5 million supported an army of 50,000—or about 3.3 percent. The Spanish monarchy, by contrast, fielded an army of 300,000 out of a population of roughly 16 million—or 1.9 percent.[11] Also impressive is the comparison of the Dutch Republic and France during their war in the 1670s. While the Dutch mustered an army of 110,000 men, France, with a population 10 times as great, fielded a scarcely larger force of 120,000 (Parker 1990, 96).

The Dutch were also able to finance a sizable navy. In the first half of the seventeenth century, the Republic possessed the largest navy in the world, measured in total warships (Modelski and Thompson 1988, 64–68). During the second phase of Eighty Years' War (1621–48), the Dutch navy outnumbered Spain's by more than two to one. Dutch dominance in this area declined only in the second half of the century, as first Britain and then France caught up.

These numbers tell only part of the story, however. The Dutch also enjoyed an advantage when it came to keeping their troops loyal and disciplined by providing steady pay. With the increasing importance of mercenary soldiers, the primary challenge facing a state was to provide sufficient funds and supplies to keep the army fighting. Poor or delinquent pay resulted in mutinies, desertion, and "movements governed not by strategic calculation but by the search for unplundered territory" (Howard 1976, 37). Governments often had only tenuous control of their troops, leading to wars that were nasty, brutish, and long.

The Dutch, however, managed to avoid these problems. As Howard observes, "there was, in western Europe, one great exception—the armies of the United Provinces; and they were exceptional for the very simple reason that they were regularly supplied and paid" (1976, 37). Although mutinies were an occasional problem in the early years of the revolt, they disappeared with the consolidation of the Republic. During the second stage of the Eighty Years' War (1621–48) the Dutch did not suffer a single mutiny despite the growing costs of the war effort (Parker 1990, 102).

Spain's experience was markedly different. The Crown's finances could not keep pace with its international ambitions. Even after borrowing at high interest rates, revenues were often not enough to cover expenditures. However, rather than scale back the military effort, Spain went into arrears on its payments:

> Faced with insufficient funds military expenditures were not so much reduced as ignored. . . . Budgets and appropriations were frequently drawn up to cover only two-thirds, one-half or even one-third of total requirements, and not a single year could have passed [from 1575 to 1607] in which the military budget was met in its entirety. (Thompson 1976, 73–74)

By 1607, total arrears owed to the military amounted to 4.8 million ducats, almost twice the military budget for that year (Thompson 1976, 73, 287).

In practice, military arrears meant that the troops were not being paid. It was common for soldiers to go two or three years without pay and sometimes as much as five or six years. And even when troops forced a settlement, generally by mutinying, they rarely received full payment. The impact of this situation on military effectiveness is predictable. Units were understaffed. Troops went hungry and had insufficient clothing. Morale and discipline were poor, with soldiers sometimes leaving their posts to go begging in the streets (Thompson 1976, 74–75; Parker 1977, 232; Parker 1990, chap. 5).

The most damaging consequence, however, came in the form of recurrent mutinies. Unpaid troops would overthrow their officers, abort their campaign, and often seize a loyal town in order to hold it for ransom. This was a recurring pattern during the Dutch Revolt. Every campaign by the Spaniards drained the Treasury, but often to little avail: mutinous troops would simply abandon their conquests and allow the rebels to reclaim whatever was lost. Moreover, because mutineers took out their vengeance on loyal towns, people in these towns often resisted paying higher taxes to buy off the army that was supposed to be protecting them. This created a vicious cycle of more mutinies and further resistance to tax increases (Parker 1977, 172–73). Under these conditions, Spain simply could not continue to prosecute the war against the rebels.

Summary

Dutch success in the seventeenth century owed a great deal to its institutions of representative government and a system of public finance that placed paramount importance on the interests of potential lenders. This system brought about a financial revolution that permitted the government to raise ever greater sums of money at diminishing rates of interest. As a result, the Dutch were able to finance longer and larger wars, which their rivals, who faced considerably higher borrowing costs, could not sustain. As Parker concludes, the Republic's innovations in government and finance "enabled the Dutch to raise an army and go on fighting, whatever the cost, until they got their own way: something no previous government had been able to do" (1990, 102).

Dutch dominance lasted until the end of the seventeenth century, when England and France replaced the Dutch Republic and Spain as the main major power rivals. As we show in the next section, the key moment in this transition occurred in 1688, when England deposed its king, enshrined the sovereignty of Parliament, and imported both a Dutch ruler, William III of Orange, and Dutch methods of public finance.

4. The Anglo-French Rivalry, 1689–1815

England's Glorious Revolution of 1688–89 put the country at war with France, beginning a rivalry for world leadership that lasted over 125 years.[12] These states fought six major wars and were at war more years than not during this period (69 of 126 years; see table 2). When the rivalry started in 1689, France had several obvious advantages over England: three times the population, an economy twice as large, and considerably more resources to draw on. And yet in two wars in quick succession—the Nine Years' War (1689–97) and the War of Spanish Succession (1701–14)—England first held off France and then defeated it. In the following century, England lost only one war to France, the War of the American Revolution.

This section reports on the institutional and financial advantages that helped England surpass France. Although England's economy was considerably smaller than France's in 1689, its new constitutional institutions underpinned a surprising ability to raise revenue via debt, greatly expanding the scale and scope of war that England could finance. These institutions formed England's "sinews of power" (Brewer 1989; Dickson 1967; North and Weingast 1989; Weingast 1997). Over the next century, Britain's financial capacity seemed almost unlimited, allowing it access to more and more credit at cheap rates, far outstripping the ability of its rival to finance wars. Indeed, by the end of the Seven Years' War (1756–63), France was financially exhausted, had lost its New World empire, and was on the verge of bankruptcy.

Political Institutions and Sovereign Debt in England and France

England's surprising financial capacity lies largely in its liberal political institutions and their effects on the creation of a credible, limited government (North and Weingast 1989; Weingast 1997). Early modern European sovereigns had considerable problems in honoring their debt agreements. Not only was the risk of default substantial, but sovereigns were significantly constrained in their ability to raise debt. The theory developed in section 2 provides the reason: because these sovereigns were above the law—often ruling by virtue of divine right, a stature that placed them above the limits of mere worldly courts—it

TABLE 2.   **Wars between Britain and France, 1689–1815**

War	Dates	Years
Nine Years' War	1689–97	9
War of Spanish Succession	1703–14	11
War of Austrian Succession	1738–47	10
Seven Years' War	1756–63	7
American Revolution	1774–83	10
Revolutionary and Napoleonic Wars	1793–1815	22
Total		69

proved difficult to impose costs on them. And, as the theory suggests, this lack of constraints curbed their access to credit. Prior to their rise as preeminent powers, both England and France faced problems with credibility and hence credit. The institutional routes taken by the two states had similar aims—to increase access to credit by "tying the king's hands" (Root 1989)—but differential effects.

France

Significant institutional innovation occurred during the reign of Louis XIV (1661–1715), greatly increasing the Crown's access to credit (see, e.g., Bien 1987; Hoffman 1994; Root 1989; and Rosenthal 1997). In terms of the theory developed in section 2, these innovations succeeded in part because they raised the punishment creditors could impose on the Crown in the event of default. Specifically, by fostering the coordination of lenders, these innovations improved the ability of the financial community to resist the Crown. This raised the punishment the community could inflict on the Crown in the event of default from $P(0)$ to $P(1)$.

The formation and expansion of the officers' corps, one of the principal institutional innovations, illustrates our contention. The officers' corps organized groups of lenders into corporate bodies that provided funds to the Crown in exchange for rights, honors, and privileges (e.g., a title, an office, and often an exemption from taxes). Corporate bodies had significant advantages in coordinating the action of lenders, raising the costs of reneging by the Crown. As our theory suggests, these institutions limited the ability of the Crown to play off subsets of financial interests one against the another. The result was substantial access to credit, as the recent work of Hoffman, Postel-Vinay, and Rosenthal (1997) on the eighteenth century reveals.

Nonetheless, France's political institutions placed significant limits in its ability to raise revenue via debt, and we note two here. First, in contrast to England, France had no centralized representative assembly to negotiate with and counterbalance the Crown. Not only were the means of deposing the Crown limited, but the Crown retained unilateral authority over the terms of the debt. Default had obvious financial costs in terms of a potential financial boycott. Still, the Crown did not need the permission of the representatives of the bondholders to default.[13] Nor did unilateral default by the Crown, in itself, risk the threat of the king being deposed.

Second, during the eighteenth century, the French king had considerable difficulty raising new taxes, particularly as it lost more wars. The inability to raise taxes increased the uncertainty over debt repayment, in part because of the "unpleasant monetarist arithmetic" (Sargent and Velde 1995), which required that all debt be paid by future taxes or wiped out via inflation or default. Limits on the ability to raise new taxes therefore translated into limits on the state's ability to raise new funds.

In part, limits on taxation reflected earlier attempts to circumvent the sovereign debt problem. During the ancien régime, an important source of revenue came from the sale of offices. Because an absolute monarch could not be trusted or forced to pay back a loan, the granting of offices provided a means to ensure that lenders would receive compensation. This technique allowed the king to tap substantial funds, but it also implied a loss of control over taxation. Indeed, the sale of offices would have failed to raise substantial revenue had it been otherwise (had the king retained this power, he would have been able to renege on his promises, greatly depreciating the value of any sale).[14]

In sum, French political institutions ultimately limited the French Crown's access to credit.[15] Although these institutions solved the problem of lender coordination, they did not solve the problem studied by Bulow and Rogoff (1989), namely, that lenders must find a means of punishing sovereigns who do not impose high costs on themselves. The relatively frequent defaults—including massive ones in 1720 and during the 1790s—reflect a public financial system inadequate for the demands placed on it by the state (Hoffman 1994; Riley 1986; Sargent and Velde 1995).

England

Following the Glorious Revolution, a series of institutional changes underpinned new limits on the English sovereign. Although these changes were aimed at resolving past problems, not at enhancing the Crown's access to debt, they had significant forward implications for public finance. In terms of the theory developed in section 2, these changes greatly enhanced the ability of lenders to impose punishments on the Crown; the latter were raised from $P(0)$ to $P(2)$. In turn, this greatly increased the government's access to credit.

The prinicpal issue of the Revolution concerned limits on the Crown's power. Although the major parties to the debate disagreed about the nature of those constraints, all agreed that they should center around Parliament and parliamentary power, notably, that Parliament should retain exclusive powers over taxation; that it should gain power over the purse; and, importantly, that parliamentary laws should be sacrosanct. The latter implied that a king—and soon thereafter his ministers—would violate parliamentary laws at their peril.

Willful violation of acts of Parliament became grounds to remove the Crown. This abstract principle had direct relevance for debt. Following the Glorious Revolution, raising debt occurred through acts of Parliament. Revising the terms of debt, including default, therefore required a new act of Parliament. The Crown no longer had unilateral authority over the terms of debt and thus could not default at will. Instead, the king had to propose revisions to the Parliament, which could then approve or disapprove them. Given that violating acts of Parliament now threatened removal, the costs to the Crown of unilateral default had increased dramatically. In the context of representation centering on wealth holders, parliamentary veto implied that, in effect, the Crown had to obtain the permission of debt holders in order to revise the terms of the debt.

In terms of our theory, it is clear why these and related institutions (such as the Bank of England; see Weingast 1997) raised the costs of default. Not only did they greatly increase the ability of lenders to coordinate, but they linked the issue of debt with parliamentary sovereignty and hence provided a large set of natural allies who sought to coordinate their behavior in order to limit the power of the Crown by defending the Parliament.[16] Unilateral default by the sovereign created a risk of deposition, lowering the costs to lenders of punishing the Crown for reneging on agreements.

Fiscal and Military Consequences

The differences in the states' political institutions led to marked differences in their access to credit and, hence, in the amount of resources each could mobilize in the event of war. Like the Dutch Republic in the seventeenth century, England enjoyed access to credit at low interest rates, even when the overall size of its debt became quite large. France, by contrast, paid relatively higher interest rates and had a harder time keeping its debt sustainable. As a result, England was consistently able to outspend France in wartime despite its smaller population and economy.

Figure 4 compares the interest rates paid by the two governments on long-term debt. Although the data for Britain during the eighteenth century are quite thorough, interest rate data on France are incomplete. This problem is compounded by partial default, where, on several occasions, the French government unilaterally cut interest rates on outstanding issues as a way of reducing its debt burden.

Two observations stand out. The first is the salutary effect of Britain's political revolution on its ability to obtain cheap credit (Dickson 1967; North and Weingast 1989). Immediately following the Glorious Revolution, interest rates were high, due in part to the uncertainty surrounding the nature of the financial mechanisms, and, prior to England's success in the Nine Years' War, the stability of the new regime. As the parliamentary system became more entrenched, interest rates dropped dramatically. The fall in interest rates in the 1720s is especially striking given that total government debt was growing throughout this period.

The second important conclusion is that, for most of the eighteenth century, French interest rates exceeded British by about two percentage points, or over 50 percent. Like Britain, France saw a downward trend in interest rates during the early part of the century. The drop to 5 percent in 1710 was dictated by the government, but market rates of 5 to 6 percent were the norm from that point on (Homer and Sylla 1991). Still, Britain had a clear advantage, with rates

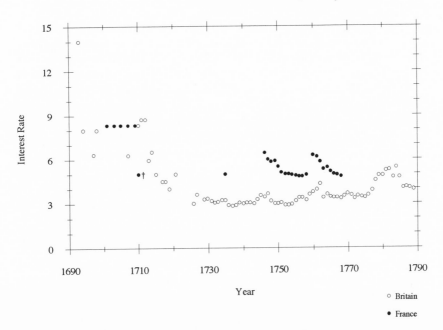

Fig. 4. British and French interest rates, 1690–1790. Dagger (†) indicates rate arbitrarily cut by government. (Data for Great Britain: 1693–1707 from North and Weingast 1989, 824; 1710–90 from Homer and Sylla 1991, 156, 161–62. Data for France: 1700–1735 from Homer and Sylla 1991, 172; 1746–68 provided by Jean-Laurent Rosenthal.)

remaining in the 3 to 4 percent range for most of the period. The rise in both countries' rates in the 1740s reflects the increased demand for debt during the War of Austrian Succession. A similar rise in the early 1760s reflects the impact of the Seven Years' War. In both instances, Britain enjoyed substantially more favorable interest rates.

This advantage meant that Britain's debt burden was generally much lighter than France's. In 1715, French debt was approximately 2,382 million livres, "the equivalent of over 30 years' ordinary revenue" (Dickson and Sperling 1970, 320), while that for England was a far more manageable 37.4 million pounds, or a little over 6 times ordinary annual revenue (see Mitchell 1988, table XI–7). Because of its relatively low debt service obligations and high political costs for default, Britain did not default on its debt obligations for the first 100 years of this rivalry.[17] France, by contrast, had three major episodes of default.

As in the Dutch case, Britain's superior access to credit permitted it to mobilize resources out of proportion to its size and population. Figure 5 compares

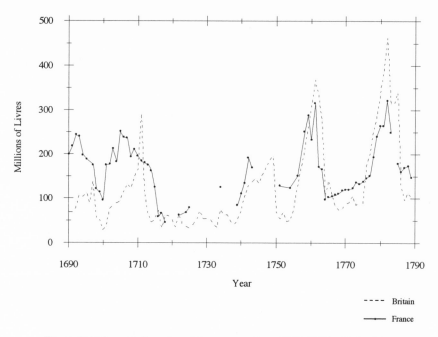

Fig. 5. British and French military spending, 1690–1789. (Data from Sargent and Velde 1995.)

military spending in Britain and France for the period 1689 to 1790. Limitations of the data aside,[18] this figure indicates that Britain was able to raise tremendous amounts of money in wartime, despite a lower national income and smaller population. This pattern is especially noteworthy when we consider that at the beginning of this period England's ordinary annual revenue was only one-fifth of France's (Dickson and Sperling 1970, 285). In the average war year, Britian's military spending amounted to 1 to 1.5 years' worth of revenue; in France, the comparable figure was only 0.5 to 0.8. This difference was especially striking during the Seven Years' War, in which France lost all of its North American colonies. The war brought France to the brink of bankruptcy, and yet Britain still outspent France by 40 percent (Sargent and Velde 1995, 489).

Finally, we observe that Britain's huge borrowing capacity allowed it to finance wars via "tax smoothing," a technique economists have shown to be optimal (Barro 1979; Lucas and Stokey 1983).[19] States have two choices for raising revenues in the face of huge increases in war expenditures. They can raise taxes or they can borrow the needed funds. Raising taxes imposes several sources of burdens on the economy relative to borrowing. First, there is considerable uncertainty over the future path of taxes. Second, taxes are very high in some years, implying excessive dead-weight losses. Economists have shown that the total tax burden is less when taxes are smooth, allowing rises in expenditures to be financed via borrowing. In brief, the pattern of expenditures demonstrates that England was able to resort to deficit finance throughout this period while France was not (Sargent and Velde 1995; Schultz and Weingast 1996).

In short, Britain's surprisingly powerful financial capacity helped provide a competitive advantage over its rival. Moreover, Britain's financial advantage was not lost on its contemporaries. In 1781, during the War of the American Revolution, French finance minister Jacques Necker lamented that "England still today can find 300 millions to borrow at 3 per cent each year, and exerts amounts of efforts and power out of proportion with its wealth and population" (quoted in Sargent and Velde 1995, 489).

Summary

The financial aspects of the eighteenth-century Anglo-French rivalry provides a significant contrast. England developed the funded debt, increasing its access to credit with each new war. At the same time, interest rates fell to a relatively low rate of 3 percent. The English system also allowed the benefits of tax smoothing. The consequence was a more efficient and predictable system of public finance. In contrast, France faced considerably higher rates of borrowing. Far less tax smoothing took place than in England, and the state's numerous defaults reflected a system taxing its limits to tap the funds of private capital holders.

The end results of the Anglo-French competition are clear, especially after the mid–eighteenth century. With the defeat of Napoleon, France ceased to be a serious military threat to England, and its influence over the continent of Europe diminished considerably. England, in contrast, emerged as the most powerful state in the world. Although finances were not the sole reason for the French defeat, superior access to credit allowed England to finance larger and longer wars, forcing France into financial turmoil and ultimately revolution.

5. Conclusions

The essays in this book reflect a growing critique of neorealism's treatment of states as unitary actors differentiated only by their position in the systemic distribution of power (e.g., Waltz 1979). The central premise of this critique is that states are led by strategic actors whose responses to the international environment depend greatly on the structure of domestic political institutions. Because institutions shape the incentives of domestic actors, institutional variation can generate variation in the way states react to a given circumstance. This reasoning implies that neorealism's exclusive emphasis on state power is at best incomplete: differences in political institutions can cause two states of identical power to behave differently.

We take this analysis one step further by arguing that domestic political institutions can also have a systematic effect on states' power. In particular, we show that institutions that impose limits on the discretion of government greatly increase the resources that a state can bring to bear in international competition. We contend that a principal—and heretofore unrecognized—advantage of states with limited government is the ability to make credible commitments. In terms of economics, this allows them to foster larger and healthier economies; in terms of finance, this allows them access to more credit. Focusing on the latter issue, we showed how the institutions of limited government, by allowing lenders to punish the state in the event of default, vastly improved these states' ability to borrow. Thus, states that possess these institutions enjoy an advantage when in competition with states that do not.

As such, our argument does not directly contradict realism's logic. Realists take the distribution of power to be exogenous and make little attempt to explain why some states do better than others in international competition. Rather, this analysis criticizes realism's scope: by ignoring the determinants of state power, realists cannot explain the outcomes of major international rivalries such as those examined here or, for that matter, the Cold War (Gaddis 1992).

We applied our approach to two cases of multidecade contests in early modern Europe: the Dutch Revolt against Spain and the 125-year Anglo-French rivalry that began with the Glorious Revolution of 1689. In both cases, debt finance helped a state with limited government out-compete an authoritarian regime. The advantage held by states with limited government is evident in later periods as well. As we show elsewhere (Schultz and Weingast 1996), although the Cold War rivalry between the United States and the Soviet Union exhibits significant differences from the contests studied here, there are also striking parallels. Moreover, Kugler and Domke (1986) show a similar effect during World War II. Although their focus is less institutional, they emphasize the importance of a state's ability to mobilize social resources in its war effort.

This argument helps us to address the paradox noted at the outset, namely, that states with limited government have often been held by international relations theorists to be weak in comparison with their authoritarian rivals. And yet they seem to succeed in international competition. We argue that limited government itself—and the attendant ability to make credible commitments—provides this advantage, one difficult to attain as efficiently by authoritarian regimes.

This conclusion suggests that state leaders engaged in military competition face a trade-off between international power and domestic autonomy. The advantages of limited government stem precisely from the fact that liberal institutions constrain state leaders and facilitate their removal from office. The fact that political leaders rarely tie their own hands in order to enjoy these advantages suggests that the quest for office and its perks often outweighs the quest for international power.[20] It is here that our argument offers it most fundamental contradiction of realism.

APPENDIX: A MODEL OF SOVEREIGN DEBT WITH UNCERTAINTY

In this appendix, we provide a formal solution for the model presented in section 2, along with its comparative statics results.

We assume that the sovereign seeks to borrow a sum D and that the lender selects the market-clearing interest rate, i. Let r be the risk-free rate of return on the lender's capital. The value of the sum to the sovereign is $v(D)$.

We represent uncertainty over the sovereign's finances by assuming that nature determines the state of the world, s, after the loan is extended but before the sovereign decides whether or not to repay. There are two possible states of the world: good and bad ($s \in \{G,B\}$). Nature's choice affects the political costs of raising taxes, which are greater in bad times than in good.

Sequence of the game. The lenders have the first move and must determine the interest rate they will charge for a loan of size D (see fig. 1). Lenders may refuse to extend a loan. Nature moves next, determining the state of the world: the state is bad with probability q and good with probability $1 - q$. Both actors observe nature's choice. The sovereign then chooses either to raise taxes and repay the loan or to default (and not alter taxes). If the sovereign defaults, the lenders can impose a penalty, P.

Payoffs. The political costs of raising taxes are a function of the amount being raised and the state of the world, s. The political costs of raising T taxes are $c(T;s)$, with $s \in \{B,G\}$. We set $c(0;s) = 0$ and assume that:

$$\frac{\partial c(T;s)}{\partial T} > 0 \quad \text{and} \quad \frac{\partial^2 c(T;s)}{\partial T^2} > 0, \tag{1}$$

meaning that both total costs and marginal costs increase with T. Raising taxes is harder in bad times than in good times: $\forall\, T,\, c(T;B) > c(T;G)$ and:

$$\frac{\partial c(T;B)}{\partial T} > \frac{\partial c(T;G)}{\partial T} \tag{2}$$

The lenders receive iD if the sovereign repays the loan and $-D$ if he does not. The sovereign receives $v(D) - c(D(1 + i);s)$ if he chooses to repay the loan and $V(D) - P$ if he defaults and the lenders impose the punishment. Notice that the sovereign's payoffs depend on the state of the world, while the lender's payoffs do not.

Equilibrium. We solve this model through backward induction. Assume that the lender imposes the punishment if and only if the sovereign defaults. The nature and credibility of this punishment is discussed in section 2. The sovereign will choose to repay the debt if and only if the penalty for default is greater than or equal to the costs of raising taxes.

Given an interest rate of i, the sovereign must raise $D(1 + i)$ to pay back the debt. Consequently, the sovereign will repay the loan in state s if and only if

$$P \geq c(D(1 + i);s). \tag{3}$$

Because $c(D(1 + i);B) > c(D(1 + i);G)$, condition 3 implies that there are three kinds of sovereign behavior, depending upon the magnitude of P. For each case, we also determine what interest rate the lender will demand ex ante. The market clears when the expected payoff for the lender equals the risk-free payoff the lender could get through alternative investments.

CASE 1: $P \geq c(D(1 + i);B)$

For sufficiently large punishments—P large relative to the costs of raising taxes—the inequality implies that the sovereign will repay the loan regardless of the state of the world. Because the sovereign always repays, the loan is risk free. Thus, the lender charges the prevailing risk-free interest rate, r.

CASE 2: $c(D(1 + i);B) > P \geq c(D(1 + i);G)$

For medium-sized punishments—those larger than the costs of taxes in good times but lower than the costs of taxes in bad times—the sovereign will repay the loan in good times but default in bad times. Competition among lenders implies that the interest rate that clears the market, i^*, equates the lender's expected payoff with its risk-free payoff, $D(1 + r)$. Setting

$$q0 + (1 - q) D(1 + i^*) = D(1 + r),$$

we find that

$$i^* = \frac{r + q}{1 - q}. \tag{4}$$

Notice that, because $q < 1$, i^* always exceeds r. Equation 4 thus implies that the sovereign must pay a risk premium when there is a prospect that he will default.

CASE 3: $P < c(D(1 + i);G)$

For relatively low punishments—less than the cost of raising taxes to repay the loan even in good times—the sovereign always defaults and is thus a poor credit risk. Given this sovereign behavior, lenders will lose money at *any interest rate,* so they do not lend money to the sovereign. This case therefore exhibits *credit rationing.*[21]

Because the boundaries between the cases are a function of the interest rate charged, we can state them in terms of r and i^*. Let

$$P^* = c(D(1 + i^*);G) \tag{5}$$

and

$$P^r = c(D(1 + r);B). \tag{6}$$

Notice that our assumptions about the cost function do not determine which of these cutoffs is higher. It might be that costs of repaying the high-interest loan in good times are less than the costs of repaying the low-interest loan in bad times, or vice versa. Nevertheless, we can make the following propositions. If $P < \min[P^*(D),P^r(D)]$, then the lenders will not extend the loan, D, at any interest rate, since the expected return is insufficient. If $P^* < P^r$ and P falls between them, then the lenders will charge an interest rate of i^*, since they will be repaid in good times at this interest rate. If $P \geq P^r$, then the lenders will charge an interest rate of r, since they will always be repaid.[22]

The core result of the analysis is illustrated in figure 2, which depicts the case in which $P^* < P^r$. As the punishment the lenders can impose increases, the interest rate that they charge decreases stepwise: the harder it is to sanction the sovereign for default, the riskier are such loans.

These results yield a seeming paradox. In terms of his ability to borrow money, the sovereign benefits from an increase in the punishment that lenders can impose on him for defaulting. *The greater that penalty, the greater his access to loans.*

Comparative statics. This approach also yields some interesting comparative statics that show what happens when the amount of money the sovereign seeks to borrow, D, increases. Notice from equations 5 and 6 that both cutoff points, P^* and P^r, are a function of D. From our assumptions about the cost function, we can specify how these cutoffs move if D changes. First, because c is an increasing function of the tax increase, it is clear that $\partial P^*/\partial D > 0$ and $\partial P^r/\partial D > 0$. Moreover, since c increases faster in bad times than in good, $\partial P^r/\partial D > \partial P^*/\partial D$. Thus, increases in D move the cutoffs higher and drive P^r and P^* further apart. For a fixed P, the costs of borrowing increase as the magnitude of the loan increases. Further, *the higher the level of debt sought, the larger is the range of credit rationing.*

The model also implies that the sovereign's debt ceilings are a function of P. To determine this relationship, we assume that the cost function described above, $c(T;s)$, is invertible. Let $\tau(c;s)$ be the tax increase that generates costs c when the state of the economy is s. The function τ is increasing in c; further, for all c, $\tau(c;G) > \tau(c;B)$.

The sovereign will repay debt at all times at interest rate r if $P \geq c(D(1 + r);B)$. We can solve for the maximum debt at this rate that the sovereign will always repay by finding the value of D that makes the two sides of the expression equal. Following our earlier notation, we will call this cut point D^r. Inverting c, we find:

$$D^r = \frac{\tau(P;B)}{1 + r} . \tag{7}$$

Any level of debt in the interval $[0,D^r]$ and with an interest rate of r will always be repaid. D^r thus represents the maximum the sovereign can borrow at the low, risk-free interest rate.

The sovereign can secure more debt only by accepting the higher interest rate, i^*. This is due to the fact that higher levels of debt are subject to default in bad times. As before, we determine this debt ceiling by noting that the sovereign will repay debt at the high interest rate in good times when $P \geq c(D(1 + i^*);G)$. Let D^* be the value of D such that the two sides of this expression are equal. We solve for D^* by inverting:

$$D^* = \frac{\tau(P;G)}{1 + i^*} . \tag{8}$$

As with earlier cutoff points, there is no guarantee that $D^* > D^r$. If $D^* < D^r$, then the sovereign can only borrow at the low interest rate to a maximum of D^r. If $D^* > D^r$, then D^* represents the maximum amount the sovereign can borrow at any interest rate. Loans in the interval $[D^r,D^*]$ carry the high interest rate, i^*.

We now derive the effect on these debt ceilings of changes in P. From expressions 7 and 8, it is clear that D^* and D^r are both increasing functions of P. Thus, *as the punishment that lenders can impose increases, the amount of credit available to the sovereign increases.*

A final set of comparative statics arises from the political costs associated with raising a given amount of taxes. As the cost of paying off a given amount of debt decreases, the punishment needed to enforce that debt also decreases. Thus, *the cutoffs* P* *and* P^r *decrease as the cost function shifts downward.* At the same time, the debt ceilings represented by *D** and *D^r* increase.

NOTES

The authors gratefully acknowledge Bruce Bueno de Mesquita, James Conklin, Kurt Taylor Gaubatz, and Jean-Laurent Rosenthal for helpful conversations. They also thank Jean-Laurent Rosenthal and François Velde for providing data. Schultz acknowledges the financial support of the Eisenhower World Affairs Institute.

1. Elsewhere we show similar results for the more recent rivalry between the United States and the Soviet Union (Schultz and Weingast 1996).

2. A formal specification of the cost terms is provided in the appendix.

3. This is a standard result in the literature on sovereign debt (see, e.g., Bulow and Rogoff 1989 and Eaton, Gersovitz, and Stiglitz 1986).

4. The appendix provides a specific formula for the relationship between q, r, and $i*$.

5. This result is standard in the literature on sovereign debt. See, for example, Bulow and Rogoff 1989; Eaton, Gersovitz, and Stiglitz 1986; and Rasmusen 1992.

6. Each of the three comparative statics results is derived formally in the appendix.

7. As Parker (1990, 100) notes, "no government could pay for a prolonged war out of current taxation: the income which sufficed for a peacetime establishment could in no way prove equal to the unpredictable but inevitably heavy expenses of a major campaign. The state therefore had to spread the costs of each war over a number of peaceful years, either by saving up in anticipation . . . or by spending in advance the income of future years with the aid of loans from bankers and merchants." For a discussion of the limitations of forced loans, see Tracy 1985, 9.

8. To be sure, these provincial estates were not representative in the democratic sense of being subject to electoral approval, but members were chosen from the class of wealth holders and merchants, and they considered this class to be their primary constituency (Parker 1977, 246–47).

9. Though they refer only to Holland, these figures reflect the creditworthiness of the entire state because the central government did most of its borrowing through Holland. At the end of the Eighty Years' War in 1648, Holland's debt stood at around 140 million guilders, while the debt of the union government was only 10 million ('t Hart 1993, 164–67). Clearly, the war was largely funded through provincial debt.

10. From the limited data available, it appears that comparable long-term interest rates in other countries were considerably higher (Homer 1977, 126–30). France sold *rentes* on and off during the seventeenth century, usually at an interest rate of 8.3 percent; the best rate achieved in this period was around 5 percent in 1679. England introduced long-term public debt in the last decade of the century at rates of 8 to 14 percent, when Holland was paying only 3 percent.

11. For manpower figures, see Parker 1990, 96. For population figures, see Wilson

and Parker 1977, 1, 37, 64, 81. Population figures for the Spanish monarchy include estimates for Portugal, Spanish Italy, and the Spanish Netherlands in addition to Spain proper; see also Stradling 1981, 33.

12. This section summarizes Schultz and Weingast 1996.

13. Root (1994) provides a good comparison of the French and English systems of negotiation between Crown and constituents, including their implications for economic growth and public finance. See also Rosenthal 1997.

14. Although the sale of offices was less prevalent during the eighteenth century, the obligations inherited from the past remained and played a significant role in the Crown's inability to pay off loans with new taxes (Sargent and Velde 1995, 483). Indeed, they constituted an important source of "privilege" excoriated during the French Revolution.

15. In addition to those limitations just noted, several additional ones could be mentioned. For example, the French actively obfuscated its total indebtedness; the Crown did not know the full extent of its obligations, raising considerable uncertainty about prospects for payment. Second, on several occasions the French decided against creating a parallel to the Bank of England.

16. As Brewer (1989) emphasizes, the English reforms were accompanied by the development of an efficient tax administration largely above corruption and politics. This contrasts strikingly with France.

17. Britain went off the gold standard during the Napoleonic campaigns, allowing some inflation.

18. These data should be read with caution because data on military spending have important limitations (see Schultz and Weingast 1996 for details).

19. This aspect of the Anglo-French rivalry is discussed at greater length in Schultz and Weingast 1996.

20. Indeed, a number of French officials, including Finance Minister Jacques Necker, understood that liberalizing reforms would be necessary to compete with England (Sargent and Velde 1995). The rejection of Necker's argument suggests that the French monarch placed a high value on his domestic autonomy.

21. This result parallels that of Eaton, Gersovitz, and Stiglitz (1986). Notice also that when case 3 applies, the formulas defining the cases also imply that there are loans smaller than D, which lenders will lend at i^*.

22. If $P^* > P^r$ and P falls within this interval, then the lenders are indifferent between the two interest rates, r and i^*. In the first case, they will always be repaid; in the second case, they will be repaid only in good times. In a competitive market, the sovereign should always be able to find lenders willing to offer the lower rate.

REFERENCES

Atkeson, Andrew. 1991. International Lending with Moral Hazard and Risk of Repudiation. *Econometrics* 59:1069–89.

Barbour, Violet. *Capitalism in Amsterdam in the 17th Century.* Ann Arbor: University of Michigan Press.

Barro, Robert. 1979. On the Determination of Public Debt. *Journal of Political Economy* 87:940–71.

Bien, David D. 1987. Offices, Corps, and a System of State Credit: The Uses of Privilege under the Ancien Régime. In *The French Revolution and the Creation of Modern Political Culture,* edited by K. Baker. Vol. 1. Oxford: Pergamon.

Brewer, John. 1989. *The Sinews of Power: War, Money, and the English State, 1688–1783.* New York: Knopf.

Bulow, Jeremy, and Kenneth Rogoff. 1989. A Constant Recontracting Model of Sovereign Debt. *Journal of Political Economy* 97:155–78.

Conklin, James. 1995. Sovereign Fiscal Commitment in Sixteenth Century Spain. Department of Economics, University of Texas. Manuscript.

De Long, J. Bradford, and Andrei Shleifer. 1993. Princes and Merchants: City Growth before the Industrial Revolution. *Journal of Law and Economics* 36:671–702.

Dickson, Peter. 1967. *The Financial Revolution in England.* London: St. Martin's.

Dickson, P., and J. Sperling. 1970. War Finance: 1689–1715. In *The New Cambridge Modern History.* Vol. 6. Cambridge: Cambridge University Press.

Eaton, Jonathan, Mark Gersovitz, and Joseph Stiglitz. 1986. The Pure Theory of Country Risk. *European Economic Review* 30:481–513.

Friedrich, Carl Joachim. 1938. *Foreign Policy in the Making.* New York: Norton.

Gaddis, John Lewis. 1992. International Relations and the End of the Cold War. *International Security* 17:5–58.

Greif, Avner, Paul Milgrom, and Barry R. Weingast. 1994. Coordination, Commitment, and Enforcement: The Case of the Merchant Guild. *Journal of Political Economy* 102:745–76.

Hoffman, Philip T. 1994. Taxes, Fiscal Crises, and Representative Institutions: The Case of Early Modern France. In *Fiscal Crises, Liberty, and Representative Government, 1450–1789,* edited by P. Hoffman and K. Norberg. Stanford: Stanford University Press.

Hoffman, Philip T., Gilles Postel-Vinay, and Jean-Laurent Rosenthal. 1997. Priceless Markets: Credit in Paris, 1660–1869. California Institute of Technology. Manuscript.

Homer, Sidney. 1977. *A History of Interest Rates.* New Brunswick, NJ: Rutgers University Press.

Homer, Sidney, and Richard Sylla. 1991. *A History of Interest Rates.* 3d ed. New Brunswick, NJ: Rutgers University Press.

Howard, Michael. 1976. *War in European History.* Oxford: Oxford University Press.

Jones, J. R. 1972. *The Revolution of 1688 in England.* New York: Norton.

Kugler, Jacek, and William Domke. 1986. Comparing the Strength of Nations. *Comparative Political Studies* 19:39–69.

Lake, David A. 1992. Powerful Pacifists: Democratic States and War. *American Political Science Review* 86:24–37.

Lippmann, Walter. 1955. *The Public Philosophy.* Boston: Little, Brown.

Lipson, Charles. 1988. The International Organization of Third World Debt. In *Toward a Political Economy of Development: A Rational Choice Perspective,* edited by R. H. Bates. Berkeley: University of California Press.

Lovett, A. W. 1980. The Castillian Bankruptcy of 1575. *Historical Journal* 23:899–911.

Lovett, A. W. 1982. The General Settlement of 1577: An Aspect of Spanish Finance in the Early Modern Period. *Historical Journal* 25:1–22.

Lucas, Robert, and Nancy Stokey. 1983. Optimal Fiscal and Monetary Policy in an Economy with Capital. *Journal of Monetary Economics* 1:55–93.

Mitchell, B. R. 1988. *British Historical Statistics.* Cambridge: Cambridge University Press.

Modelski, George, and William R. Thompson. 1988. *Seapower in Global Politics, 1494–1993.* Seattle: University of Washington Press.

Morgenthau, Hans J. 1973. *Politics among Nations.* New York: Knopf.

North, Douglass C. 1990. *Institutions, Institutional Change, and Economic Performance.* Cambridge: Cambridge University Press.

North, Douglass C., and Robert Paul Thomas. 1973. *The Rise of the Western World.* Cambridge: Cambridge University Press.

North, Douglass C., and Barry R. Weingast. 1989. Constitutions and Commitment: The Evolution of Institutions Governing Public Choice in 17th Century England. *Journal of Economic History* 49:803–32.

Olson, Mancur. 1982. *The Rise and Decline of Nations.* New Have: Yale University Press.

Parker, Geoffrey. 1974. The Emergence of Modern Finance in Europe, 1500–1730. In *The Fontana Economic History of Europe,* edited by C. M. Cippolla. Glasgow: Collins/Fontana Press.

Parker, Geoffrey, 1977. *The Dutch Revolt.* Ithaca: Cornell University Press.

Parker, Geoffrey. 1988. *The Military Revolution.* Cambridge: Cambridge University Press.

Parker, Geoffrey. 1990. *Spain and the Netherlands: 1559–1659.* Glasgow: Fontana Press.

Rasmusen, Eric B. 1992. The Strategy of Sovereign-Debt Renegotiation. In *Country-Risk Analysis: A Handbook,* edited by Ronald L. Solberg. London: Routledge.

Riley, James C. 1986. *The Seven Years War and the Old Regime in France.* Princeton: Princeton University Press.

Root, Hilton L. 1989. Tying the King's Hands: Credible Commitments and Royal Fiscal Policy during the Old Regime. *Rationality and Society* 1:240–58.

Root, Hilton L. 1994. *The Fountain of Privilege: Institutional Innovation and Social Choice in Old Regime France and England.* Berkeley: University of California Press.

Rosenthal, Jean-Laurent. 1997. The Political-Economy of Absolutism Reconsidered: England and France, 1600–1789. In *Analytical Narratives,* edited by Robert Bates, Avner Greif, Margaret Levi, Jean-Laurent Rosenthal, and Barry R. Weingast. Manuscript.

Sargent, Thomas, and François Velde. 1995. Macroeconomic Features of the French Revolution. *Journal of Political Economy* 103:474–518.

Schultz, Kenneth A., and Barry R. Weingast. 1996. The Democratic Advantage: The Institutional Sources of State Power in International Competition. Essays in Public Policy, no. 67. Stanford, CA: Hoover Institution Press.

Stradling, R. A. 1981. *Europe and the Decline of Spain.* London: George Allen & Unwin.

Taylor, A. J. P. 1961. *The Origins of the Second World War.* New York: Atheneum.

't Hart, Marjolein C. 1993. *The Making of a Bourgeois State: War, Politics, and Finance during the Dutch Revolt.* Manchester: Manchester University Press.

Thompson, I. A. A. 1976. *War and Government in Habsburg Spain, 1560–1620.* London: Athlone.

Thompson, I. A. A. 1994. Castile: Polity, Fiscality, and Fiscal Crises. In *Fiscal Crises, Liberty, and Representative Government, 1450–1789,* edited by P. Hoffman and K. Norberg, Stanford: Stanford University Press.

Tracy, James D. 1985. *A Financial Revolution in the Habsburg Netherlands.* Berkeley: University of California Press.

Waltz, Kenneth N. 1979. *Theory of International Politics.* New York: McGraw-Hill.

Weingast, Barry R. 1995. The Economic Role of Political Institutions: Market-Preserving Federalism and Economic Development. *Journal of Law, Economics, and Organizations* 11:1–31.

Weingast, Barry R. 1997. The Political Foundations of Limited Government: Parliament and Sovereign Debt in 17th and 18th Century England. In *Frontiers of the New Institutional Economics,* edited by John V. C. Nye and John N. Drobak. San Diego: Academic.

Wilson, Charles, and Geoffrey Parker, eds. 1977. *An Introduction to the Sources of European Economic History, 1500–1800.* Ithaca: Cornell University Press.

Evasive Maneuvers? Reconsidering Presidential Use of Executive Agreements

Lisa L. Martin

The Problem of Ratification

The popularity of Robert Putnam's two-level game metaphor (Putnam 1988; Evans, Jacobson, and Putnam 1993) and a general desire to bring domestic politics systematically into the study of international relations has rekindled interest in the importance of ratification processes. Variation in the methods used to ratify international agreements may serve as an organizing device for analyzing the impact of domestic political arrangements on the efficiency and distributional characteristics of international bargaining. *Ratification,* as it is used here, simply refers to the procedures necessary to gain domestic approval of an international agreement. Ratification processes may be formal or informal; they may involve just a few actors or many; they may use majority, supermajority, or consensus requirements.

In this essay I concentrate on ratification in the United States. While ratification procedures for trade agreements have received extensive attention (Lohmann and O'Halloran 1994; O'Halloran 1994; Haggard 1988), few analysts have considered the impact of ratification procedures in areas other than trade (for an exception, see McGillivray in this volume). As a step in this direction, I focus on the use of executive agreements and treaties. Treaties, as provided by the Constitution, must receive the approval of two-thirds of voting senators to go into effect. Executive agreements, in comparison, are not mentioned in the Constitution. They are approved through a number of different mechanisms, from a formal legislative vote to sole executive approval. However, they have the same legal effect as treaties (Millett 1990).[1] While Congress has attempted to specify criteria for determining the form of international agreements, the president continues to make these decisions unilaterally in response to various internal and external pressures. Explaining variation in the use of agreements thus allows us to gain insight into the executive's strategic calculations about the use of domestic institutions.

51

Due to the striking difference in the role of Congress under these procedures, most studies of executive agreements have argued that they provide the
president with a way to evade congressional constraints on his ability to make
commitments to other countries. The use of executive agreements has sky-
rocketed since the mid–twentieth century, while the number of treaties has remained about constant. With this evidence in hand, the image of executive
agreements as providing the president with a way to get around Congress has
led to expressions of concern and attempts to limit the use of such agreements.

In this essay I question this understanding of executive agreements. Two
lines of argument should lead us to suspect that they do not provide the president with an effective way to avoid Congress. First, Congress is not as easy to
evade as would be necessary for the evasion perspective to have much force.
Even without the formalities of treaty ratification, the president operates within
the boundaries of congressional consent. While these boundaries most likely
vary under different ratification procedures, they do not disappear. Second, considerations of making credible commitments to other states should lead us to
question the value of executive agreements that are intended simply to avoid
Congress. If other states understand that evasion is the purpose of executive
agreements, they should question the credibility of the commitment made by
the executive in such agreements and therefore be reluctant to accept them.

If the evasion argument were correct, we would expect to see predictable
patterns in the use of executive agreements and treaties. However, the data presented here suggest that such patterns provide only minimal explanatory leverage. They lend support to the notion that executive agreements are not effective evasive devices. While the president may try to use them in this manner,
congressional constraints and the need to make credible commitments to other
countries put limits on his ability to do so. Alternative explanations for the
choice of institutional form lie in considerations of credibility as well as the
need to deal with increasing complexity in the international environment. Additional evidence of congressional influence and its interaction with credibility
comes from examining congressional reactions to executive agreements over
time, particularly congressional attempts to force the president to provide information about such agreements.

The examination of executive agreements and treaties provides an illuminating window on strategic politicians and institutions in foreign policy. Ratification procedures are one of the key domestic institutions that may influence
the course of U.S. relations with other states. An additional institutional dimension arises in examining the effect of interbranch competition and party
control of the two branches of government. What I call the "evasion hypothesis" is one assumption about the strategic behavior of presidents. I conclude in
this essay that the notion that the president is strategizing only against Congress
is too narrow. Additional strategic constraints arise from his need to interact

with other states, particularly to make credible commitments to them. A more fully strategic president, therefore, will be modest in his attempts to circumvent Congress. As the two-level games metaphor suggests, bringing domestic politics into the study of international negotiations does not imply merely a return to studies of the domestic politics of foreign policy. Instead, it forces us to consider the interaction of domestic politics with the international strategic environment, as the essays in this volume attest.

The Logic of Evasion

In traditional U.S. foreign policy analysis, the relationship between Congress and the executive branch has been conceptualized as a "struggle for power" (Crabb and Holt 1992). Most analysts find that the executive branch is privileged in this struggle. The powers of the executive branch, its task of negotiating with other countries, and congressional weakness all contribute to an executive branch that is able to get its way on foreign policy issues. While most analysts see a resurgence of congressional activism since the early 1970s, they conclude that the executive retains a dominant position (Peterson 1994). This analysis, however, stands in contrast to that of comparative foreign policy analysts. When put in comparative perspective, the United States invariably is singled out for having a strong legislature and an activist Congress (Katzenstein 1978).

As this discussion suggests, our understanding of executive-legislative relations in U.S. foreign policy remains plagued by a number of unexplained anomalies. How can we resolve the conflicting perspectives of those who concentrate on American politics versus comparative foreign policy analysis? If the dominance of the executive has in fact changed over time, how can we explain these changes? Does executive dominance vary across issues? These questions all demand an analytical framework that will allow us to identify and make sense of the patterns of legislative influence on foreign policy.

The understanding of legislative influence on *domestic* policy, both its mechanisms and degree, has undergone a sea change in the last decade. Legislative scholars, drawing on the new economics of organization, have developed numerous models that suggest that Congress exerts influence on policy in many nonobvious ways and therefore has not abdicated authority to the executive as previous analyses have suggested (Weingast and Moran 1983; Kiewiet and McCubbins 1991). Too often, observers mistake action for influence (Calvert, McCubbins, and Weingast 1989, 590). Because the executive branch takes many actions without explicit legislative consultation or approval, it is easy to infer mistakenly that the executive is acting without any effective legislative constraints. If we wish to examine influence, we must turn to patterns of variation other than a simple count of presidential versus legislative actions, such as variation in the use of different institutions.

Applying models of delegation and legislative organization to foreign policy issues may help resolve some of these anomalies. While it is possible that Congress cannot exert similar mechanisms of control in the domestic and foreign policy areas, this proposition should be treated as a hypothesis rather than an assumption. In foreign policy, even more than in domestic policy, the locus of activity is in the executive rather than the legislative branch. But this does not necessarily imply that legislative influence is absent. Models of delegation suggest that congressional activity could even be negatively correlated with congressional influence. Only when more subtle, effective mechanisms of influence fail is Congress likely to take the difficult and perhaps costly steps of holding hearings, overturning executive decisions, and otherwise "micromanaging" foreign policy.

One oft-cited piece of evidence to support the claim of congressional lack of influence is the use of executive agreements as a method for making binding commitments to other countries. Such agreements are not mentioned in the Constitution. Because they do not involve the Senate in its prescribed "advise and consent" role, they are seen as a method for the president to make commitments independent of the wishes of Congress. Thus, increasing use of executive agreements, according to the evasion hypothesis, is evidence of decreasing legislative influence.

As figure 1 shows, the use of executive agreements has increased from very low levels in 1930 to 300 to 400 per year by the 1990s. At the same time, the number of treaties has remained about constant, at approximately 14 per year.[2] Prior to 1930, executive agreements were used only infrequently. The Congressional Research Service (CRS 1993, 14), citing a study by Borchard (1946), calculates that between 1789 and 1929 the United States signed a total of 667 treaties and 1,028 executive agreements. Today, the United States typically signs this many executive agreements in less than three years. Their use particularly accelerated in the late 1940s, as the United States assumed a more active role in international affairs. The numbers continued to grow until the mid-1970s and appear to have settled into a fairly constant rate since then.

The trend toward increasing use of executive agreements has worried most interested observers, whether legal scholars, senators, or political analysts. The legal community engaged in a spirited debate in the 1970s about the constitutionality of such executive agreements (Millett 1990; Paige 1977). The conclusion of this debate, and of Supreme Court cases, was that the president did indeed have the power to bind the United States through the use of executive agreements. Like treaties, they became the "supreme law of the land" once the president agreed to them. Only if an international commitment were to come into conflict with specific provisions of the Constitution would problems arise. In the Senate, as will be discussed further, many expressed concern that the use

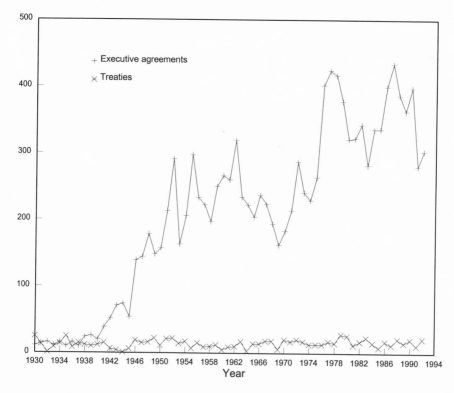

Fig. 1. Number of agreements, 1930–92. (Data from CRS 1993, 14.)

of executive agreements further diminished the Senate's already questionable ability to influence the content of international agreements.

The consensus view among political scientists is expressed well by Nathan and Oliver (1994, 99): "Presidents . . . have developed and employed the executive agreement to circumvent Senate involvement in international agreements almost altogether." The trend toward using these agreements is considered part of the development of the "imperial presidency" during the Cold War. Executive agreements were also "a potent device in the hands of activist presidents who sought means to further their conception of an energetic presidency" (99). Because members of Congress are not by law involved in consultations during the negotiation of executive agreements, and often do not have to vote on them, it seems plausible to interpret them as one of the tools presidents use when they wish to avoid congressional scrutiny. Executive agreements are thus perhaps antidemocratic, a way for the president to avoid keeping international commitments within the range acceptable to Congress. This perspective from students of U.S. foreign policy is consistent with arguments that see international co-operation as a kind of "executive cartel" designed to strengthen the exective at the expense of the legislature (Moravcsik 1994; Vaubel 1986; Kaiser 1971).

Why question this common-sense view? I do so because it neglects con-straints on the president's ability to evade Congress. Recent studies of domes-tic political issues have taught us that such inferences frequently mischaracter-ize the actual nature of legislative influence. In the case of executive agreements in particular, I would suggest two sets of reasons why we should look more carefully at the claims made by the executive dominance school. One set of rea-sons lies in mechanisms of influence that remain in the hands of members of Congress even in the case of executive agreements. To argue that the president can make far-reaching commitments without taking note of these mechanisms requires a demonstration that they have no effect. If Congress retains mecha-nisms of influence, it has far-reaching implications. In particular, it implies that a president using the executive agreement procedure to avoid a Congress that will refuse to implement an international agreement or will overturn it through legislation will bring the credibility of any U.S. commitment into question. Such questions about credibility are a second reason why we should examine the evasion hypothesis more deeply.

Congress has in its hands a number of mechanisms by which it can exert influence on international agreements, even if they do not take the form of treaties. Executive agreements come in a number of varieties, including con-gressional-executive agreements, agreements pursuant to treaties, and sole ex-ecutive agreements. Congressional-executive agreements, which include most executive agreements, are "either explicitly or implicitly authorized in advance by Congress or submitted to Congress for approval" (CRS 1993, xvii). In some areas, such as the relatively technical area of postal conventions or occasion-ally the more politicized areas of foreign trade and military assistance, Con-gress explicitly has authorized the conclusion of international agreements. The Reciprocal Trade Agreements Act of 1934 is a good example, wherein the presi-dent was authorized to negotiate reciprocal reductions in trade barriers within limits set in legislation. At other times, such as the fast-track procedures used to approve most recent trade agreements, the president is required to submit negotiated agreements for congressional approval.

Agreements pursuant to treaties include those that have either been ex-pressly authorized in a treaty or are clearly implied by a treaty's provisions. For example, the president has concluded a large number of executive agreements under the terms of the NATO treaty without explicitly coming back to Congress for approval. Sole executive agreements are those that do not have any explicit or underlying implicit authorization from Congress. Legally, the president in-vokes constitutional authority such as that as commander in chief to justify the conclusion of sole executive agreements. While the legal status of sole executive agreements remains fuzzy, it appears that they cannot supersede a prior act of Congress (CRS 1993, xvii).

When agreements are explicitly or implicitly authorized in advance by Congress, it is difficult to sustain the argument that Congress has no influence on their content. Such delegation of authority does give the president room to maneuver, for example, by creating issue linkages not anticipated by Congress but that Congress finds difficult to reject. But, since Congress does explicitly delegate negotiating authority, it is highly unlikely that such a procedure could leave the median legislator worse off than she was under the status quo. Thus, congressional preferences continue to set the boundaries for executive action. Similarly, when the president concludes agreements pursuant to treaties, the Senate's preferences have been taken into account during the initial ratification process. If the president's action pursuant to the treaty goes beyond the bounds of what the Senate anticipated, the power to abrogate the treaty or otherwise punish the president remains.

Johnson (1984), in a comprehensive study of international agreements, distinguishes between statutory agreements (what I have called congressional-executive agreements or agreements pursuant to treaties) and sole executive agreements. He concludes that the conventional wisdom that executive agreements have replaced treaties is incorrect, since almost 87 percent of all U.S. international agreements are statutory (10–12). He finds that sole executive agreements account for only about the same number of agreements as treaties (7 and 6 percent, respectively). Johnson concludes that the notion that Congress has been closed out of the process of international negotiation is therefore misplaced. Another estimate puts the number of executive agreements that involve some legislative action at 97 percent (Stevens 1977, 907; see also Pyle and Pious 1984, 274).

Sole executive agreements present the greatest opportunity for the president to evade the congressional will. But, beyond the formal approval mechanisms that apply to the first two categories of executive agreements, other legislative powers provide the opportunity for influence on most types of international agreements. The keys are powers of implementation and appropriation. Many international agreements require changes in domestic law, so that implementation engages normal legislative processes. Not only does this implementation stage provide some congressional influence, but it brings in the House as well as the Senate (CRS 1993, xxxii–xxxiii). The possibility of exerting influence on the content of negotiations through anticipation of the implementation stage has been shown in the case of agreements within the European Union (Martin 1994). A similar pattern surely should apply in the United States, with its more powerful legislature. In addition, any international agreement that requires appropriation of funds will be scrutinized and can be overturned, de facto, by the House. The need to appropriate funds has been used to exert leverage over executive agreements, for example, when the president has tied foreign assistance to various political commitments from recipient states. Since all foreign aid appropriations pass through the House, and are often closely scrutinized, the potential exists at this stage for a de facto legislative veto. Anticipating such problems, the president should take congressional preferences into account. In addition, many international negotiations involve congressional representatives in a formal or informal consultative role, often due to anticipation of a potential legislative veto.

These factors suggest that at the domestic level there are reasons to expect the president to be sensitive to congressional concerns. While it is surely incorrect to assert that Congress "controls" international negotiations, the numerous methods by which the two houses of Congress effectively can veto or otherwise complicate implementation of an international agreement should suggest that it is not easy to circumvent congressional wishes entirely. Further reasons to question the evasion hypothesis arise when we model the problem of strategic interaction with other states. Strategic interaction is a central factor when we consider international relations, but it has not been taken seriously by those who consider executive-legislative relations on domestic policy issues. Models of domestic delegation assume that, after delegation, the executive sets policy. However, in international issues, delegation leads to negotiations (tacit or explicit) with other states rather than to unilateral setting of policy. It is reasonable to expect that this change in the structure of the situation will lead to differences in patterns and effects of delegation.

In particular, the United States' negotiating partners must consider whether the commitments made by the United States are credible. Concern that commitments will be overturned by Congress are reasonable and not infrequently expressed by other states. Knowledge that the president is using executive agreements to circumvent congressional opposition surely would add to concerns about credibility. Since Congress often has the power effectively to abrogate executive agreements, through the appropriations process or by otherwise refusing to implement an agreement, other countries will not take the president's word at face value in such situations. Unless other mechanisms make the commitment credible, states should be reluctant to commit themselves to take costly steps through executive agreements if they are primarily evasive devices. Other states may have incentives to demand more explicit and formal ratification processes such as fast-track procedures. The most far-reaching commitments are precisely those for which concerns about evasion are most likely to arise, so that the executive agreement would become less effective as an evasive technique as U.S. credibility becomes more questionable.

The evasion hypothesis, consistent with the executive dominance approach to foreign policy, suggests that executive agreements provide the president with an effective means of circumventing congressional opposition. Those who prefer to see congressional influence on international commitments therefore find the increasing use of executive agreements threatening. However, the logic of this approach may not be sound. Congress appears to retain indirect mechanisms of influence even in the case of executive agreements. These mechanisms should not only constrain the president, but they should make other states skeptical of U.S. commitments that are made through executive agreements designed only to circumvent Congress. They should therefore lead to a different pattern in the use of executive agreements than that predicted by the evasion hypothesis.

Alternative Explanations for the Use of Executive Agreements

As long as Congress retains some capacity to overturn or undercut international commitments with which it disagrees, negotiating partners suspecting congressional disagreement with a commitment will question its sincerity. They may demand a more formal approval process, such as a treaty, to establish credibility. One well-known example of such a demand came in the process of establishing military bases in Spain. Beginning in the 1960s, the United States committed to bases there through secret executive agreements. When these agreements came to light in 1970, they caused an uproar in the Senate. Congress nevertheless agreed to renew funding. By 1975, after a series of complaints, the renewal agreement for the bases was submitted as a treaty. What is interesting here is that demands for moving toward a treaty came not only from the Senate. Spain also pushed for the more formal treaty procedure (Atwood 1981, 218).

The logic of interbranch regulations suggests that we need to go beyond the evasion perspective if we are to understand the use of executive agreements. In this section, I suggest two alternative frameworks for explaining variation in the use of ratification procedures: complexity and credibility. Both of these arguments are more consistent with the logic of congressional influence than is the evasion perspective, and both consider the impact of the international strategic environment in addition to the domestic political strategies of the president.

The rationale originally given for the use of executive agreements was the complexity of U.S. relations with the rest of the world. Complexity often provides the fundamental incentive for delegation in principal-agent settings, and there is no reason to rule it out as an explanation here. While most authors acknowledge that complexity is an important motivation for executive agreements, the implications of this insight for understanding patterns in their use have not been explored.

The literature on agency problems and the solution of informational dilemmas may provide some leverage. For example, this literature suggests that delegation is most effective when the agent has preferences similar to those of the principal. If true, we should see extensive use of executive agreements on those issues on which a consensus on basic policy has been reached. For example, after the debate about Spanish bases was settled with the 1975 treaty, and Spain became a more attractive alliance partner in the post-Franco era, Congress explicitly gave the president the authority to conclude executive agreements relating to military bases in Spain pursuant to the treaty. More controversial issues, on the other hand, should be those dealt with by more formal ratification procedures.

Some preliminary evidence in support of the complexity explanation comes from a simple examination of the number of executive agreements used over time. Prior to the twentieth century, U.S. engagement with the rest of the world was minimal, and the number of international agreements negotiated reflected that. In contrast, after World War II the frequency and complexity of U.S. international relations increased suddenly. If this rapid increase in interactions with other countries had been dealt with solely through treaties, the sheer difficulty of getting them all through the cumbersome ratification process would have brought the Senate machinery to a halt and put a straitjacket on the United States' ability to play the active role in the world it has played ever since. Not surprisingly, this upsurge in international engagement is reflected in an increased use of executive agreements. While it is possible for such a movement to limit legislative influence on foreign policy, models of delegation show that delegation for reasons of complexity can preserve legislative influence (Krehbiel 1991). Delegation is not equivalent to abdication.

A complementary perspective could consider how the use of executive agreements is related to the general problem of making credible commitments in foreign policy. Models of credible commitment are now being applied to foreign policy in democracies (Schultz and Weingast 1994). The major drawback of an executive agreement is that the commitment inherent in it is, ceteris paribus, not as credible as one that has been ratified in a treaty. The reasons lie in two analytically distinct, although practically intertwined, considerations: signaling and commitment.

Signaling considerations refer to the information that actors send one another about their preferences and intentions. A state concluding an international agreement with the United States requires information that will allow it to assess the probability that the agreement has received widespread consent and that the U.S. government intends to abide by it. More open, formal ratification mechanisms, particularly those that involve a vote in the legislature, send more information about the preferences and intentions of those who will be responsible for implementing the agreement. A president who chooses to use the executive agreement mechanism for a potentially controversial agreement may be sending precisely the wrong signal, telling other states that there is not much support for the agreement in the legislature. Such a signal would raise legitimate doubts about the credibility of the U.S. commitment expressed in the agreement.

In contrast to signaling, considerations of commitment need not rely on the assumption of uncertainty about preferences. Commitment mechanisms allow actors to bind themselves to a particular course of action, even one that all parties involved know will be difficult to sustain when the time comes. Ulysses binding himself to the mast, or Schelling's teenage driver throwing his steering wheel out of the window during a game of chicken, exemplify commitment mechanisms that do not rely on a signaling logic. In both, there is little doubt about preferences. The problem instead is time inconsistency, where actors know that they will not be able to live up to desirable courses of action in the future unless they take some drastic action today.

Choosing to undergo the rigors of a treaty ratification process can serve as a commitment mechanism as well as a signaling device. Gaining ratification of a treaty is a course that is not lightly reversed in the future, even by a new executive. Systems like that in the United States, with multiple veto points, induce a status quo bias. Once put in place, policies are difficult to change. This is certainly the case with treaties. Once senators have gone on record by ratifying a treaty, they will be more reluctant to allow a president to abrogate it than if they had not gone through the ratification process. Part of the logic of commitment lies simply in the complexity of the legislative process. Another dimension lies in audience costs, the notion that an actor that has publicly approved an agreement will suffer costs to its reputation for backing down from that commitment unless circumstances have changed substantially.

Whether treaties serve as signaling devices, commitment mechanisms, or both, there is good reason to expect that they are more credible indicators of future U.S. behavior than simple executive agreements are. While gaining treaty ratification is certainly more difficult than simply signing an agreement, the costs of ratification will result in more credible commitments. While credibility may not be an overriding issue in all international interactions (such as one-shot assistance deals or actions that are entirely noncontroversial), it is extremely important in most long-term interactions and provides a justification for forgoing the easier executive agreement path in such circumstances. The credibility of commitments, as well as the complexity of international relations, provide potential explanations for variation in the use of ratification procedures that are consistent with current understandings of legislative influence.

Testing the Evasion Hypothesis

Since indirect legislative influence is, by definition, difficult to observe directly, we must look for other methods to sort out the logic behind the use of executive agreements. Simply noting congressional oversight activity, or pointing to cases in which the president has taken actions not explicitly authorized by Congress, cannot settle this debate. Instead, we need to turn to aggregate evidence on patterns in the use of executive agreements and treaties.

If the evasion hypothesis is correct, it has clear implications for the frequency with which executive agreements are used. If their intent is to circumvent Congress, we should see them used most frequently when the president is confronted with a Congress with preferences different from his own. When the Senate tends to agree with the president's foreign policies, there will be a reduced need to use the escape route provided by executive agreements. Instead, we should see a shift to the use of treaties when the Senate is in agreement with the president's foreign policies.

To test this hypothesis, I begin by considering the percentage of executive agreements as a function of party control of the Senate and presidency. When the Senate is controlled by the same party as the presidency, we can assume that it generally has preferences closer to those of the president than when it is controlled by the opposition party. Even if there is some divergence in foreign policy preferences within the party, the constraints of party membership provide the president with a source of support within Congress under unified government (Cox and McCubbins 1993). Margolis (1986) finds evidence that the use of executive agreements increases under divided government and argues that this is convincing support for the evasion hypothesis. However, his tests are only bivariate, do not control for time trends, and do not consider problems of statistical significance. The following models correct for these flaws. They use data from the Congressional Research Service (1993, 14) on agreements between 1930 and 1992.

Margolis (1986, 45–47) argues that the best indicator for the evasion hypothesis is the percentage of all international agreements that are negotiated as executive agreements in each year. Table 1 shows a model of the percentage of all agreements as executive agreements that tests for the effects of divided government and different points in the electoral cycle.

The key independent variable is SENNUMB, the number of senators from the president's party. If the evasion hypothesis is correct, we should see decreasing use of executive agreements when SENNUMB increases, since there will be a reduced need to circumvent the Senate under these conditions. Therefore, SENNUMB should have a negative coefficient.

I also include a dummy, FIRSTYR. This variable takes on the value one when the president is in his first year of office. A new president, learning how to deal with a new Congress, might be expected to rely more heavily on the use of executive agreements than one who, through experience, has learned the ropes in Washington. The third independent variable, ELECT, is a dummy for election years. Those who see executive agreements as an evasive device have also argued that presidents will use a higher percentage of executive agreements in election years (King and Ragsdale 1988, 115). The rationale is that since executive agreements provide autonomy they are particularly useful tools for presidents engaged in an election campaign. Therefore, the evasion hypothesis suggests that ELECT should have a positive coefficient. The data on treaties and, especially, executive agreements show strong time-series effects. To control for these, the following models have been estimated with two parameters for autoregression and model the first difference effects in the dependent variable.

The results in table 1 appear to be quite encouraging for the evasion hypothesis. I use a one-tailed *t*-test as a measure of statistical significance, since we have strong priors about the direction of effects. As predicted, an increase in the number of senators from the president's party leads to a significant decrease in the percentage of executive agreements concluded. In addition, we see a significant increase in the percentage of executive agreements negotiated in election years. These results suggest that the president turns to the use of executive agreements in order to avoid partisan opposition in the Senate and to provide room for foreign policy accomplishments during election years.

One potential objection to this preliminary model as a test of the evasion hypothesis is that the number of senators from the president's party is an extremely crude measure of support. Party unity varies over time, so that party membership may often a poor indicator of willingness to support the president. For much of this period, the Democratic Party was split into its northern liberal wing and a more conservative southern wing, suggesting that, for Democrats in particular, party membership is not a good measure of support. In addition, if the parties are internally split on foreign policy issues, we should find alternative measures of support for the president.

TABLE 1. Percentage of International Agreements as Executive Agreements, 1930–92

Variable	Estimated Coefficient	Standard Error	*t*-Statistic
SENNUMB*	−0.003	0.0018	−1.693
FIRSTYR	0.0162	0.0288	0.564
ELECT*	0.0385	0.0227	1.698
AR1*	−0.461	0.134	−3.438
AR2	−0.16	0.132	−1.214
Constant	0.0077	0.0082	0.941

Number of observations	63
Standard error	0.103
Log likelihood	55.61

One measure of support comes from analysis of patterns of congressional voting. A common measure of congressional support is the number of congressional votes supporting the president divided by the total number of votes on which the president took a position. *Congressional Quarterly* collects these data (Stanley and Niemi 1994, 276–77), and in table 2 I include them in the model as the variable SUPPORT. Because support data are only available beginning in 1953, the following models are limited to the period 1953–92.

This model suggests that SUPPORT does predict presidential choices better than a measure of party membership did. We find a significant negative coefficient on SUPPORT, which is consistent with the evasion hypothesis. When congressional support for the president increases, he less frequently turns to executive agreements. However, the effect of SENNUMB disappears, suggesting that SUPPORT is picking up the relevant variation in congressional support. In the following models, to avoid problems of multicollinearity, I include only SUPPORT, dropping SENNUMB.

This alternative specification of congressional support also shows an interesting change in the effects of the election cycle. Now, the effect of election years has disappeared. Instead, we find that the president tends to negotiate a larger percentage of executive agreements during his first year. This is an effect not predicted by the evasion hypothesis. It suggests that regular fluctuations in support for the president during the electoral cycle produced a spurious positive result in the former model. The increase in use of executive agreements during election years seems to have been caused by fluctuations in congressional support during these years. Once we control for support, we do not find the president turning to executive agreements as an electoral device.

While congressional support for the president seems to have a statistically

TABLE 2.   Percentage of International Agreements as Executive Agreements, 1953–92

Variable	Estimated Coefficient	Standard Error	t-Statistic
SENNUMB	0.0005	0.0004	1.174
FIRSTYR*	0.0241	0.0076	3.172
ELECT	0.0002	0.0055	0.0363
SUPPORT*	−0.0974	0.0434	−2.242
AR1*	−0.8883	0.1642	−5.409
AR2*	−0.3865	0.1608	−2.403
Constant	−0.0002	0.0015	−0.1154

Number of observations	40
Standard error	0.020
Log likelihood	100.3

significant effect on the percentage of executive agreements used, we also need to ask about the substantive significance of this result. A contrast between the years 1959 and 1965 provides an illuminating perspective. In 1959, Eisenhower received the lowest support score in this data set, 52.9 percent. In 1965, Johnson received one of the highest support scores, 93.1 percent. We should therefore expect to see a dramatic difference in the percentage of executive agreements used in these two years, according to the evasion hypothesis.

In fact, however, the predicted percentages for these two years are not very far apart. The model predicts that in 1959 Eisenhower would have negotiated 96.1 percent of total agreements as executive agreements, while in contrast Johnson would have negotiated 94.4 percent as executive agreements.[3] This difference, of less than two percentage points, is disappointing evidence for the evasion perspective. A dramatic shift in levels of congressional support gives rise to only a minor shift in the use of executive agreements. These results imply that while presidents predictably attempt to use executive agreements to evade congressional opposition, their ability to do so effectively is quite constrained.

These results necessitate a reevaluation of the evasion hypothesis. The predicted effect on electoral behavior does not appear once we control for levels of congressional support. And, while congressional support does have a regular effect, leading to a shift toward the use of a higher percentage of executive agreements, the size of this effect is small. It seems appropriate to further disaggregate these results to determine whether some other framework for analysis provides more leverage than the imperial presidency approach.

The percentage of executive agreements negotiated may not, in fact, be the best indicator of executive behavior. Changes in percentages can result from a number of underlying trends, obscuring the real influences at work. The evasion hypothesis offers a clear prediction about the causes of change in these percentages. It predicts that a president attempting to evade congressional restraints would both increase his use of executive agreements and decrease his use of treaties, since executive agreements effectively substitute for treaties. Both effects would lead to an increase in the percentage of executive agreements. However, testing these separate predictions about the *number* of treaties and executive agreements may provide a more sensitive test of alternative theories.

Tables 3 and 4 present estimations of the effects of congressional support and the electoral cycle on executive agreements and treaties, respectively. Table 3, examining the number of executive agreements, shows no statistically significant effects whatsoever. While we find a large negative coefficient on SUPPORT, the standard error of this coefficient is very large, so that the effect of congressional support cannot reliably be distinguished from zero. Similarly, we find the predicted positive coefficient on ELECT, but it is not statistically sig-

TABLE 3.   Executive Agreements, 1953–92

Variable	Estimated Coefficient	Standard Error	t-Statistic
SUPPORT	−61.94	98.95	−0.0361
FIRSTYR	−13.49	14.79	−0.912
ELECT	10.05	12.52	0.803
AR1	−0.0062	0.172	−0.0361
AR2	−0.164	0.186	−0.882
Constant	2.385	7.149	0.333

Number of observations	40
Standard error	51.46
Log likelihood	−206.1

nificant. These results are a challenge to the evasion hypothesis. It does not appear that an increase in the percentage of executive agreements negotiated when congressional support is low results from an increased number of executive agreements, as predicted.

Turning to the evaluation of treaties in table 4, we find a potential solution to the puzzle of how to account for changes in the percentage of executive agreements. This table shows that we find a significant increase in the number of treaties negotiated when levels of congressional support are high. We also see a decrease in the number of treaties negotiated during a president's first year in office. To gain a sense of the magnitude of the congressional support effect, compare the years 1959 and 1965. In 1959, Eisenhower's low level of congressional support leads to a predicted 7.7 treaties being negotiated. In contrast,

TABLE 4.   Treaties, 1953–92

Variable	Estimated Coefficient	Standard Error	t-Statistic
SUPPORT*	18.76	8.426	2.227
FIRSTYR*	−7.093	1.804	−3.931
ELECT	1.181	1.426	0.829
AR1*	−0.8322	0.1629	−5.11
AR2	−0.303	0.1636	−1.85
Constant	0.1557	0.3998	0.3895

Number of observations	40
Standard error	5.14
Log likelihood	−116.5

the model predicts that Johnson would negotiate 14.9 treaties in 1965, more than double the number predicted for Eisenhower.[4] This is a sizable effect, suggesting that the president finds it quite difficult to conclude treaties when he lacks overall congressional support. The increased percentage of executive agreements used when congressional support is low appears to result not from a regular increase in the use of executive agreements but from a reduced ability to conclude treaties. This decrease does not reliably show up as a shift to using more executive agreements, contrary to the evasion hypothesis.

Because the number of treaties negotiated each year is fairly small, ordinary least squares (OLS) may not provide a good statistical model for this dependent variable. To check for this possibility, table 5 illustrates a Poisson model of the number of treaties. A generalized event count model showed no evidence of overdispersion, so that a negative binomial model is not required. The variable YEAR is included to control for some time-series effects. The results are consistent with those found in the OLS model: an increased use of treaties when congressional support is high and fewer treaties concluded during presidents' first year in office.

What do these results suggest about alternative frameworks for understanding institutional choice? While the initial results appeared consistent with the evasion hypothesis, deeper probing makes a credibility story appear more persuasive. While we see an increased percentage of agreements being negotiated as executive agreements when congressional support is low, the size of this effect is small. We find no evidence of increased use of executive agreements during election years once we properly control for congressional support. The significant effect is not increased use of executive agreements but diminished ability to conclude treaties when congressional support is low. The effect contradicts the imperial presidency argument. The president's ability to conclude treaties depends heavily on his level of support in Congress, and he is not able to substitute executive agreements for treaties, at least not robustly.

TABLE 5.   Treaties, 1953–92, Poisson Regression

Variable	Estimated Coefficient	Robust Standard Error	*t*-Statistic
SUPPORT*	1.162	0.4548	2.555
FIRSTYR*	−0.4048	0.1539	−2.63
ELECT	0.0483	0.1149	0.4204
YEAR*	0.0206	0.0056	3.679
Constant	−38.8	11.22	3.458
Number of observations	40		
Log likelihood	1009.6		

The results are, instead, entirely consistent with credibility arguments. When congressional support is low, the president finds it more difficult to conclude treaties, as other nations question his ability to get them ratified back home. However, the inconclusive results on the number of executive agreements suggest that other states are not generally willing to accept executive agreements in place of treaties. As the credibility framework suggests, institutional maneuvers designed solely to evade congressional intent are not effective.

Further evidence in support of the credibility argument comes from considering other mechanisms that might establish credibility in international negotiations. Ratification is only one factor that lends credibility to a commitment. If commitment has been established through another mechanism, or if it is not an issue for some other reason, then we may see less pressure to negotiate a formal treaty.

Consideration of the credibility problem suggests that the use of executive agreements and treaties should vary across the type of issue. Where other mechanisms exist to establish commitment, we should see relatively frequent use of executive agreements. Political observers have often noted that military commitments, in particular, are made credible through mechanisms other than ratification. Overseas bases are established; joint planning and military maneuvers take place; extensive military assistance programs are put in place. All of these should tie the hands of the United States more surely than any ratification procedure would. Therefore, we should expect to see more extensive use of executive agreements on military matters than on those in which such alternative commitment mechanisms are hard to identify.

Margolis (1986) collects data on the type of agreements negotiated from 1943 to 1977, providing a preliminary assessment of the use of different types of agreements on different issues. He divides international agreements into three types: goods (economic agreements), military, and procedural. Figure 2 shows the percentage of each type of agreement that takes the form of an executive agreement. We should, if the credibility perspective is correct, expect to see a relatively high percentage of executive agreements on military issues. Procedural issues, on the other hand, may be those in which commitment mechanisms are difficult to identify, so we should see a low percentage of executive agreements here. Figure 2 supports this expectation, with procedural agreements consistently having a higher percentage of treaties than those on military issues or on goods. In this period, 90 percent of procedural agreements were executive agreements, compared with 97 percent of military and virtually 100 percent of economic agreements.

One type of military agreement, however, does not have built-in commitment mechanisms: those on arms control. Arms control agreements are difficult to monitor effectively. In addition, undetected cheating on an arms control agreement could have devastating consequences, so credibility is an important

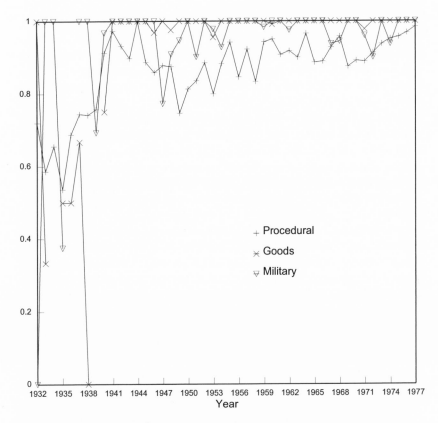

Fig. 2. Executive agreements as a percentage of all agreements, by type. Gaps in lines represent years in which there were no agreements of this type. (Data from Margolis 1986, 106–7.)

issue. Given these considerations, we should expect that arms control agreements should more often take the form of treaties than do other military agreements. And this is precisely what the CRS (1993, xxx, 203) has found.

Students of divided government have looked at ratification of treaties as one of the primary indicators of its impact (Fiorina 1992). We might expect that such evidence would be relevant to the evasion hypothesis. However, consideration of the president's ability to anticipate congressional action suggests that Senate rejection of treaties will not be a good indicator. If the president anticipates that a treaty will be rejected, he often simply refuses to submit it to Congress. If a controversial treaty is submitted, Senate leaders will usually prevent it from coming to a vote rather than subjecting the president to the embarrassment associated with a formal rejection, which is a severe blow to U.S. credibility. The occasions on which the Senate has actually rejected a treaty are few, although they include dramatic examples such as the rejection of the Versailles Treaty (Nelson 1989, 1101). These strategic considerations suggest that there is little reason to expect that evidence on the formal rejection of treaties under divided government will be very enlightening. In fact, Fiorina (1992) finds no effect of divided government.

Our inability to use evidence of failed ratification to test the effects of divided government is a specific example of the general problem of selection effects in data like these. Because sophisticated political actors anticipate the outcome of ratification processes, looking at the number of agreements rejected is a poor indicator. Instead, we can examine the number of agreements actually concluded, as this essay does. The credibility hypothesis recognizes that these numbers are the result of sophisticated political action and so show selection effects. When deciding whether to turn to an executive agreement to evade congressional opposition to a treaty, the president and other states will consider whether such an agreement will, in fact, provide a credible commitment. Often it will not, and so no agreement at all is concluded. Thus, we end up with the observed pattern: decreased use of treaties in the face of congressional opposition, but no corresponding increase in the number of executive agreements.

The statistical patterns found here show stronger evidence for considerations of credibility than for the evasion hypothesis. When we look at the percentage of all agreements negotiated as executive agreements, we initially seem to find support for the evasion hypothesis. It does appear that as congressional support for the president goes up he less frequently turns to the executive agreement mechanism. However, the size of this effect is small, with even large movements in congressional support leading to only a couple of percentage point shifts in the use of executive agreements. This effect appears to be the result of a decreased ability to conclude treaties rather than increased use of executive agreements. We can conclude that, while the president is occasionally tempted to use executive agreements as an evasive device, his ability to do so is tightly constrained by considerations of credibility necessitated by the international strategic environment.

Constraining the Executive: Congressional Mechanisms

Empirically, the hypothesis that executive agreements provide the president with an efficient means of evading congressional opposition does not find much support. While there are reasons to suspect that the president attempts to use executive agreements in this manner, the extent to which he is able to do so is limited. Earlier, I suggested two related sets of constraints. The first lies in the mechanisms that Congress maintains to exercise influence on agreements other than treaties. The second lies in the fact that negotiating partners can appreciate these constraints and by anticipating them will be reluctant to make commitments to executive agreements that are intended solely to circumvent Congress. In this section, I examine congressional oversight of executive actions. Such oversight is a necessary condition for indirect mechanisms of congressional influence to have any effect. If they do, strategic presidents should strategize vis-à-vis other states as well as Congress, leading to patterns of use of various procedural instruments different from those predicted by the evasion hypothesis.

Congressional concern about the use of executive agreements has led to two concentrated efforts to reform the system. The first, in the 1950s, led to near passage of a constitutional amendment that would have severely restricted the president's ability to negotiate executive agreements. The second, in the 1970s, was more modest in its ambitions but ultimately more successful in establishing a clear and formalized role for Congress.

The two major attempts to reform procedures could hardly have come from more different ideological backgrounds. The first, led by Senator John W. Bricker (R-Ohio), was grounded in conservative political principles, especially the isolationist variety of conservatism. It was motivated by fears that U.S. commitments to multilateral institutions would override traditional visions of states' rights. The 1970s reforms were part of a more general revolt against the "imperial presidency." They were led by liberals, especially those who opposed U.S. involvement in Vietnam. The Brickerites were protesting the actions of a fellow Republican president, Eisenhower, and the debate tended to split each party between its isolationist and internationalist wings. The 1970s debate split somewhat more along party lines, although its major emphasis was on the powers of the legislative versus the executive branch of government. It therefore involved both houses of Congress, while the 1950s debate took place solely in the Senate.

The Bricker revolt aimed to put strict limitations on presidential authority to reach international agreements. It also sought to minimize the effects of such agreements on domestic law, especially the prerogatives of the individual states.[5] The main focus of concern was that U.S. participation in the United Nations would increase presidential control of policy at the expense of the states. The debate became framed as one of human rights versus states' rights, as fears were expressed that the UN's Genocide Convention and other human rights agreements would severely curtail the autonomy of states. In response to such concerns, in 1951 Bricker began efforts to limit the president's ability to commit the United States to multilateral organizations. His proposed amendment would have specified issues on which the United States was not allowed to enter into international agreements, particularly issues involving individual rights. It also prevented delegation of any legislative, executive, or judicial powers to any international organization or foreign country. It sought to prevent the president from substituting executive agreements for treaties and would have required all executive agreements to be publicized and in effect for only a limited period.

By 1953, the Senate Committee on the Judiciary began holding hearings. The Eisenhower administration first tried to sink the amendment while avoiding open confrontation, but eventually it pulled out all stops in an attempt to fend off Bricker's challenges to its authority. According to Tananbaum (1988), this effort represented one of Eisenhower's most effective uses of the "hidden-hand presidency." After the Judiciary Committee reported an amendment that would have put severe constraints on the executive favorably to the floor, the president put his support behind an alternative, weaker amendment introduced by Senator William F. Knowland (R-Calif.), the majority leader. The Knowland amendment was significantly weaker than the Bricker, merely making explicit already existing conditions, for example, that treaties that conflict with the Constitution would have no force.

By the time floor debate began on the Bricker amendment in 1954, it appeared that Bricker had gained enough support to get his amendment through Congress. Eisenhower moved to open confrontation now, for example, putting an open letter in the *Congressional Record* stating that he was "unalterably" opposed to the Bricker amendment. After much maneuvering, introduction of amendments, and administration lobbying, the Bricker amendment was defeated by a vote of 42 to 50 on February 25, 1954. However, this was not the end of the story. The Bricker forces regrouped and threw their weight behind a slightly weaker amendment introduced by Senator Walter George (D-Ga.). This amendment focused less on states' rights, but required that Congress explicitly approve all executive agreements. Since this was a proposed constitutional amendment, it would have required 61 votes (two-thirds of those senators present at the time) for passage. In the end, the administration managed to find the single necessary defector, and the amendment was defeated by a vote of 60 to 31. While similar amendments were on occasion introduced in later years, none went very far.

By the 1970s, concern about the use of executive agreements resurfaced as part of a general concern about the aggrandizement of executive power. However, this time reform attempts concentrated on gaining information from the executive rather than changing voting procedures. They were more successful. This pattern of success and failure may tell us something about congressional incentives and influence and the logic behind the use of executive agreements. As argued, Congress has a number of mechanisms by which to influence agreements besides formal ratification power. However, none of these mechanisms will be very effective if the administration can successfully keep agreements secret from Congress. Much information about agreements comes through leaks and other nonofficial channels, as is predicted by a "fire-alarm" understanding of congressional oversight (McCubbins and Schwartz 1984). However, to supplement these sources of information, in 1972 Congress passed the Case Act requiring the State Department to notify Congress of all executive agreements within 60 days of their entry into force.[6]

This second round of attempts to revise the usage of executive agreements began in 1969, when Senator Stuart Symington (D-Mo.) began an investigation of U.S. international agreements in the Foreign Relations Committee. This investigation was stimulated by U.S. involvement in Vietnam and general military commitments in Southeast Asia (Stevens 1977). The hearings of the Symington subcommittee (formally known as the Subcommittee on U.S. Security Agreements and Commitments Abroad) uncovered information about previously unknown executive military commitments. These findings led Congress to pass the National Commitments Resolution, which reaffirmed that commitments to other nations should require affirmative action by both the executive and legislative branches (Nincic 1992, 87–88). However, this resolution was not binding, and it did not appear to have much impact on executive behavior.

Senator Clifford Case (R-N.J.) introduced legislation in 1970 to require notification within sixty days of any international agreement not submitted to the Senate as a treaty. This bill became law in 1972. Classified as well as unclassified agreements are transmitted, although through a different procedure designed to assure their secrecy. It took a number of years for the provisions of the Case Act to be implemented effectively, but consistent oversight by Sen. Case and a series of amendments led to what appears to be a more consistent flow of information about executive agreements to Congress. One initial problem came more from lack of cooperation among executive agencies than outright executive noncompliance. The State Department apparently complied immediately. But many international agreements are negotiated by agencies other than State, and State did not have information about these agreements to transmit to Congress. A system was set up within a few years to require agencies to send their information to the State Department. State appeared to cooperate quite enthusiastically in this endeavor, as it enhanced its role as the central actor coordinating U.S. activities overseas. While there have been a series of investigations that have turned up some failures to notify Congress about agreements, these investigations appear to have had the intended effect of increasing compliance with the Case Act (CRS 1993, 185).

What impact has the Case Act had? The evasion hypothesis would lead us to expect that it would have a negative impact on the use of executive agreements. If such agreements are intended to circumvent Congress, being forced to make them public should curtail their use. However, I see no evidence of this in the numbers of executive agreements concluded, as is shown in figure 1. In fact, beginning in 1976, at about the time the Case Act gained effectiveness, we see what appears to be a large jump in the number of executive agreements used. We probably should not make too much of this increase, since it may have resulted in part from improved counting procedures, with more international commitments being considered executive agreements as a result of Case Act procedures. However, there is no sign that the president is now less willing to use executive agreements than he was prior to 1972. This pattern suggests that the logic of such agreements throughout the entire period rests on much more than attempts to circumvent congressional oversight.

What does this brief legislative history suggest about the logic of executive agreements and the powers of Congress? It provides some support for the "struggle for power" perspective, and it is clear that at times the executive branch has attempted to evade congressional oversight by using executive agreements. However, it also suggests that Congress has mechanisms to discover such uses and has now institutionalized a procedure to facilitate the flow of information about international commitments. This information provides Congress with the means to create more indirect mechanisms of influence, such as denying appropriations or taking legislative action to overturn commitments, effective. Anticipating such actions, the president is likely to be more sensitive to congressional concerns in negotiating agreements with other countries (Stevens 1977, 929). In fact, we do see increasing provisions for consultation with members of Congress during important international negotiations (CRS 1993, 201). In spite of congressional action and oversight, the use of executive agreements continues at high levels. Therefore, we should consider alternative explanations for their use such as the complexity and credibility frameworks suggested in this essay.

Conclusion

Ratification mechanisms are one of the key domestic institutional variables that could affect international commitments. Most foreign policy literature argues for the dominance of the executive branch. From this perspective, a strategic executive uses informal ratification procedures to avoid legislative constraints. However, modern understandings of legislative influence suggest that the evasion hypothesis may be mistaken. The legislature maintains numerous mechanisms to influence international agreements, particularly during their implementation, and so it is not as easily circumvented as the image of an imperial presidency implies. Therefore, executive agreements used as evasive devices can cast serious doubt on the credibility of international commitments.

The evidence presented in this essay generates little support for an evasion perspective. Shifts in the use of executive agreements and treaties seem to be accounted for by a reduced ability to conclude treaties when congressional support is low. The evasion hypothesis expects any reduced ability to conclude treaties to lead to increased use of executive agreements, but we do not find this in the data. If we reject the evasion hypothesis, the question arises of alternative explanations for the use of executive agreements. I suggest two. The first is the demands of complexity. This perspective is consistent with the increased use of executive agreements as the United States has become more actively involved in international affairs. The second is the need to make credible commitments. Reduced use of treaties in the face of congressional opposition, and the inability to substitute executive agreements for these treaties, are consistent with a credibility framework.

Overall, the evidence and logic presented here drive home the need for an integrated approach to understanding international negotiations and cooperation. A purely systemic approach is inadequate; domestic factors have predictable, measurable effects. But we cannot simply return to traditional foreign policy analysis, neglecting what we know about the international strategic demands put on states. Instead, we need to develop an understanding of how domestic politics interacts with these demands. Considerations of credibility provide one lens through which to begin developing such an understanding.

NOTES

My thanks for comments and suggestions go to John Conybeare, Steph Haggard, Bob Keohane, and participants in this project.

1. Agreements that have been reached on sole executive authority, not pursuant to legislation or otherwise involving the legislature, may not in fact have the same legal standing as treaties. See Congressional Research Service (CRS) 1993, xvii.

2. Figures are from CRS 1993, 14. The CRS obtained these data from the Office of the Assistant Legal Adviser for Treaty Affairs in the Department of State. Figures do not include classified agreements, and the criteria for reporting an international understanding as an executive agreement occasionally change. For example, the decrease in the number of executive agreements in 1991 and 1992 resulted from a change in reporting rules. In 1990, the State Department decided to discontinue reporting agricultural assistance agreements under Public Law 480 as executive agreements (CRS 1993, xxxvii).

3. In practice, in 1959 the measure of executive agreements was 95.4 percent, while in 1965 it was 93.6 percent. While somewhat off scale, the difference between these two years is the same size as is predicted by the model.

4. The actual numbers of treaties concluded were 12 in 1959 and 14 in 1965.

5. The following discussion of the Bricker amendment is drawn largely from Johnson 1984 and Tananbaum 1988.

6. For a discussion of the background and effects of the Case Act, see CRS 1993, 169–202.

REFERENCES

Atwood, J. Brian. 1981. Downtown Perspective: Lessons on Liaison with Congress. In *The Tethered Presidency,* edited by Thomas M. Franck. New York: New York University Press.

Borchard, Edwin M. 1946. Treaties and Executive Agreements. *American Political Science Review* 40, no. 4 (August): 729–39.

Calvert, Randall L., Mathew D. McCubbins, and Barry R. Weingast. 1989. A Theory of Political Control and Agency Discretion. *American Journal of Political Science* 33:588–611.

Cox, Gary, and Mathew McCubbins. 1993. *Legislative Leviathan: Party Government in the House.* Berkeley: University of California Press.

Crabb, Cecil V., Jr., and Pat M. Holt. 1992. *Invitation to Struggle: Congress, the President, and Foreign Policy.* Washington, DC: Congressional Quarterly Press.

CRS [Congressional Research Service]. 1993. *Treaties and Other International Agreements: The Role of the United States Senate.* Washington, DC: Government Printing Office.

Evans, Peter B., Harold K. Jacobson, and Robert D. Putnam. 1993. *Double-Edged Diplomacy: International Bargaining and Domestic Politics.* Berkeley: University of California Press.

Fiorina, Morris P. 1992. *Divided Government.* New York: Macmillan.

Haggard, Stephan. 1988. The Institutional Foundations of Hegemony. *International Organization* 42 (Winter): 91–119.

Johnson, Loch K. 1984. *The Making of International Agreements: Congress Confronts the Executive.* New York: New York University Press.

Kaiser, K. 1971. Transnational Relations as a Threat to the Democratic Process. *International Organization* 25:706–20.

Katzenstein, Peter J. 1978. *Between Power and Plenty: Foreign Economic Policies of Advanced Industrial States.* Madison: University of Wisconsin Press.

Kiewiet, D. Roderick, and Mathew D. McCubbins. 1991. *The Logic of Delegation: Congressional Parties and the Appropriations Process.* Chicago: University of Chicago Press.

King, Gary, and Lyn Ragsdale. 1988. *The Elusive Executive: Discovering Statistical Patterns in the Presidency.* Washington, DC: Congressional Quarterly Press.

Krehbiel, Keith. 1991. *Information and Legislative Organization.* Ann Arbor: University of Michigan Press.

Lohmann, Susanne, and Sharyn O'Halloran. 1994. Divided Government and U.S. Trade Policy: Theory and Evidence. *International Organization* 48, no. 4 (Autumn): 595–632.

Margolis, Lawrence. 1986. *Executive Agreements and Presidential Power in Foreign Policy.* New York: Praeger.

Martin, Lisa L. 1994. The Influence of National Parliaments on European Integration. Working Papers, no. 94–10. Center for International Affairs, Harvard University.

McCubbins, Mathew D., and Thomas Schwartz. 1984. Congressional Oversight Overlooked: Police Patrols versus Fire Alarms. *American Journal of Political Science* 28 (February): 165–79.

McGillivray, Fiona. 1997. How Voters Shape the Institutional Framework of International Negotiations. This volume.

Millett, Stephen M. 1990. *The Constitutionality of Executive Agreements: An Analysis of United States v. Belmont.* New York: Grand.

Moravcsik, Andrew. 1994. Why the European Community Strengthens the State. Paper presented at the annual meeting of the American Political Science Association, New York, September.

Nathan, James A., and James K. Oliver. 1994. *Foreign Policy Making and the American Political System.* 3d ed. Baltimore: Johns Hopkins University Press.

Nelson, Michael, ed. 1989. *Congressional Quarterly's Guide to the Presidency.* Washington, DC: Congressional Quarterly Press.

Nincic, Miroslav. 1992. *Democracy and Foreign Policy: The Fallacy of Political Realism.* New York: Columbia University Press.

O'Halloran, Sharyn. 1994. *Politics, Process, and American Trade Policy.* Ann Arbor: University of Michigan Press.

Paige, Joseph. 1977. *The Law Nobody Knows: Enlargement of the Constitution—Treaties and Executive Agreements.* New York: Vantage.

Peterson, Paul E. 1994. The President's Dominance in Foreign Policy Making. *Political Science Quarterly* 109, no. 2: 215–34.

Pyle, Christopher H., and Richard M. Pious. 1984. *The President, Congress, and the Constitution: Power and Legitimacy in American Politics.* New York: Free Press.

Putnam, Robert D. 1988. Diplomacy and Domestic Politics: The Logic of Two-Level Games. *International Organization* 42, no. 3 (Summer): 427–60.

Schultz, Kenneth A., and Barry R. Weingast. 1994. The Democratic Advantage: The Institutional Sources of State Power in International Competition. Presented at the annual meeting of the American Political Science Association, New York, September.

Stanley, Harold W., and Richard G. Niemi. 1994. *Vital Statistics on American Politics.* 4th ed. Washington, DC: Congressional Quarterly Press.

Stevens, Charles J. 1977. The Use and Control of Executive Agreements: Recent Congressional Initiatives. *Orbis* 20, no. 4 (Winter): 905–31.

Tananbaum, Duane. 1988. *The Bricker Amendment Controversy: A Test of Eisenhower's Political Leadership.* Ithaca: Cornell University Press.

Vaubel, Roland. 1986. A Public Choice Approach to International Organization. *Public Choice* 51:39–57.

Weingast, Barry R., and Mark J. Moran. 1983. Bureaucratic Discretion or Congressional Control? Regulatory Policymaking by the Federal Trade Commission. *Journal of Political Economy* 91: 765–800.

How Voters Shape the Institutional Framework of International Negotiations

Fiona McGillivray

This essay explores the strategic linkages between domestic politics and international negotiations. Rather than focus on the negotiation process, it explores how governments choose the "rules of the game" used to structure negotiations.[1] Before the bargaining begins, political leaders choose the institutional framework for interstate negotiations. Among the questions they consider are: will the negotiations be public or private, when is the "best" time for the negotiations, will the final agreement be ratified in the legislature, and where will the negotiations be held?

The French and U.S. governments made a number of such choices during the 1986–94 Uruguay round of the General Agreement on Tariffs and Trade (GATT) negotiations. For example, the French chose to make public the nature of their demands during ongoing talks on agricultural subsidies with the United States. The United States, however, chose to give these negotiations a low public profile. They frequently denied negotiations on agriculture were taking place, only to unveil agreements during the last stages of the GATT round.[2] This issue was politically sensitive in both countries; why did one country prefer an open negotiation process and the other a closed one?

Another choice the French government faced was the type of settlement format to use for the final agreement. In the United States, GATT agreements negotiated by the executive must, by law, be approved by the legislature. In France, GATT treaties are, by convention, executive agreements. However, on December 2, 1994, French prime minister Edouard Balladur demanded that the GATT trade deal be completed by the sixth, so he could ratify the final draft before the French National Assembly. Because the agreement was not yet an international treaty, the National Assembly could only vote on the draft as a matter of general policy. To get a legislative agreement, Balladur had to tie the vote to a motion of confidence in the government.[3] The National Assembly had never voted on any part of GATT negotiations since France joined the GATT in 1947. Why did the parliamentary leader change the settlement format from an executive to a legislative agreement?

In part, the answers to these questions depend on the details of the situation. However, when the motivation for these choices is strategic, more general arguments can be developed. This essay builds on recent work examining how the strategic choice of institutional framework affects the content and credibility of international agreements (Chayes and Chayes 1993; Lipson 1991; Martin 1995; Pahre 1995). Much of this work focuses on the U.S. president's attempts to use institutional constraints to increase his bargaining leverage and make international agreements more credible.[4] Taking a comparative perspective, I model the choices made by a parliamentary government with strong parties. Instead of assuming that governments seek to increase their bargaining leverage and the credibility of the agreement, I model how the "rules of the game" affect the saliency of issues and the information revealed to voters about party policy and party unity on these issues. The government chooses the settlement format and negotiation process given the information it wants revealed and the issues it wants to be politically salient. One implication of the findings is that many of the international agreements made by parliamentary governments are long-lasting and reliable because they are designed to be easily negotiated. The findings also challenge the popular conception that democratic governments negotiate politically sensitive issues as secretly as possible. The electoral model predicts that holding open negotiations over unpopular agreements can sometimes help the government's reelection chances.

What are these "rules of the game"? Governments can choose from a variety of organizing frameworks on which to base international negotiations. I focus on features of the negotiation process and the settlement format. In this stylized framework, governments can choose a negotiation process that is open or closed. The public is aware that negotiations are ongoing if the negotiation process is open. If the process is closed, the public is unaware that negotiations are taking place. For example, in 1986 President Reagan and General Secretary Gorbachev chose to negotiate arms control agreements through media press releases rather than behind closed doors (Department of State Bulletin 1986). In the Uruguay round example described earlier, the U.S. chose a closed process, the French an open one.

The government also has a choice of settlement format. It can choose to make an executive or a legislative agreement. A legislative agreement is an agreement that is ratified by the legislature and passed into law. An executive agreement is an agreement signed by the government as an executive order. For example, in 1993 and 1994, President Clinton preferred to use executive orders rather than legislate most favored nation status with the Chinese (Lampton 1994). In the Uruguay round example, the French switched from an executive agreement to a legislative one.

In this stylized framework there are four possible institutional arrangements for international negotiations. These are diagramed in table 1. There are examples of executive agreements that are closed (e.g., Prime Minister Major's 1995 cease-fire negotiations with Sinn Fein); legislative agreements that are closed (e.g., President Nixon's peace treaty with the North Vietnamese); legislative agreements that are open (e.g., the French agricultural negotiations during the Uruguay round of GATT negotiations); and executive agreements that are open (e.g., President Clinton's 1995 negotiations with the Chinese government over intellectual property rights). None of these four institutional arrangements are strategically equivalent. I explore how electoral incentives lead political leaders to choose one institutional framework over another.

The essay has two sections. In the first I discuss how this essay builds on the literature on international political economy. In the second I compare the choice of negotiation process and settlement format made by office-seeking and policy-seeking governments in parliamentary systems with strong parties. The basic approach is as follows. International negotiations are modeled as a two-level bargaining process. I suppose that two countries are entering into international negotiations. One is a foreign government. For clarity of explanation, assume that the foreign government is a unitary actor. The other country has a democratic government. It is not modeled as a unitary actor. Instead, I am interested in how the preferences of different domestic actors in the democratic nation affect outcomes. I begin with this sparse framework: a party in government, an opposition party, a median voter in the electorate, and a foreign government. I diagram hypothetical sets of preferences to describe how the strategic interaction of these actors affects the choice of negotiation process and settlement format. In the electoral model, the government is office seeking. This model characterizes negotiations over politically salient issues in competitive electoral races. The policy model portrays negotiations about nonsalient political issues and/or noncompetitive electoral races. Whether the issue is politically salient or not is found to be important in determining the predictions about the government's choice of negotiation process and settlement format. The last section concludes by reviewing the findings and discussing their empirical implications for future research.

TABLE 1.   Institutional Arrangements by Type of Settlement Format and Type of Negotiation Process

	Type of Settlement Format	
Type of Negotiation Process	Executive Agreement	Legislative Agreement
Open negotiation process	open, executive	open, legislative
Closed negotiation process	closed, executive	closed, legislative

Previous Work

The approach taken here is based on Putnam's (1988) two-level game framework and Lipson's (1991) analysis of the state leader's decision to choose "formal" or 'informal' international agreements. The essay builds on these works in a number of ways. Both Putnam and Lipson examine why leaders choose different types of institutional arrangements for international negotiations. Lipson and Putnam assume that the government cares about reelection and behaves strategically. The voters, however, do not behave strategically. For example, Lipson hypothesizes that domestically sensitive issues are dealt with as informally as possible. In the stylized framework I use, this is by closed executive agreement. By choosing a closed, executive agreement the government can avoid being punished by voters who dislike the government's policy. The implicit assumption here is that voters are politically naive. Politically naive voters punish or reward the government's actions at the polls without reference to the policy preferences of the opposition parties.

However, governments often hold open negotiations over domestically sensitive issues and frequently go on to make legislative agreements: for example, France's actions during the Uruguay round of the GATT talks. Governments often hold closed negotiations and make executive agreements when they anticipate that the final agreement will be domestically popular, (e.g., Prime Minister John Major's 1995 cease-fire negotiations with Sinn Fein). The choice of negotiation process and settlement format does not depend on the public popularity of the issue under negotiation. What matters is the relative popularity of the parties' policy positions: whether voters prefer the agreement negotiated by the government or the agreement the opposition party would renegotiate if it got into office.

I assume a strategic government and a sophisticated voter. The latter do not naively punish or reward the government on the basis of the policy content of the agreement. Voters compare the government's policy preferences with those of the opposition parties. They consider: what will the opposition party do if it gets into office? What is its policy position? Will it drive as hard a bargain? Voters do not choose the agreement. Their only choice is which political party to elect. Their relevant consideration in choosing a government at election time is which agreement each party would form.

Another feature that distinguishes this essay from previous work is the theoretical explanation for the government's choice of settlement format. Putnam (1988) argues that domestically constrained governments will be able to drive harder bargains if they adopt a legislative settlement format. Putnam's most widely cited hypothesis is that domestically constrained governments have greater bargaining leverage because they must satisfy their domestic constituencies and can credibly claim that they are restricted in the set of bargains they can make. If the government is domestically constrained, the threat of ratification in the legislature decreases the size of the government's win set. This cuts the government's maneuverability on bargaining issues while enhancing its bargaining power.

One of the conclusions in the Evans, Jacobson, and Putnam (1993) edited volume, however, is that this tactic is rarely attempted and infrequently succeeds, in part because political leaders misestimate whether or not agreements will be ratified within their own legislatures.[5] In political systems outside of the United States there is another reason this tactic seldom succeeds. In most parliamentary systems, there is little difference between the win set of the executive and the majority of representatives in the legislature. More importantly, with majority government and strong parties, the executive can pass virtually any agreement it wants. If the party is divided the government can always put the legislation through on a vote of confidence. The party typically unites behind the government rather than face an early election. There is no misperception involved here; the threat that treaties are less likely to be approved if ratified in the legislature simply is not tenable in most parliamentary systems.

Lipson (1991) and Martin (1995) argue that legislative agreements are used by the government not to increase bargaining leverage but to enable the government to credibly commit to the international agreement. Lipson argues that legislative agreements are more public than executive agreements are. By signing a legislative agreement the government puts its political reputation on the line. If the government reneges on the deal the damage to its political reputation is costly. The government will lose votes and find it harder to make international agreements in the future. However, international agreements hold only as long as the government that negotiated the agreement is in office. At the next election a new party could enter office. Reneging on an agreement made by the previous government will not adversely affect this party's political reputation. For any agreement to be credible, the government must be able to tie its hands on the issue and those of the next party that gets into office.

Martin (1995) argues that legislative agreements can, in such a way, be used by the U.S. president to credibly commit to international agreements. The argument focuses on the legislature as an institutional constraint. If a new president gets elected or a new party gets into Congress, the multiple veto points in the U.S. system make it difficult for the new government to overturn legislative agreements. Martin also points out that, given the division of power within the United States, congressional approval is needed during the implementation process. If the agreement is to become effective, Congress needs to affirm the bargain. Finally, if all branches of government are behind the agreement, it is less likely to get overturned when a new government wins office. This is particularly true in the United States, where getting legislative and executive support often means getting the support of both the Republican and Democratic Parties.

Can countries with parliamentary systems and strong parties also use legislative ratification to credibly commit to international agreements? Most parliamentary systems have strong parties and majority government. In these systems legislative support simply confirms support for the party in government. The government can always use a vote of confidence to contain debate on a bill and speed it through Parliament if there is division among its members. However, there are costs to renegotiating a legislative agreement even in a parliamentary system.[6] There are opportunity costs associated with renegotiating the agreement. The government only has a certain amount of legislative time in Parliament. If the government tries to overturn an international agreement, valuable time on the floor of the house will be taken up in parliamentary debate. Using the vote of confidence is costly for the government. Huber (1995) points out it generates negative publicity, in part because it sends a signal to voters that the government does not have a majority on this issue. Instead of hiding division by suppressing debate, the vote of confidence signals division within the party. The costs of renegotiating an agreement ratified in the legislature are not as high as in the U.S. presidential system; nevertheless a parliamentary government with strong parties is also able to use a legislative settlement format to credibly commit.[7]

Although one could argue that parliamentary governments use legislative agreements purely as a device to credibly commit, I consider other electoral motivations for using legislative agreements to "tie the hands" of the government and opposition parties. Suppose the government is office seeking and the voters sophisticated. Parties have fixed policy positions. I argue that the executive wants to tie her hands, and those of the opposition party, when doing so removes a politically costly issue from the political arena. For example, when the opposition party's policy preferences are more popular than those of the government, the government will want to make a legislative agreement. This ties the opposition's hands should it get into office, making it costly for the opposition party to renegotiate the agreement. If voters do not expect the opposition party to renegotiate the agreement when in power, they will not consider the opposition party or the government's policy preferences on this issue when they vote. In other words, the government removes an issue on which it is relatively unpopular from political debate in the forthcoming election. However, the government is less likely to want to remove an issue from the agenda if its policy position is more popular. In this case the government will want an executive agreement. The opposition's hands are not tied on this issue should it get into office. Voters know this. Voters will reelect the government because they dislike the agreement the opposition party would renegotiate should it get elected. In this case making an executive agreement keeps the issue on the political agenda and the opposition party out of government.

Whether or not the government chooses a legislative or executive agreement also depends on how unified the government and opposition parties are.

Using a legislative agreement gives the government the chance to embarrass a politically divided opposition party. If the electorate learns that the opposition party is internally divided over this issue, this will cost the opposition party votes. A party that is internally divided has an ambiguous policy position. This makes it difficult to negotiate an international agreement. Voters do not want to elect a party incapable of entering international negotiations. If the government is internally divided, it will prefer to use an executive agreement. It could choose the legislative agreement and tie the issue to a vote of confidence; however, as mentioned, this is costly for the government because it signals division within the party.

Finally, previous work focuses on the government's choice of executive or legislative settlement format. However, in the stylized framework depicted in table 1, I differentiate between the choice of settlement format (legislative or executive) and the choice of negotiation process (open or closed). The type of negotiation process is distinguished from the type of final contract because this helps clarify the structure of electoral incentives. The settlement format affects which issues are salient in the political arena. The negotiation process affects what information voters receive on these issues.

Open negotiations reveal information about the policy positions of the government and the opposition parties to voters and the foreign government. If the government anticipates that the opposition party's policy position will be less popular with the voters, open negotiations are a useful way of informing voters. The foreign government also receives information about the parties' policy positions and the preferences of voters over parties' policy positions. Open negotiations allow the voters and the opposition party to comment on the ongoing negotiations. Closed negotiations allow the government to surprise voters and the opposition party with a "done deal." If voters would prefer the opposition's policy position, a closed negotiation allows the government to hide the opposition parties' preferences from voters and curtails public debate. If the party in government is internally divided, the government prefers a closed process. The government does not want voters to learn of the political divisions within the party. However, if the party in opposition is internally divided, the government prefers an open process. The government wants to reveal the political divisions within the opposition party.

To summarize: I offer a strategic explanation for the choice of settlement format and negotiation process. I focus on what information is revealed to voters, how voters interpret that information, and how this affects the government's reelection chances. I distinguish between the choice of settlement format (legislative and executive) and the choice of negotiation process (open or closed). I assume that voters do not naively punish or reward the incumbent government; sophisticated voters compare the government's preferences with those of the opposition party.

In the next part of the essay I examine how reelection incentives affect the choice of negotiation process and settlement format for strategic politicians in a more rigorous manner. This electoral model applies when the issue is politically salient and the electoral race is party-competitive. Cease-fire talks, agricultural subsidies, and intellectual property rights are a few of the issues that, in recent years, have captured the public's interest. I contrast the electoral model with a policy model in which the government is under no electoral pressure and is free to pursue its policy preferences. This model applies when the issue is not politically salient. Many issues under negotiation are of no interest to the general public. Open or closed, negotiations on extradition treaties rarely make the news. The policy model also applies when the government is extremely popular or extremely unpopular; the international agreement does not affect its electoral fate. The findings reveal that whether the issue is politically salient or not is important in determining the predictions about the government's choice of negotiation process and settlement format.

The Theory

I use diagrams to describe the strategic interaction of domestic actors in different situations. In the diagrams I represent each actor's most preferred deal with a letter: for example, F represents the foreign nation's ideal point. Each actor would most like to see its favorite agreement implemented. As agreements move further from an actor's ideal point the actor likes the deal less. If a deal is far from an actor's ideal point, then the actor prefers that no agreement is reached. What happens if no agreement is reached? This depends upon the issue being negotiated. In many instances it means that the status quo prevails. In the diagrams the curves represent the set of agreements that make actors indifferent between that agreement and the status quo (SQ). Actors prefer agreements inside this curve to the status quo. However, an actor would rather have the status quo than a deal that is outside of this indifference curve.

Suppose there are two parties, R and L. R and L have different foreign policy positions. R is in power. R plans to negotiate with F, a unitary foreign government. R's bargain set contains the set of policy positions that R's core voters would like to implement. Likewise with L. The leadership of party R will have considerable difficulty persuading voters it can make an agreement that its core party members do not support. This credibility problem is modeled by assuming that party leaders cannot change policy without the consent of their core supporters. Therefore, party R can only credibly agree to policies inside its bargain set. When the policy position of the median voter is included, there are strategic incentives for government R to make agreements outside that bargain set (Hayes and Smith 1994). However, for the credibility of implementing these deals I assume that agreements must be inside indifference curves.[8] Similarly, L has a "fixed" policy position. F has no information about the preferences of the median voter or those of R and L's core supporters. If the negotiation process is open, this information is revealed to F.

Suppose that R is in government and is thinking about negotiating with F. Why does it care about the choice of negotiation process and settlement format? First, I present the policy model. I assume that the next government is randomly chosen and that the international negotiation does not affect the election outcome. Parties care only about policy, both its immediate and long-term consequences. I assume that R cares about negotiating an agreement as close as possible to its ideal policy point.

Next, I incorporate electoral incentives. I assume that R cares about how the choice of negotiation strategy and settlement format affects its reelection chances. I assume an office-seeking government and a sophisticated voter. The government wants to maximize its chances of getting reelected. If voters are sophisticated, the government wants to maximize the differential between its vote and that of the opposition party. Sophisticated voters compare the government's preferences with those of the opposition party. I also consider how the degree of consensus within the opposition and within the government party affects the hypotheses derived from the electoral model.

The Policy Model

Assume that parties care only about policy outcomes. The government is randomly chosen. Figures 1 and 2 depict hypothetical sets of policy preferences. In figure 1, L's policy preferences are closer to F's than R's. In fact, R has only a narrow set of policy preferences that overlap with F's preferences. The predictions in this set of circumstances are as follows.

1. R desires a closed process. R does not want F to know that L's policy preferences are closer to F than R's. Otherwise, F may choose not to bargain with R but wait and take its chances with a new government.
2. R desires a legislative agreement. Legislative agreements are costlier to renegotiate. If L gets into office, the agreement L renegotiates is further from R's ideal point. R wants to make it as costly as possible for L to renegotiate the agreement.

In figure 2, R, L, and F have different sets of policy preferences. R is closer to F in policy position. However, the bargain set of both R and L overlaps with that of F. The predictions in this example are as follows.

1. R wants an open process. The threat that L might get into office after the next election makes R a stronger negotiator. R wants F to know L's policy preferences. R can use this information as bargaining leverage against F.

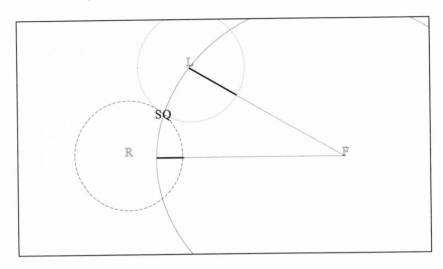

Fig. 1. Example of a policy space where party L's preferences are closer to the foreign government than party R's

2. R desires an executive agreement. L is able to negotiate a policy deal closer to R's ideal point than R can. R does not want to tie L's hands on this issue. R wants an executive agreement because it lowers the cost of renegotiating the agreement for L.

To summarize: whether or not R prefers an open executive or a closed legislative agreement depends on the policy preferences of L, R, and F. In figure 2, R's preferences are closer to F than L's and R wants an open executive agreement. In figure 1, L's preferences are closer to F than R's and R wants a closed legislative agreement.

The Electoral Model

Next, I consider the role of electoral effects in shaping the choice of institutional format. As in model 1, L and R have fixed policy positions. These reflect the policy preferences of their core party supporters. However, L and R are also concerned over how the negotiations will affect their popularity in the electorate more generally. I introduce M, the median voter. M is a sophisticated voter. He does not punish or reward R without considering L as the alternative choice of government.

Figure 3 depicts a hypothetical example. The preferences of the median voter and the foreign government are extremely far apart. The parties L and R lie between the median voter and the foreign government. R's preferences lie

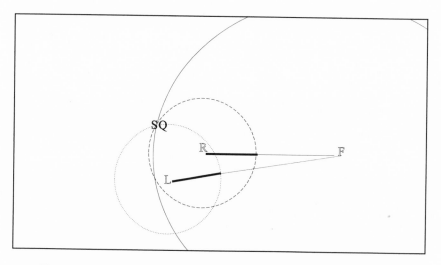

Fig. 2. Example of a policy space where party R's preferences are closer to the foreign government than party L's

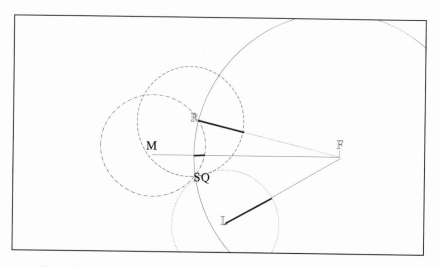

Fig. 3. Example of a policy space where party R's preferences lie closer to the median voter than party L's. The foreign government's preferences, however, lie closer to party L's.

closer to the median voter than L's does. There is a small area of overlap in the bargaining set of R, F, and M. As in figure 1, F prefers to bargain with L. Suppose that voters are sophisticated: what are the officeholding effects?

1. R bargains hard to make an agreement close to its ideal point, rather than the median voter's ideal point. R will make the agreement even if it lies outside the set of agreements preferred by M to the status quo. This is because voters do not get to choose the agreement. They only get to choose a political party, and voters prefer the agreement R would make to the deal L would make.
2. R wants an open agreement because the opposition party's policy position is less popular than the government's. R wants the voters to know L's extreme policy preferences so they will realize that they are better off with the party in power. However, the open agreement reveals the opposition party's policy position to F. R will find it difficult to reach a bargain if F realizes that it could get a better deal from the opposition party. It might try to draw out negotiations before the election (Morrow 1991). However, if the negotiations are open, voters will return R to office because they prefer the deal R will make to the one L will make. If F anticipates that R is going to get reelected it has little incentive to drag out the negotiations before the election.
3. R wants an executive agreement. The costs for L to renegotiate the deal, if it gets into office, are low. However, M does not want L to renegotiate! M prefers R's policy position and fears what L would do in office. This is why R does not want to tie L's hands on this issue. R wants an executive agreement because it wants this issue to remain important in the upcoming election. Hopefully, voters will return R to office because they fear how L would renegotiate the agreement if elected.

The degree of internal political consensus within L and R affects these predictions. In figure 3, the median sophisticated voter prefers R's policy position to that of L. R chooses an open process. However, if party R is internally divided, R may prefer a closed process. If the process is open, R risks appearing incompetent. The party's policy position is ambiguous, which makes it difficult to negotiate an agreement. R's leadership does not want voters observing the bargaining process, and it does not want its party membership getting involved in the negotiation process. In figure 3, R still prefers an executive format when it is internally divided. If R uses a legislative format then voters will learn that the government does not have the full support of its party on this issue. This will cost R votes. If R is internally divided it prefers a closed, executive format.

To summarize; in figure 3, when voters are politically sophisticated, agreements will be open, executive. The government chooses an open process because

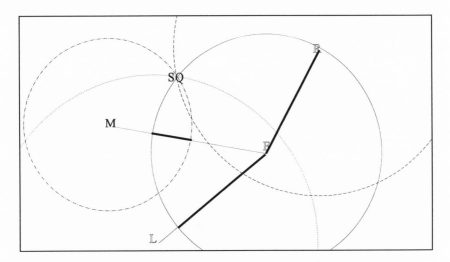

Fig. 4. Example of a policy space where party L's preferences lie closer to the median voter than party R's. The foreign government's preferences, however, lie closer to party R's.

its policy position is relatively more popular. It chooses an executive format because it wants voters to fear what deal the opposition party would renegotiate if in office. If, however, the government's party is internally divided, it prefers a closed, executive agreement. This hides dissention within the governing party.

In figure 4, there is a small range of possible agreements with F that M favors. The two parties, R and L, lie much farther away from M and F. L's preferences lie closer to the median voter's than R's. As in figure 2, however, F prefers to negotiate with R. Suppose voters are sophisticated: what are the office holding effects?

1. R wants a closed agreement. The government's policy position is relatively unpopular. If the process is closed, there is little time for different domestic pressure groups to organize and inform voters. In addition, there is little time for the opposition party to organize its objections or present a unified, competent, alternative to the party in government. The legislative agreement surprises the opposition party, which has a more popular policy position but hasn't had the time to put a coherent opposition together.

2. R wants a legislative agreement. The opposition party's preferences are more popular than R's. The closed process will minimize public debate, and the legislative agreement will remove a potentially politically costly agreement from the agenda in the next election.

The government also chooses a closed, legislative agreement when it wants to present a "package deal" to the voters and the legislature. This package may include both popular and unpopular measures. A closed, executive agreement will prevent legislators and pressure groups from picking apart the agreement and force the public and the legislature to vote up or down on the final deal. If the agreement, on aggregate, benefits voters, a closed legislative agreement is one way of avoiding political division on redistributive issues.[9]

The degree of internal political consensus within L and R affects the predictions. Currently M prefers L's policy position to that of R. R chooses a closed process. However, if party L is internally divided, R may prefer an open process. An open negotiation will reveal L to be internally divided. L's policy position is unclear. L will appear incompetent, incapable of reaching an agreement with F. R loses the element of surprise associated with the closed process, but no surprise is needed to throw the opposition party into disarray if it is already internally divided. R still wants a legislative agreement. L will be politically embarrassed if a faction within the party supports R, the government. Admittedly, an executive format would keep an issue on which the opposition is divided on the political agenda. However, the government policy position is less popular than the opposition's policy position, and as the election approaches the opposition party typically unifies as party discipline increases. In figure 4, the government prefers an open, legislative agreement if the opposition party is internally divided.

In summary for figure 4; the government chooses a closed, legislative format. R wants to remove a politically costly issue from public debate. If the opposition party is internally divided, R prefers an open, legislative agreement. R wants to create as many opportunities as possible to reveal information to the voters about L's divisions.

Conclusion

In this essay I use the choice of settlement format and negotiation strategy to explore how voters affect the rules used to structure international agreements. Rather than focusing on U.S. institutions, I model the choice of institutional arrangement made by parliamentary governments with strong parties. The choice of settlement format and negotiation process affects the content and credibility of international negotiations. However, these choices also determine which issues are salient in the political arena and the information voters receive about the parties' issue positions and internal political divisions.

I diagram hypothetical sets of preferences to depict the strategic interaction of the government, opposition party, and foreign government. The baseline for comparison with the electoral model is the policy model. In the latter there are no electoral incentives and the government pursues policy goals. In figure 1, the policy model predicts that the government chooses a closed, legislative agreement. The legislative agreement is costly to renegotiate and is used to discourage the opposition party from renegotiating the agreement farther from the government's ideal point. The process is closed because the government does not want the foreign government to discover that it could negotiate a better deal with the opposition party. Recognizing this, the foreign government may drag out negotiations until after the election, hoping that the opposition party gains office.

Figure 3 is similar to figure 1; however, the preferences of the median voter have been added. In the electoral model, the government is office seeking and the median voter is sophisticated. It is predicted that the government prefers an open, executive process. The government wants an executive process because the opposition party would renegotiate a less popular agreement if elected. The electorate, fearing the deal the opposition party would renegotiate if in office, votes for the government party. In this case the government does not care that an executive agreement makes it less costly for the opposition party to renegotiate a deal farther from the government's ideal point. After all, the government thinks this tactic will get it reelected and the opposition party will not get a chance to renegotiate the agreement. The government wants an open negotiation process despite the lack of public support for its policy position. What matters is that the government's policy preferences are relatively more popular than those of the opposition party. The government wants the electorate to know that it would get a worse deal if the opposition were in power. If the government is internally divided, however, it prefers a closed, executive agreement. The closed process hides the political dissention within the party from the electorate and the foreign government.

In figure 2, the policy model predicts that the government prefers an open, executive agreement. An open negotiation process is used to help the government drive a harder bargain. The government wants the foreign government to realize that it can get a better deal with the party in government than it could with the opposition party. The government chooses an executive agreement because, in this example, the opposition could renegotiate a deal closer to the government's ideal point. The preferences of the government, opposition party, and foreign government are similar in figure 4; however, the median voter has been added. In the electoral model, the government prefers a closed, legislative process. The government uses the legislative agreement because it anticipates that the opposition party will renegotiate a more popular agreement if elected. By making it costly for the opposition party to renegotiate the agreement, the government removes the issue from the political debate in the forthcoming election. A closed process gives little time for domestic pressure groups or the opposition party to organize and inform voters. It allows the government to surprise the voters and the opposition party with a "done deal." A closed process gives the opposition party little time to organize opposition to the legislative agreement. If the opposition party is internally divided, however, the government prefers an open, legislative agreement. This gives the government the chance to embarrass a politically divided opposition party.

To make comparisons easier, these predictions are summarized in tables 2 and 3. There are many other hypothetical preference arrangements not depicted diagrammatically. I have sampled only a few possible situations. Nonetheless, these four simple examples yield interesting implications. One consequence of the findings is that international agreements made by parliamentary governments with strong parties are long-lasting and reliable, although they are often designed to fail. When the government's policy position is more popular than the opposition party's, it chooses a settlement format that lowers the costs for the opposition party to renegotiate the agreement if elected. The possibility that the agreement could collapse and be renegotiated helps the government's reelection chances against the opposition party. All else being equal, the government gets reelected and the original agreement stands. This implies that many of the international agreements made by parliamentary governments are long lasting and reliable because they are designed to be easily renegotiated.

The predictions challenge the popular conception that democratic governments are forced to negotiate politically sensitive issues as secretly as possible. It is believed that holding unpopular negotiations publicly is political suicide. However, the electoral model predicts that holding open negotiations over unpopular agreements can actually help the government's reelection chances. The issue under negotiation may be unpopular, but if the government's policy position is prefered to that of the opposition it wants negotiations to be open. Voters do not get to choose the agreement. Their only choice is which political party to elect.

More generally, the predictions in tables 2 and 3 yield empirically falsifiable hypotheses. The electoral model applies when the issue is politically salient and the electoral race is party-competitive. The policy model characterizes negotiations over nonsalient political issues or noncompetitive elections. Although there is a danger of selecting on the dependent variable, public opinion data can be used to create a data set of politically salient and nonsalient international agreements for parliamentary systems with strong governments.[10] Public opinion and party manifesto data will reveal the relative positions of the

TABLE 2.   Summary of Predictions for Figures 1 and 3

Actors' Preferences[a]	Predictions
Policy model: figure 1	closed, legislative
Electoral model: figure 3	open, executive
Electoral model: figure 3[b]	closed, executive

[a]L's ideal point is closer to F than R's is.
[b]R is internally divided.

TABLE 3. Summary of Predictions for Figures 2 and 4

Actors' Preferences[a]	Predictions
Policy model: figure 2	open, executive
Electoral model: figure 4	closed, legislative
Electoral model: figure 4[b]	open, legislative

[a]R's ideal point is closer to F than L's is.
[b]L is internally divided.

government and opposition parties on these issues. It is then possible to test, in a rigorous way, the predictions of the two models.[11] These predictions do not provide a test of the assumptions; however, they do provide a test of the strategic behavior described in this essay.

NOTES

I would like to thank Bruce Bueno de Mesquita, Jim Morrow, Alastair Smith, Andrew Sobel, and participants at the conference Strategic Politicians, Institutions, and Foreign Policy for their helpful comments.

1. There is a growing literature that examines in a rigorous way the interaction of electoral politics and the outcomes of international negotiations. See Friman 1993; Hayes and Smith 1994; Iida 1993; Lohmann 1994; Mo 1994; Morrow 1991; Paarlberg 1993; and Schoppa 1992.

2. See *Financial Times,* December 1–7, 1994.

3. See *Financial Times,* November 26, 1992, and December 2, 1992.

4. A notable exception is Pahre 1995.

5. See also Iida 1993 and Mo 1994.

6. See Pahre's (1995) discussion of parliamentary oversight in Denmark.

7. Note that no commitment is completely reliable. If the next party that gets elected has strong and extreme preferences, the benefits of renegotiating the agreement may be greater than the costs.

8. For example, in the United Kingdom in the 1970s and 1980s, Labour Party members included the security policy of unilateral disarmament in the party manifesto. This was an extremely unpopular policy with voters. Although the Labour leadership tried to persuade voters it would not unilaterally disarm if it got into office, voters did not trust Labour not to implement such a policy when in power.

9. Thanks to Lisa Martin for making this point.

10. Although I model a two-party system, the number of political parties in the parliamentary system with strong parties does not affect the predictions.

11. One problem with this empirical test is that outcomes are some compromise of the things R wants and the things F wants. However, because of informational asymmetries, it is possible for R and F to be in negotiations and for R to have a closed, legislative agreement and F an open, executive agreement.

REFERENCES

Chayes, A., and A. H. Chayes. 1993. On Compliance. *International Organization* 47:175–217.

Department of State Bulletin. 1996. Office of Public Communication, Bureau of Public Affairs, Washington, DC.

Evans, P. B., H. K. Jacobson, and R. D. Putnam, eds. 1993. *Double-Edged Diplomacy.* Berkeley: University of California Press.

Friman, R. H. 1993. Side Payments versus Security Cards: Domestic Bargaining Tactics in International Economic Negotiations. *International Organization* 47: 387–410.

Hayes, D. R., and A. Smith. 1994. The Shadow of the Polls: Electoral Effects on International Agreements. Working Paper, Center of Political Economy. Washington University, St. Louis.

Huber, J. 1995. The Impact of Confidence Votes on Legislative Politics in Parliamentary Systems. Manuscript.

Lampton, D. M. 1994. America's China Policy in the Age of the Finance Minister: Clinton Ends Linkage. *China Quarterly* 3:597–621.

Iida, K. 1993. When and How Do Domestic Constraints Matter? Two-level Games With Uncertainty. *Journal of Conflict Resolution* 37:403–26.

Lehman, H. P., and J. L. McCoy. 1992. The Dynamics of the Two-Level Bargaining Game. *World Politics* 44:600–644.

Lipson, C. 1991. Why Are Some International Agreements Informal? *International Organization* 45:495–58.

Lohmann, S. 1994. Electoral Cycles and International Policy Cooperation. *European Economic Review* 36:1–19.

Martin, Lisa. 1995. Evasive Maneuvers? Reconsidering Presidential Use of Executive Agreements. Paper presented at the conference, Strategic Politicians, Institutions, and Foreign Policy, University of California, Davis, April.

Mo, J. 1994. The Logic of Two-Level Games with Endogenous Domestic Coalitions. *Journal of Conflict Resolution* 38:402–22.

Morrow, J. D. 1991. Electoral and Congressional Incentives and Arms Control. *Journal of Conflict Resolution* 35:245–65.

Paarlberg, R. L. 1993. Why Agriculture Blocked the Uruguay Round: Evolving Strategies in a Two-Level Game. In *World Agriculture and the GATT,* edited by W. Avery. Boulder, CO: Lynne Rienner.

Pahre, R. 1995. Endogenous Domestic Institutions in Two-Level Games: Parliamentary Oversight in Denmark and Elsewhere. Paper presented at the annual meeting of the American Political Science Association, Chicago.

Putnam, R. D. 1988. Diplomacy and Domestic Politics: The Logic of Two-Level Games. *International Organization* 42:427–60.

Schoppa, L. J. 1993. Two-Level Games and Bargaining Outcomes: Why Gaiatsu Succeeds in Japan in Some Cases but Not Others. *International Organization* 47:353–86.

Strategic Actors or Passive Reactors?
The Political Economy of U.S.-Japanese
Monetary Relations

Keisuke Iida

One of the common themes in this volume is the impact of electoral incentives on foreign policy. Gaubatz and Smith theoretically examine the impact of electoral incentives on foreign policy. Gilligan and Hunt empirically explore the impact of government change, including nonelectoral turnovers. This essay shares this common theme with the others but takes a different angle. In particular, it examines the cross-border impact of elections on economic policy.

In political economy, the study of elections and economic policy has a long tradition. It is well known that in many democracies electoral results are, to a significant degree, determined by macroeconomic outcomes such as unemployment, economic growth, and inflation (Fair 1978, 1982, 1988; Kiewiet 1983; Kramer 1971, 1983). Given this well-established relationship, a natural question is to ask whether governments try to manipulate the economy through economic policy to improve their electoral fortunes. This is known as the political business cycle (PBC) hypothesis, and it has been a source of controversy over the years. First evidence was provided by Nordhaus (1975) and Tufte (1978), but on closer examination follow-up studies cast doubt upon the hypothesis. Theoretical argument based on rational expectations has also undermined the PBC hypothesis: markets will adjust their behavior in anticipation of policy manipulation, and that will undermine the effectiveness of manipulation. In recent years, however, additional empirical evidence for the cycle has been offered (Grier 1989; Suzuki 1992), and theoretically it has been shown that PBC is possible even under the operation of rational expectations (Rogoff 1990). Thus, this debate in domestic political economy is still unsettled.

Despite intensive research devoted to this problem, political economists have not paid much attention to the international dimension of this problem. In other words, will elections in country A possibly affect economic policy of country B? Very few studies have addressed this question. This essay intends to fill this gap. In particular, it will examine whether or not elections in the

United States affect monetary policy in Japan. To preempt the conclusion, the results seem to show that U.S. elections moderately affect Japanese monetary policy but in a rather complicated way. The only evidence that I can find is that when Democratic administrations are facing a reelection campaign, Japanese monetary policy is tightened, ceteris paribus. Also, this essay tries to see if this effect comes from a "strategic" motive or from a passive reaction to U.S. economic and political pressures. Evidence exists in favor of both interpretations.

Strategic Actors and Passive Reactors

When one examines the interrelationships between domestic and international politics, two approaches are possible: passive and strategic interpretations of governmental behavior. Under the passive actor model, governments take either domestic or international "pressures"[1] as given and adjust their policies accordingly. Thus, these policy adjustments are explained as a "result" of these pressures. Typically, students of domestic politics take international "pressures" (e.g., pressures from powerful foreign countries, international organizations, or international economic developments) as given and explain domestic policy as a result of these external pressures. Similarly, students of foreign policy take domestic pressures (e.g., political pressures from interest groups or public opinion) as given and explain foreign policy as a result of these internal pressures.

These passive reactions can be rational or nonrational. When governments are assumed to be rational, they are assumed to have a well-defined set of objectives and to try to attain those objectives in an efficient manner. Thus, when the situation changes, hitherto optimal policies are no longer optimal in terms of their objectives and require some adjustments. On the other hand, these adjustments could be interpreted as nonrational. Since governments are actually composed of many individuals and complex organizations, it is hard to find a well-defined governmental "utility function," to use economists' language, or "the national interest," to use realists' language. When the analyst assumes that there is no well-defined set of governmental objectives, the interpretation of the above-mentioned policy adjustments is nonrational. Such adjustments may be based on standard operating procedures of bureaucracy or instinctive human reactions.

While a definitive statement is hazardous to make, it seems fair to say that a majority of the existing studies of economic policy making have been some variant of this passive actor model, whether rational or nonrational. But it should be clear that this is not the only possible interpretation when a government changes its policy seemingly in reaction to external or internal pressures. Another, ulterior or preemptive, motive may be lurking behind the surface.

The other possible interpretation is one of strategic behavior. A precise definition of strategic behavior is hard to make, but the standard one seems to be that of "interactive decision making." Others prefer to add another element, which is the existence of a preconceived plan, whether explicit or implicit (Calder 1993, chap. 1, n. 3).

Since our concern is how to detect strategic behavior if it exists, the latter element of the definition would be particularly helpful if the preconceived plan is indeed explicit and preferably written. Then, one's task is to find such a plan and see whether behavior indeed follows it. But in reality most of what is seemingly strategic behavior is based on an implicit or hidden plan, if any.

There are other elements that are often associated with strategic behavior:

1. Behavior is forward looking as opposed to backward looking. That is, behavior is meant to improve (or prevent a deterioration of) the actor's future welfare rather than simply reacting to past events. This could be considered a consequence of a preconceived contingent plan. In macroeconomics, market agents are more "strategic" if they form forward-looking expectations, while they are less strategic if they form expectations in a backward-looking manner, simply adjusting their expectations incrementally in response to the past realization of shocks. A similar distinction can be made about voting behavior: retrospective voting (passive behavior) and prospective voting (strategic behavior).

2. Strategic behavior often involves intentional manipulation of information to one's advantage. As long as there is incomplete information about some aspects of the environment, actors are expected to use that information even if that requires a distortion of information. Thus, "strategic voting," for instance, refers to the existence of this aspect of strategic behavior where voters do not reveal their preferences in a straightforward manner. Wilson (1994) documents a case in which the Costa Rican government feigned that it had been "instructed" by the U.S. Agency for International Development (USAID) to undertake banking reform, which it wanted to achieve despite domestic opposition, while USAID had not actually made that demand.

3. Actors know that their behavior has reverberations: one's behavior affects the other players' behavior, which in turn affects the former's behavior. Actors are assumed to know and take these interactive effects into account when making a decision. While this may seem like a straightforward consequence of the interactive decision-making part of the definition, theoretically and empirically the lack of this aspect is possible even if actors are objectively situated in an environment of interactive decision making.

4. Similarly, strategic actors are assumed to know that their behavior (at least potentially) affects the very political survival of other actors,

whose fate in turn may affect theirs. The classical theory of balance of power takes this aspect of international politics seriously. Ito's hypothesis, to be explained shortly, may be interpreted as "strategic" in this sense.

For the remainder of the essay, we take these features as essential components of strategic behavior, and the lack of these features will be deemed indications of nonstrategic or passive behavior.

Ito's Hypothesis: Internationally Strategic Behavior of the Japanese Government

The discussion of these aspects of strategic behavior is in part motivated by the recent finding by a Japanese economist, Takatoshi Ito (1991), about Japanese macroeconomic policy. Through a vector autoregression (VAR) analysis, he found that the Japanese macroeconomy expands faster and inflation is slower during a quarter before each U.S. presidential election, ceteris paribus. Furthermore, his interpretation of this finding is one of strategic behavior by the Japanese government:

> [T]he Japanese will increase growth just before the U.S. election, presumably to be a "locomotive" for the U.S. economy. To be a locomotive, growth has to be attained by the [*sic*] Japanese domestic demand stimulation rather than by exports. This observation combined with the fact that inflation goes·down at the same time suggests that the yen had been appreciated to help keep inflation down. This is just opposite of the "beggar-thy-neighbor" policy, which may be a first thought on the international aspect of elections, a result of a special kind of policy coordination. (S85)

In other words, the Japanese are helping the incumbent president to be reelected by stimulating their economy before the presidential election. If it proves to be true, this is a tremendous finding, since it had not been known that the Japanese government engages in such internationally strategic behavior in terms of macroeconomic policy.

There are three major problems with Ito's approach, however. First, he only examines economic aggregates such as real gross national product (GNP) growth and price inflation, but the interpretation he provides has to do with governmental policy, either fiscal or monetary. Therefore, it would seem preferable to look at specific policy instruments to see if they are used in the expected way. For this reason, I will focus on Japanese and U.S. monetary policy instruments in this essay.

Second, as has been suggested, there is an alternative interpretation of the same phenomenon that he discovers: one of passive behavior. It may well be the case that the Japanese government adjusts its macroeconomic policy in response to economic and political developments in the United States. Some researchers have found that both U.S. monetary (Grier 1989) and fiscal policies (Laney and Willett 1983) are used for electoral purposes. Therefore, if the Japanese government reacts to these electoral cycles in the United States in a predictable way, that may result in the kind of economic outcomes that Ito observes. Thus, before one confirms Ito's hypothesis, it is necessary to test for passive as well as strategic behavior. That is exactly what we attempt to do here.

Third, since good economic performance in the United States and abroad presumably advantages the incumbent president rather than the challenger, the natural question that arises from Ito's interpretation is why the Japanese government prefers to see the incumbent president reelected. One possible answer may be the maintenance of a cooperative relationship with the U.S. administration. Since cooperation requires a long time horizon (Oye 1986), it is advantageous to have a long-term administration in the United States if the Japanese government's primary goal is to maintain a cooperative relationship with Washington. But the Japanese government has difficulty getting along with some administrations, and in such a case it may prefer to see the incumbent president replaced rather than reelected. It may be interesting to see if such a possibility exists.

Testing for Passive and Strategic Behavior

As suggested previously, we use monetary policy instruments as dependent variables in this chapter. The first thing we have to test is whether or not there is any influence by U.S. presidential elections on Japanese monetary policy. Supposing that there is an effect, then we can test for passive behavior in the following way.

First, we regress Japanese monetary policy variables on U.S. monetary and fiscal policies. If the latter have statistically significant effects, it indicates that Japanese monetary policy is simply reacting to U.S. economic policies. That will support the passive reactor interpretation. However, that does not rule out strategic behavior: we may be simply tracing the reaction function of Japanese monetary policy in the neighborhood of a Nash equilibrium. Since Nash equilibria arise from strategic behavior, the fact that U.S. monetary (or fiscal) policy has an effect on Japanese monetary policy is perfectly consistent with both passive and strategic behavior assumptions.

Thus, a second test would be to see if the effects of U.S. presidential elections on Japanese monetary policy vanish if one controls for U.S. monetary and fiscal policy. If that were the case, it would reinforce the conclusion that the Japanese monetary electoral cycle is simply a reaction to the political business cycle in the United States.

Furthermore, passive behavior could arise in response to U.S. political pressures.[2] Very often U.S. administrations pressure the Japanese government to stimulate the economy so that it will be an "engine of growth" for the rest of the world. Also, such pressures come with an implied or explicit threat that if the Japanese do not comply the dollar will decline, hurting Japanese exporters, who are an important constituency of the ruling Liberal Democratic Party (LDP). If the Japanese indeed expand their economy, that would be "cooperative" behavior in line with Ito's interpretation, but such behavior does not seem to be particularly strategic.

Next, to test for strategic behavior, we conduct the following tests. First, we regress U.S. monetary policy variables on Japanese monetary policy variables. If there is an indication of simultaneous effects, that means that U.S. and Japanese monetary policies constitute interactive decision making in line with the definition of strategic behavior just described. If U.S. monetary policy affects Japanese monetary policy but not vice versa, that would support the passive behavior interpretation. If neither affects the other, they are simply independent.

Another test for Ito's interpretation is to see if Japanese monetary policy has an impact on U.S. electoral results. Since the number of presidential elections we can examine is limited, we will use presidential popularity as a surrogate for electoral results. If Japanese monetary easing has a positive effect on presidential popularity, that will indirectly support Ito's hypothesis.

Finally, we can measure the effects of Japanese monetary policy on Japanese electoral politics. If Japanese monetary policy is politically costly in Japan, a rational government may think twice.

All the data (except U.S. unemployment and political data) are taken from *International Financial Statistics* of the International Monetary Fund. All the reported regressions use monthly series; similar regressions with quarterly data give more or less the same results. Both the federal funds rate and the discount rate are used as U.S. monetary policy instruments, although experts say the role of the discount rate is only symbolic. The call rate (an overnight interbank rate similar to the federal funds rate) and the discount rate are used as Japanese monetary policy instruments. Compared with its U.S. counterpart, the Japanese discount rate plays a more substantive role, especially in the earlier period.

As suggested, we start by regressing Japanese monetary policy variables on the dummy variable for U.S. presidential elections as well as other possibly relevant variables. Economic forecast variables are generated by a VAR described in appendix A. As argued by Abrams et al. (1980), it is theoretically compelling and empirically sound to use forecast variables rather than lagged or current economic variables. Although it is generally assumed that monetary authorities watch real gross domestic product (GDP) growth as well as inflation, GDP data are reported only on a quarterly basis. Therefore, output growth is measured instead via industrial production, which is reported every month. Inflation is the rate of increase in consumer prices (CPI).

Parallel to that on the United States, there has been scholarly debate on the political business cycle in Japan. One complication in the case of Japan is that election timing is endogenous: the government can call a general election any time it wants (Ito 1990). About a month before election day, the election is called, and there is only a two-week campaign period. Therefore, using the leads of election dummy variables as in the case of the United States makes little theoretical sense. However, there is a constitutional limit on the term of each lower-house session; an election has to be called within 48 months of the previous election. As time elapses since the previous election, the probability that an election will be called increases monotonically. Thus, the number of months since the last election is used as a proxy for the probability of an election being held.

Table 1 shows the instrumental variable (IV) estimates of the Japanese monetary policy reaction function. The two monetary policy variables, the federal funds rate and the discount rate, are taken to be endogenous, and their lags are used as instrumental variables. U.S. fiscal policy, measured by government debt as a percentage of GDP, on the other hand, is taken to be exogenous.

The coefficients on the lagged dependent variables show that the call rate is stationary, but the discount rate may have a unit root (hence nonstationary). I have conducted several tests to see if there is evidence for unit roots, but most tests reject the hypothesis of unit roots. The economic variables have the predicted effects: prospects of higher growth and higher inflation elicit monetary tightening (higher interest rates).

There is clear evidence that Japanese monetary policy reacts to both U.S. monetary and fiscal policies. The federal funds rate, the discount rate, and U.S. public debt have statistically significant effects on Japanese monetary policy instruments. But this is not enough to conclude that Japanese monetary policy is entirely passive.

There is no statistical evidence for the political monetary cycle in the domestic sense: the Japanese monetary authorities do not seem to ease monetary policy as the prospect of an election looms large. Nor is there evidence that U.S. presidential elections per se influence Japanese monetary policy; while the dummy variable for the U.S. presidential election year[3] has the expected sign, in neither equation can the null hypothesis of zero effect be rejected.

The only statistically discernible effect of the United States upon Japan, however, is that of the interaction term between the presidential election dummy and the dummy for Democratic incumbent presidents. Both equations indicate that Japanese monetary policy is tightened if Democrats are up for reelection. And this is *after* controlling for the effects of U.S. economic policy. However, there are only three elections in which Democratic presidents were up for reelection in the sample period, and in 1968 Johnson withdrew from the campaign in the spring. Therefore, it is likely that this effect is mostly driven by the 1980 election, in which every major country, including Japan, was battling inflation that had been trigged by the second oil shock.

U.S. political pressures have been measured by coding Japanese newspaper articles on U.S. "demands" on Japanese macroeconomic policies. Three dummy variables have been coded; one indicating U.S. pressures on monetary policy, the second coding pressures on fiscal and other policies to reflate the economy, and the third being the composite of the first two. Unfortunately, due

TABLE 1.   Instrumental Variable Estimates of Japanese Monetary Policy Reaction Functions

Explanatory Variables	Dependent Variable: Call Rate (percentage)	Dependent Variable: Discount Rate (percentage)
Constant	−0.82	−0.32
	(−2.78)**	(−2.40)*
Dependent variable	0.61	0.94
(lagged by one period)	(13.12)**	(17.77)**
Dependent variable	0.16	−0.05
(lagged by two periods)	(2.99)**	(−0.76)
Dependent variable	0.12	0.04
(lagged by three periods)	(2.73)**	(0.89)
Growth in industrial production	0.02	0.01
(three-month forecast)	(4.23)**	(3.93)**
Consumer price inflation	0.08	0.04
(three-month forecast)	(5.47)**	(6.60)**
Federal funds rate	0.05	
(percentage)	(4.04)**	
U.S. discount rate		0.03
(percentage)		(5.11)**
U.S. government debt as	0.02	0.01
percentage of GDP	(3.47)**	(2.73)**
Time elapsed since last	−0.00	0.00
election	(−0.75)	(0.54)
U.S. presidential election	−0.10	−0.03
year	(−1.07)	(−0.73)
Democrats × U.S.	0.53	0.20
presidential election year	(3.33)**	(3.13)**
Sample period	June 1958 to September 1995	February 1964 to September 1995
Degrees of freedom	437	369
Adjusted R^2	0.93	0.98
Durbin-Watson	2.00	1.99

Note: t-ratios are in parentheses.
*$p < .05$ **$p < .01$ (two-tailed)

to limitations of the sources at hand, I have been able to get these data only back to 1976. Estimation results only adding the third variable to the equations of table 1 are shown in table A2 in appendix B. A detailed description of these dummy variables can be also found in appendix B.

Next, we estimate the U.S. monetary policy reaction functions, first to see if Japanese monetary policy also influences U.S. monetary policy and second to see if there is any electoral cycle in U.S. monetary policy.

Table 2 shows the IV estimates of U.S. monetary policy reaction functions. In this estimation, the Japanese call rate is the endogenous explanatory variable and the instrumental variable is its one-month lag. The lagged values

TABLE 2.   Instrumental Variable Estimates of U.S. Monetary Policy Reaction Functions

Explanatory Variables	Dependent Variable: Federal Funds Rate (percentage)	Dependent Variable: Discount Rate (percentage)
Constant	−0.04	0.06
	(−0.17)	(0.54)
Dependent variable	1.32	1.12
(lagged by one period)	(28.19)**	(21.75)**
Dependent variable	−0.56	−0.18
(lagged by two periods)	(−7.68)**	(−2.33)*
Dependent variable	0.19	0.03
(lagged by three periods)	(4.20)**	(0.60)
Growth in industrial production	0.04	0.02
(three-month forecast)	(4.82)**	(5.66)**
Consumer price inflation	0.08	0.05
(three-month forecast)	(4.85)**	(5.93)**
Japanese call rate	−0.02	—
(percentage)	(−1.57)	
Japanese discount rate	—	−0.03
(percentage)		(−2.88)**
U.S. government debt as	0.00	−0.00
percentage of GDP	(0.47)	(−0.46)
U.S. presidential election	−0.17	−0.12
year	(−2.24)*	(−3.10)**
Democrats × U.S.	0.16	0.12
presidential election year	(1.32)	(2.05)*
Sample period	June 1958 to September 1995	April 1964 to September 1995
Degrees of freedom	438	368
Adjusted R^2	0.97	0.99
Durbin-Watson	1.98	1.99

Note: t-ratios are in parentheses.
*$p < .05$ **$p < .01$ (two-tailed)

of the dependent variables show that the one-month lag has an unusually large impact.

There is some evidence of a political monetary cycle in both equations: the coefficient on the election dummy shows the expected negative sign, and it is statistically discernible from zero at the standard levels of significance.

Japanese monetary policy, as measured by the call rate, does not seem to influence U.S. monetary policy in a statistically significant way, but the coefficient on the discount rate shows statistical significance. Thus, "strategicness" in the sense of interactive decision making is partly confirmed.

To summarize the findings so far, there is clear evidence that Japan reacts to U.S. monetary and fiscal policies, and this supports the passive behavior assumption. The reaction of U.S. monetary policy to Japanese monetary policy is somewhat more ambiguous, but there is some evidence of two-way interaction. Thus, this is consistent with both strategic and passive interpretations of Japanese monetary policy making.

On the other hand, evidence is weak that Japanese monetary policy is changed during the presidential election year. And, if there is anything like the internationalized political business cycle discovered by Ito, Japanese monetary policy is not implicated, except through an indirect influence of Japanese reactions to electorally motivated macroeconomic policy in the United States.

We have already seen that the reaction of U.S. monetary policy to Japanese policy is weak at best, but this does not deny the possibility that Japanese monetary policy is proactive or forward looking in Ito's sense. One way to see if Japanese monetary policy is strategic in this sense is to measure the political effects of Japanese monetary policy in the United States. As indicated previously, presidential popularity will be used as an indicator of the electoral effects of Japanese policy in the United States. Table 3 shows the ordinary least squares (OLS) estimates of presidential popularity determination equations. Gallup asks: "Do you approve of the way that President X is handling his job?" every month. Here the last poll results are taken if there are more than one in a given month. The first equation uses the gross approval rate (the proportion of respondents who "approve"), and the second equation uses the net approval rate (the gross approval rate minus the disapproval rate).

Inflation and unemployment (each lagged by one period) are known to affect presidential popularity (Nordhaus 1989), but in this estimation only inflation shows a statistically discernible impact. Monetary policy variables were entered in terms of levels, and the only variable of interest that seems to show statistically significant effects is, somewhat surprisingly, the lagged Japanese call rate. The current levels of the call rate and the current and lagged values of the federal funds rate do not show statistical significance. Furthermore, the coefficients on the lagged and current levels of the Japanese call rate are of opposite signs. Thus, this may suggest that it is *changes* rather than *levels* in interest rates that affect presidential popularity. This is partly borne out by evidence. If one estimates the same equations as in table 3 but replaces the monetary policy variables of the two countries with changes, the current change (in other words, the current level minus the lagged level) in the Japanese call rate has statistically discernible effects on presidential popularity in the United States, but the change in the federal funds rate shows no comparable impact. Therefore, the results suggest that there is some room for Japanese manipulation of U.S. electoral politics in line with Ito's hypothesis.

Finally, we estimate the effects of Japanese monetary policy on Japanese electoral politics. Even if the Japanese are interested in manipulating U.S. electoral politics through monetary policy, it would be irrational to do so if the domestic costs of manipulation were too high. A rational government would weigh international benefits against domestic costs (if any) before attempting such manipulation. Thus, by estimating the electoral effects of monetary policy, one can indirectly check the plausibility of such a scenario.

Since 1978, *Yomiuri Shimbun,* a major Japanese daily newspaper, has been conducting a monthly survey of public opinion, asking: "Do you or do you not

TABLE 3. OLS Estimates of the Determinants of Presidential Popularity (sample period: February 1958 to December 1994)

Explanatory Variables	Dependent Variable: Approval Rate	Dependent Variable: Net Approval Rate
Constant	5.43	0.70
	(2.98)**	(0.29)
Lagged dependent	0.88	0.89
variable	(33.95)**	(34.00)**
Current Japanese call	−0.57	−0.96
rate (percentage)	(−1.65)	(−1.69)
Lagged Japanese call	0.84	1.50
rate (percentage)	(2.41)*	(2.54)*
Current federal funds	−0.03	0.02
rate (percentage)	(−0.08)	(0.03)
Lagged federal funds	0.21	0.27
rate (percentage)	(0.59)	(0.38)
Unemployment (lagged)	−0.06	−0.19
	(−0.39)	(−0.59)
Consumer price inflation	−0.45	−0.81
(lagged)	(−3.02)**	(−2.96)**
Degrees of freedeom	389	389
Adjusted R^2	0.86	0.87
Durbin-Watson	2.01	1.98

Note: t-ratios using heteroskedasticity- and autocorrelation-consistent standard errors are in parentheses.
*$p < .05$ **$p < .01$ (two-tailed)

support the XX cabinet?" where XX refers to the prime minister currently in office.[4] Thus, the proportion of the respondents who say they support the cabinet is called the "support" rate. The net support rate can be calculated by subtracting the proportion of the nonsupporting respondents from the support rate.

I have run more or less the same regressions as those for U.S. presidential popularity, as shown in table 4. In these regressions, the current and lagged levels of the Japanese call rate have coefficients of more or less the same signs as in the U.S. equations, but they are not statistically significant. The federal funds rate seems to show no discernible effect, either. From this, one could tentatively conclude that the costs of monetary manipulation, if tried, would not be particularly high in Japan.

These regression results suggest that there is at least some potential for the Japanese government to engage in strategic behavior with respect to U.S. government. But some caveats are in order.

First, the estimation of these political effects of monetary policy is nothing more than a highly indirect test of strategic behavior. Confirmation of strategic behavior will require that the Japanese government is fully aware of and

TABLE 4.   OLS Estimates of the Determinants of Support for Japanese Cabinets (sample period: April 1978 to December 1995)

Explanatory Variables	Dependent Variable: Support Rate	Dependent Variable: Net Support Rate
Constant	0.23	−3.78
	(0.11)	(−1.49)
Lagged dependent	0.95	0.97
variable	(21.91)**	(21.35)**
Current Japanese call	−0.99	−1.54
rate (percentage)	(−1.34)	(−1.03)
Lagged Japanese call	1.07	1.63
rate (percentage)	(1.40)	(1.07)
Current federal funds	−0.14	−0.30
rate (percentage)	(−0.36)	(−0.40)
Lagged federal funds	0.15	0.33
rate (percentage)	(0.39)	(0.46)
Industrial production	0.15	0.32
growth (lagged)	(1.98)*	(2.07)*
Consumer price inflation	0.03	0.14
(lagged)	(0.07)	(0.19)
Degrees of freedom	159	159
Adjusted R^2	0.86	0.85
Durbin-Watson	2.02	1.92

Note: t-ratios using heteroskedasticity- and autocorrelation-consistent standard errors are in parentheses.
$*p < .05$ $**p < .01$ (two-tailed)

intends to exploit these effects. That is very hard to do within the framework of this current work: for corroboration, one would need in-depth interviews with policymakers.

Second, although one can find political effects of Japanese monetary policy in the United States, the effects are relatively small. Therefore, one should expect that such manipulation will happen only infrequently. It is not surprising, then, that we have not found that Japanese monetary policy is *routinely* used in every U.S. presidential election year.

Third, rational expectations may undermine the argument that assumes highly passive and unsophisticated electorates. The effects of monetary policy, both domestically and internationally, depend largely on the gap between the actual and expected course of monetary policy. If one assumes that electorates are highly rational, well informed, and forward looking, they can see through the political gambit behind monetary policy, thereby nullifying most of the political and economic benefits of manipulative behavior by governments. This argument, which can undermine the domestic PBC hypothesis, applies to the internationalized PBC as well. This essay does not have space to pass judgments on the highly complex issue of voter sophistication, but this argument also suggests that manipulative, strategic behavior should be relatively infrequent.

Conclusions

I have drawn a distinction between passive and strategic behavior and devised a few tests to make judgments on this distinction, using the case of U.S.-Japanese monetary relations. The results are highly consistent with the passive behavior interpretation of Japanese monetary policy: Japanese monetary policy reacts to U.S. fiscal and monetary policy in a predictable way. Therefore, if U.S. macroeconomic policy were used for electoral purposes (and, indeed, there is some evidence for this), such an electoral cycle would be "exported" to Japan.

The only negative result for passive behavior is that there is no statistical evidence that Japanese monetary policy reacts to U.S. *political* pressures in a simple way. But this lack of evidence may be due to coding error.

The results are highly mixed for the strategic behavior interpretation. First, there is only weak evidence that the United States reacts to Japanese monetary policy in a systematic manner, while the Japanese reactions are quite consistent. Therefore, the interpretation of interactive decision making is only weakly supported. This does not rule out the possibility, however, that the Japanese government uses monetary policy strategically with respect to the political survival of the U.S. government along the lines of Ito's hypothesis.

Another negative result is that there is little evidence that Japanese monetary policy is manipulated in every presidential election year. The only finding in this respect is that when Democratic presidents are in office and up for reelection Japanese monetary policy is changed. But this result may be driven by the 1980 election, which occurred when all the central banks in the industrial world were tightening monetary policy in the aftermath of the second oil crisis.[5]

On the other hand, the estimation of the political effects of Japanese monetary policy in the United States and Japan suggests that there is room for the manipulation of Japanese monetary policy envisaged in Ito's hypothesis. There is some evidence that Japanese monetary policy affects U.S. presidential popularity, hence electoral results as well. Therefore, if the Japanese government is well informed about this effect, this potentially could be exploited.

If anything, this study shows that the distinction between passive and strategic behavior, often implicitly made in the literature, is very subtle and hard to make empirically. The problem is that the same behavior can be interpreted either way, and the empirical judgments are highly elusive. In fact, the same problem exists, to some extent, on the issue of voting. Since governments' behavior is expected to differ, depending on whether electorates are passive or strategic, as McGillivray argues in this volume, judging whether governments are strategic or passive also hinges on the nature of electorates' behavior. We may have to wait for future research to devise more discriminating tests on both fronts.

APPENDIX A: DESCRIPTION OF VAR USED TO GENERATE
ECONOMIC FORECASTS

This appendix briefly describes the vector autoregression used to generate forecasts of economic variables that are in turn used as regressors. Suppose that the two-country world economy can be reasonably described by the following VAR(p):

$$\mathbf{y}_t = c + \Phi_1 \mathbf{y}_{t-1} + \Phi_2 \mathbf{y}_{t-2} + \ldots + \Phi_p \mathbf{y}_{t-p} + \varepsilon_t,$$

where $\mathbf{y}_t$ is an $(n \times 1)$ vector of endogenous variables, c is an $(n \times 1)$ vector of constants, and ε_t is an i.i.d. $(n \times 1)$ innovation vector with mean zero and variance-covariance matrix Ω. In particular, we have set $p = 6$ and $n = 4$:

$$\mathbf{Y}_t = \begin{bmatrix} \text{UGR}_t \\ \text{UINF}_t \\ \text{JGR}_t \\ \text{JINF}_t \end{bmatrix},$$

where UGR is the year-on-year growth rate of U.S. industrial production, UINF is the year-on-year rate of U.S. consumer price inflation, JGR is the year-on-year growth rate of Japanese industrial production, and JINF is the year-on-year rate of Japanese consumer price inflation.

By estimating this VAR separately for two subperiods, that is, the fixed exchange rate period until March 1973 and thereafter, three-month forecasts were generated.

The correlation coefficients between the forecasts and the actual values are shown in table A1.

APPENDIX B: CODING RULES OF THE U.S. POLITICAL
PRESSURE VARIABLES

Three dummy variables used to measure U.S. political pressure on Japanese monetary policy have been coded. One variable codes U.S. demands for interest rate cuts in Japan. The other codes generalized U.S. pressure for demand stimulus or reflation. In these pressures, monetary policy is not specifically mentioned, but often fiscal measures, such as tax cuts, are either mentioned or implied. Admittedly, this is only indirect pressure on monetary policy, but it is important in Japan since the Finance Ministry, when it is pressured by the United States to adopt an expansionary *fiscal* policy, often diverts the pressure to monetary policy, considering that monetary easing is a substitute (albeit an imperfect one) for a fiscal stimulus to the economy. Finally, the third is a composite of the first two, taking the value of one if either one of the two dummies takes the value of one, and zero otherwise (table A2).

The source is *Nihon Keizai Shimbun.* The headlines of articles found under the heading *United States* were looked up in the index. If the headlines of the articles were ambiguous, the articles themselves were consulted.

TABLE A1. Correlation Coefficients between Forecast and Actual Values of the Economic Variables

	Fixed Exchange Rate Period (1957–73)	Floating Exchange Rate Period (1973–96)
U.S. industrial production growth rate (UGR)	0.84	0.93
U.S. consumer price inflation rate (UINF)	0.96	0.98
Japanese industrial production growth rate (JGR)	0.95	0.93
Japanese consumer inflation rate (JINF)	0.77	0.98

Several criteria had to be met for an article to be coded as an indication of U.S. political pressure. First, the article had to include a direct or indirect quote and it could not be merely journalists' conjectures on U.S. intentions. Second, the sources of such public statements had to be government officials currently in office (in the Treasury Department, the Federal Reserve, Congress, and so on). Third, statements had to refer to future actions and not past events. For example, U.S. government officials often make statements welcoming or approving recent policy actions such as rate cuts in Japan. Those statements were not counted as pressures.

TABLE A2.   Instrumental Variable Estimates of Japanese Monetary Policy Raction Functions with U.S. Political Pressure Variables (sample period: February 1977 to September 1995)

Explanatory Variables	Dependent Variable: Call Rate (percentage)	Dependent Variable: Discount Rate (percentage)
Constant	−0.41	−0.47
	(−2.15)*	(−2.61)**
Dependent variable (lagged	1.16	0.95
by one period)	(17.13)**	(13.96)**
Dependent variable (lagged	−0.16	−0.11
by two periods)	(−1.57)	(−1.21)
Dependent variable (lagged	−0.07	0.07
by three periods)	(−1.00)	(1.12)
U.S. political pressure	0.03	0.00
(lagged)	(0.56)	(0.02)
Growth in industrial production	0.01	0.00
(three-month forecast)	(1.17)	(0.73)
Consumer price inflation	0.03	0.03
(three-month forecast)	(1.81)	(1.97)
Federal funds rate (percentage)	0.04	
	(3.34)**	
U.S. discount rate (percentage)		0.05
		(3.68)**
U.S. government debt as	0.01	0.01
percentage of U.S. GDP	(2.47)*	(2.84)**
Time elapsed since last	0.00	0.00
election	(1.39)	(1.01)
U.S. presidential election	−0.02	−0.01
year	(−0.31)	(−0.27)
Democrats × U.S. presidential	0.48	0.37
election year	(3.39)**	(3.21)**
Degrees of freedom	212	212
Adjusted R^2	0.98	0.98
Durbin-Watson	1.96	1.94

Note: t-ratios are in parentheses.
*$p < .05$ **$p < .01$ (two-tailed)

The variables were coded on a monthly basis. In other words, the variables took the value of one whenever one or more articles met the criteria during the month. Otherwise, they were coded zero.

NOTES

I would like to thank Mukul Kumar for research assistance.

1. The meaning of this word is deliberately vague to accommodate many different combinations of factors.

2. I owe this point to Lisa Martin.

3. To be precise, the presidential election "year" is taken to be the 12-month period preceding the election, or, in other words, November of the preceding year through October of the election year.

4. The survey had been conducted before 1978, but it was on a quarterly basis.

5. Of course, one may note that 1996 would be a perfect occasion for testing the validity of this hypothesis, but as of this writing the results are unclear.

REFERENCES

Abrams, R. K., R. Froyen, and R. N. Waud. 1980. Monetary Policy Reaction Functions, Consistent Expectations, and the Burns Era. *Journal of Money, Credit, and Banking* 12:30–42.

Calder, K. E. 1993. *Strategic Capitalism: Private Business and Public Purpose in Japanese Industrial Finance*. Princeton: Princeton University Press.

Fair, R. 1978. The Effects of Economic Events on Votes for President. *Review of Economics and Statistics* 60:159–72.

Fair, R. 1982. The Effects of Economic Events on Votes for President: 1980 Results. *Journal of Economics and Statistics* 64:322–25.

Fair, R. 1988. The Effects of Economic Events on Votes for President: 1984 Update. *Political Behavior* 10:168–79.

Grier, K. B. 1989. On the Existence of a Political Monetary Cycle. *American Journal of Political Science* 33:376–89.

Ito, T. 1990. The Timing of Elections and Political Business Cycles in Japan. *Journal of Asian Economics* 1:135–56.

Ito, T. 1991. International Impacts on Domestic Political Economy: A Case of Japanese General Elections. *Journal of International Money and Finance* 10:S73–89.

Kiewiet, D. R. 1983. *Macroeconomics and Micropolitics*. Chicago: University of Chicago Press.

Kramer, G. H. 1971. Short-Term Fluctuations in U.S. Voting Behavior. *American Political Science Review* 65:131–43.

Kramer, G. H. 1983. The Ecological Fallacy Revisited: Aggregate- versus Individual-Level Findings on Economics and Elections, and Sociotropic Voting. *American Political Science Review* 77:92–111.

Laney, L. O., and T. D. Willett. 1983. Presidential Politics, Budget Deficits, and Monetary Policy in the United States; 1960–1976. *Public Choice* 40:53–69.

Nordhaus, W. D. 1975. The Political Business Cycle. *Review of Economic Studies* 42:169–90.

Nordhaus, W. D. 1989. Alternative Approaches to the Political Business Cycle. *Brookings Papers on Economic Activity* 2:1–68.

Oye, K. A. 1986. Explaining Cooperation under Anarchy: Hypotheses and Strategies. In *Cooperation under Anarchy,* edited by Kenneth A. Oye. Princeton: Princeton University Press.

Rogoff, K. 1990. Equilibrium Political Budget Cycles. *American Economic Review* 80:21–36.

Suzuki, M. 1992. Political Business Cycles in the Public Mind. *American Political Science Review* 86:989–96.

Tufte, E. R. 1978. *Political Control of the Economy.* Princeton: Princeton University Press.

Wilson, B. M. 1994. When Social Democrats Choose Neoliberal Economic Policies. *Comparative Politics* 26:149–68.

International Conflict

None Dare Call It Reason: Domestic Incentives and the Politics of War and Peace

Kurt Taylor Gaubatz

[T]he representative betrays his constituents if he sacrifices his judgement to their opinions.

—Edmund Burke

Politics, the saying goes, stops at the water's edge. Faced with external enemies, we have long believed, or perhaps just hoped, that domestic political battles could be put aside. But it is often the case that the demands of the international system are not so clear-cut, and disagreements about the proper course of action in the international sphere exacerbate other domestic divisions. When such disagreements occur, political leaders may well be forced to choose between policies that maximize their personal political fortunes and those that in their view maximize the national interest. The possibility that leaders might make such choices cuts to the foundations of the state and the use of state-centric analysis in the study of international relations. If political actors are making decisions in the face of trade-offs between their personal political prospects and the national interest, then we will need to explore more carefully and systematically the interaction of domestic and international politics in order to build a more effective understanding of politics on the international stage.

Toward this end, I present here a model of decision making by strategic politicians who must make decisions that simultaneously affect their domestic political fortunes and the security of the nation as a whole. I develop a single framework that connects models of domestic and international politics. At the international level, I consider the foreign policy position selected by the governing party and the interaction of that policy with the policy choices of another state. At the domestic level, I consider the effects of different models of decision making by the voters and the position taking of an opposition party.

Political Pandering: The Temptation to Treason

Philosophically, there is considerable debate about how we should respond to the trade-off of the national interest for domestic political interests. The title of this essay and the famous quote from Burke allude to treason or betrayal when the national interest is knowingly sacrificed to the personal interests of political actors. Burke's provocative assertion that representatives should follow their consciences rather than simply transmitting some sense of constituent demands has traditionally characterized one pole in a debate about the sources of the national interest. At the other pole are those who advocate a close connection between the demands of the wider public and the definition of state interests. Democratic values, in this view, are best realized when representatives directly express the wishes of their constituents.[1] Whichever way this debate is resolved, it will be useful to better understand the dynamics that make political leaders more or less likely to compromise their sense of the national interest for political gains.

Following the Burkean line, which provides a nicer alliteration, I will label the incentive to pander to domestic interests "the treason temptation." Understanding the sources and nature of the treason temptation is important to the study of foreign policy and international relations. There has long been considerable dissatisfaction with the treatment of states as unitary rational actors. The search for the so-called microfoundations of the state as an actor in the international arena has yielded much in the way of heat but relatively less light. Despite widespread acknowledgment of the levels of analysis issue, many scholars have simply ignored the problem, working either at the level of states in some variant of the realist tradition or simply pursuing a domestic politics model that focuses on the creation of foreign policy in the internal battles of national political actors. Policy analysts have tended to be even more cavalier about the levels of analysis issue, pursuing an intuitive balance between the demands of the international system and the vagaries of domestic incentives. Historians, meanwhile, have been moving toward an increasingly domestic politics view of international relations (Levy 1988).

There has been a resurgence of interest in the notion that international relations may be better understood by reference to the interaction of domestic and international politics (see Putnam 1988). One example of this development can be seen in the work of Bruce Bueno de Mesquita and David Lalman (1992), who have recently shown the importance of this problem within a rationalist framework. Bueno de Mesquita's early work (1981) left the sources of utility indeterminate—they could be domestic, international, or even personal—while building his models on the assumption that a single leader plays a gatekeeping role that ensures that foreign policy will reflect the transitive preferences required of rational actors. More recently, working with David Lalman, he has argued that international incentives alone are insufficient for explaining the foreign policy choices of states and the international outcomes to which they lead (Bueno de Mesquita and Lalman 1992).[2] Nonetheless, their models still put domestic politics within a black box.

The Model

The central problem in moving away from the unitary rational actor mode of analysis remains the formidable challenge of linking the domestic and international incentives faced by state leaders in a coherent single model. My goal in this essay is to develop a model that can illustrate the simultaneous impact of domestic and international influences on the foreign policy choices of domestic actors. The international influence I look at is the effect of the foreign policy choice on the probability of war with another state. The domestic influence is the effect of the foreign policy choice on the probability that the government will be reelected. This model, then, pulls together the core phenomena at the domestic and international levels—elections and war, respectively. I proceed by developing a model of electoral dynamics and then one of conflict dynamics. I then put the two models together to provide a tool for analyzing the interaction of the two realms.

The Domestic Politics Model

I build the domestic component of my model around the electoral process. Elections are a particularly transparent form of leadership selection in polities. This does not mean, however, that the analysis has to be restricted to democratic states. Nearly all leaders have to satisfy some level of domestic constraint and selection process, whether it be by the general populace, elites in a monolithic political party, or a set of powerful colonels in a military dictatorship. While I refer here to the electorate, the appellation "selectorate" could be applied to refer to the selecting body in almost any political setting. The political dynamics of selection I identify in the democratic context should still largely apply.

Foreign Policy and Elections

The domestic component of this model involves two parties—a governing party and an opposition party—competing for an election victory through their choice of a foreign policy. The influence of foreign policy positions on presidential elections is a subject of considerable controversy (see Page and Shapiro 1992; and Aldrich, Sullivan, and Borgida 1989). At a minimum, this model requires foreign policy to have at least a marginal influence on election outcomes. As long as the influence of foreign policy on elections is not zero, then to the degree that government leaders want to maximize their electoral prospects, they will need to select foreign policy choices with an eye toward the electoral consequences. More realistically, my focus here on the relationship between wars and elections looks at foreign policy issues that have a very high profile and thus suggests circumstances in which foreign policy should prove more salient in the electoral environment.

Voting Behavior

Thinking about elections requires a consideration of the behavior of voters. For the purposes of the model, I focus on a single voter, who can be thought of as the median voter. Modeling the behavior of this voter requires some consideration of the large literature on the motivations and decision processes of voters. At the risk of some simplification, we can reduce this literature to three main streams of thought. These streams focus, respectively, on party identification, the evaluation of outcomes, and the evaluation of policies.

In the tradition that emphasizes party identification, voters are seen as quite limited in their capabilities. Party identification is a useful heuristic that saves voters the trouble of monitoring either the performance or the positions of the parties on individual issues (see Berelson, et al. 1954). In my model party line voting can also be seen as reflecting the behavior of voters who focus on other issues besides foreign affairs. Single issue pro-life voters, for example, are also saved the trouble of monitoring positions and performance on foreign policy issues in making their voting decision.

In the retrospective voting literature, voters focus on outcomes (Fiorina 1981). The advocates of this position have primarily addressed economic issues. Voters who observe that the economy is doing well—either in terms of their personal economic well-being or in terms of the general well-being of the economy—will vote for the government. When things are not going well, it will be time for a change. These voters do not have to know anything about the policies of the government or opposition party. Nor do they need to concern themselves with theories about the relationship between policies and outcomes. They do, however, require more information than in the party identification model, since they have to form some impression about economic conditions.

It is important to note, however, that retrospective voting may be less tenable for issues involving international relations than it is for the domestic economy. Retrospective voters interested in economic performance can look either in their own pocketbooks or at some widely agreed upon indicators of the health of the domestic economy. The question of whether war is more or less likely, or a state is more or less secure, is a much more difficult assessment to make. Often, this assessment will be made only through the lens of policy debates. Kennedy's missile gap in the 1960 election was a product of the policy debate, not an objective reality that voters could directly assess through their personal experiences. Was the Gulf War a bad result?—the Bush administration was asleep at the switch and war happened. Or was it a good result?—Saddam Hussein was stopped with a minimal loss of American lives before he could develop nuclear weapons and realize his vision of revitalizing the greater Babylonian empire. Consider the central international conflict for the United States in the latter half of the Cold War. Was the Soviet Union behaving responsibly and cooperatively throughout the period of détente? Or was it systematically exploiting Western good will? Were the SALT agreements good results or bad results? Right up until the fall of the Berlin Wall, there was still significant debate over whether the changes in Gorbachev's foreign policy were serious or just the clever tactics of an ambitious politician jockeying for domestic power and trying to lull the West into complacency.[3]

This brings us to the third voting model, which portrays voters as *prospective* in their voting decisions. In this view, voters form expectations about the future impact of the policies of the competing parties. Prospective voting makes the greatest demands on the abilities of voters. Voters have to be aware of the policy differences of the parties and make connections between those differences and their expectations for the future. Nonetheless, as I have suggested, on many international issues this may be the only way for voters to actually evaluate outcomes.

My approach here is to build a model that incorporates all three of these views of individual voting behavior. This approach allows me to examine the impact of these different views within the framework of the model. The intuition behind this approach is that voters are motivated by some combination of all three factors. Voters do have party biases, but they also form preferences over policies and outcomes.

I describe the median voter with five variables.[4] First, the voter can have a relative attitude toward war and peace. This attitude, A, will be represented by a point on a scale from $A = 1$ for a strong pro-war bias to $A = -1$ for a strong antiwar bias. In this model, this attitude will apply to both policies and outcomes.

The second variable that describes the preferences of the voter represents the party identification component of the vote. The voter has an underlying preference for the government or the opposition. The party bias, P, will also be measured on the $[-1, 1]$ interval, with 1 a strong bias toward the government and -1 representing the strongest bias in favor of the opposition. Again, P can also be thought of as representing the influence of other issues—the domestic economy, abortion, whatever—that the voter may like or dislike about the government and the opposition.

In addition to these two preference variables, there are the three weighting variables that determine the relative role of party, outcomes, and policy differences in the voter's decision making. v_P represents the relative weight of the party bias. v_R represents the weight of the concern with outcomes (R for results). v_D represents the relative weight the voter puts on the policy differences between the government and the opposition (D for differences).

I should digress for a moment here to say that the difference between policy-based voting and outcome-based voting is particularly important in this model. As I discuss at greater length below, the security dilemma plays a significant role in the international component of my analysis. The security dilemma forces us to recognize that under different international conditions the same policy might lead to quite different outcomes (Jervis 1971). In this regard, it is important to note that the voter in this model is not sophisticated about the security dilemma. Voters prefer belligerent policies when they are basically in favor of war, and they prefer conciliatory policies when they are basically in favor of peace. This bars me from including the important possibility that the median voter likes a belligerent policy in order to avoid war. I do, however, allow policymakers to pursue this more sophisticated course.[5]

The Voting Decision

We can now describe the voting decision. The median voter reelects the government when that voter makes a net positive evaluation of the government compared with the opposition in accordance with the relative weight that voter puts on outcomes, policy differences, and party membership. In formal terms, the median voter reelects the government if and only if:

$$ADv_D + ARv_R + Pv_P \geq 0, \tag{1}$$

where

> A = attitude of the median voter toward war
> D = difference between policy of government and policy of opposition
> R = results of government policy in the international arena
> P = party bias of median voter
> v_D = voter's weight on policy difference
> v_R = voter's weight on result of government policy
> v_P = voter's weight on underlying party bias

and subject to:

$$A,D,R,P \in [-1,1]$$

$$v_D + v_R + v_P = 1.$$

Equation 1 will yield a result that falls into the range $[-1, 1]$. We can map this outcome into the $[0, 1]$ space and then use it to represent the probability that the government will be elected (e) as in equation 2:

$$e = .5(ADv_D + ARv_R + Pv_P) + .5. \tag{2}$$

The government and the opposition will want to choose policies to optimize their respective probabilities of being elected. The government will want to maximize e, while the opposition will want to minimize it. They will both be constrained in their attempts to do this, however, by the realization that their foreign policy choices also have international effects. To fully specify the behavior of the government and the opposition, we will now need to develop a corresponding model of that arena.

The International Conflict Model

The international arena encompasses the foreign policy choices of two states: state A and state B. The domestic politics in state A will be modeled as in equation 2. Two parties will choose foreign policies that have effects on both their electoral prospects and the international environment. The governing party's foreign policy is actually pursued and leads to results in the real world. The foreign policy of the opposition party is a policy statement that only affects real world results to the degree that other states pay attention to this electoral competition.

State B and the Security Dilemma

I will model state B as a unitary rational actor. State B will choose whether or not there will be a war based on its reactions to the foreign policy dynamics within state A. The decision process for state B is defined by two variables. The first is the degree to which state B can be deterred. Following the logic of the security dilemma, state B will either be deterred or provoked by a belligerent foreign policy line in state A. We can think of nature choosing a type for state B—either deterrable or provokable—and the variable d can represent a belief about the probability that state B is deterrable. A deterrable state B ($d = 1$) will choose peace if state A chooses belligerence, but it will be tempted to exploit state A or start a war if state A chooses a conciliatory policy. A provokable state B ($d = 0$) will choose war if state A chooses belligerence and will choose peace if state A chooses a conciliatory policy.

State B and the Domestic Politics of State A

The second variable that will describe state B is the degree to which it observes the internal political process in state A. In this model, this observation will be represented by state B's attention to the foreign policy line of the opposition party in state A. The variable *t*—for *transparency*—will capture this effect, varying from 0 when state B pays no attention at all to state A's domestic opposition to 1 when state B is obsessed with the policy line of state A's domestic opposition and ignores the foreign policy of the government.[6]

The attention that state B pays to the opposition party in state A will likely be a function of two factors. First, and most commonly discussed, is the likelihood that the opposition party will soon become the governing party. State B might pay considerable attention to domestic politics in state A if the opposition party is advocating a dramatically different foreign policy line than the government and if there are indicators that the opposition party is highly likely to take over from the governing party. The importance of this phenomenon is often seen most clearly when states fail to pay adequate attention to domestic opposition forces in other states. Consider the failure of the United States to adequately assess the frailties of the regime of the Shah of Iran and the vitriolic anti-Americanism of the Ayatollah Khomeini.

A second kind of transparency comes into play to the degree that domestic politics are seen as a part of state A's overall foreign policy. This kind of transparency has not garnered much discussion in the international relations literature. It is not difficult, however, to think of cases that raise this issue. A state that is trying to present a highly aggressive foreign policy in order to deter an enemy may find such a policy less effective to the degree that an enemy finds comfort in the opposition's lack of support for such a foreign policy line. In the months leading up to the Gulf War, Saddam Hussein seemed to take considerable, if misplaced, solace in the belief that the Democratic Congress would not support George Bush's more forceful foreign policy line.

From the other direction, a state trying to present a conciliatory front may be stymied to the degree that domestic opposition forces advocate a hard line policy. Current American policy toward Russia is surely predicated on a sense of both of these sources of transparency. American defense policy toward Russia has to be based on attempt to assess the relative weakness of the current Yeltsin government. No matter how friendly Yeltsin may seem, American leaders are unlikely to too quickly draw down American forces in light of the hard line voices that so seriously threaten his power. In a little bit different scenario, George Bush's primary battle against the right wing of the Republican Party in 1988 forced him to take a more belligerent foreign policy line than he would have preferred. He attempted to mitigate the effects of this rhetoric outside of the domestic arena by telling Gorbachev that President Reagan was surrounded by "marginal intellectual thugs" who would try to portray Bush as a closet liberal. He assured Gorbachev that once he was elected he would work to improve U.S.-Soviet relations. In the meantime, he urged Gorbachev to ignore the many things he might have to do and say to get elected. Gorbachev later recalled this discussion as the most important talk he ever had with George Bush (Beschloss and Talbott 1993, 3–4).

The Probability of War

The foreign policy positions of the government and the opposition in state A will be defined in terms of a probability of pursuing a belligerent policy. Thus, $g = 1$ will reflect certainty that the government is going to pursue a belligerent foreign policy, while $g = 0$ will reflect certainty that the government will pursue a policy of conciliation. b will play the corresponding role for the opposition. Once the government and the opposition choose their foreign policies, the probability of war will depend on whether state B is deterrable or provokable and the amount of attention state B pays respectively to the government and the opposition in state A. This can be expressed as in equation 3:

$$p = (1 - d)[(1 - t)g + tb] + d[(1 - t)(1 - g) + t(1 - b)], \qquad (3)$$

where

p = probability of war
d = probability that state B is deterrable or provokable
t = weight that state B gives to opposition's policies in state A (transparency)
g = probability that the government will choose a belligerent foreign policy
b = probability that the opposition will choose a belligerent foreign policy
$p,d,t,g,b \in [0,1]$

In equation 3 the probability of war is the sum of the probability that a provokable state will be provoked and the probability that a deterrable state will be tempted. More specifically, the probability of provoking a state is the probability that state B is provokable $(1 - d)$ multiplied by the probabilities that the government and/or the opposition will be belligerent (g and b, respectively). These latter probabilities are weighted by the attention state B pays to government and opposition policies ($(1 - t)$ and t, respectively). The probability that state B will be tempted to exploit state A is the probability that state B will be deterrable (d) multiplied by the sum of the probabilities that the government and/or the opposition will be conciliatory ($(1 - g)$ and $(1 - b)$, respectively). Again, these probabilities are weighted by the relative attention that state B pays to the government and the opposition ($(1 - t)$ and t, respectively).

Equation 3 can be rearranged to focus attention on the policies of the government and opposition, as in equation 4:

$$p = g(1 - t)(1 - 2d) + bt(1 - 2d) + d. \tag{4}$$

As discussed previously, the intuition behind equation 4 is that belligerence will count for more—either in provoking or deterring state B—when the government is backed up by the opposition. Likewise, to the degree that state B pays attention to the opposition in state A, it will be more likely to react to a conciliatory policy from state A that reflects a foreign policy consensus.

The Combined Model

I now turn to the task of integrating the domestic and international models. Beginning with the electoral model (eq. 2), there are two variables that connect foreign policy and the international environment. First, we need to define D for the difference between the policy of the government and the policy of the opposition. I use the simple expression $(g - b)$—the difference between the policy of the government and the policy of the opposition—in that role here. There are more complex ways to describe the policy difference that are more satisfying as general functions, but $(g - b)$ offers some computational advantages and is adequate for the analysis that follows here.[7] As with D, $(g - b)$ will span the $[-1, 1]$ interval. It will take the -1 value when the government is maximally conciliatory ($g = 0$) and the opposition is maximally belligerent ($b = 1$) and will equal 1 when the government is maximally belligerent and the opposition is maximally conciliatory. When the government and the opposition take the same position, it will equal zero. It will be positive when the government is more belligerent than the opposition and negative when the opposition is more belligerent than the government.

The primary point of connection between the international and domestic models is the role of the probability of war as a central indicator of the results of foreign policy choices. This brings us to the second variable needed in the election model (eq. 2), which is the result variable, R. I approximate R from the probability of war by mapping the probability of war from the $[0, 1]$ range to the $[-1, 1]$ range with a simple linear transformation:

$$R = 2p - 1. \tag{5}$$

When the probability of war is greater than .5, R is positive. R is negative when the probability of war is less than .5. When war is a certainty, $R = 1$. When peace is a certainty, $R = -1$.

Substituting the probability of war from equation 4, into equation 5 we get:

$$R = g2(1 - t)(1 - 2d) + b2t(1 - 2d) + 2d - 1. \tag{6}$$

We can now rewrite the election equation (eq. 2) with the substitutions for D and R as in equation 7:

$$e = .5\{A(g - b)v_D + A[g2(1 - t)(1 - 2d) + b\,2t(1 - 2d)$$

$$+ 2d - 1]v_R + Pv_P\} + .5. \tag{7}$$

Rearranging terms to put the focus on the foreign policy choices of the government and the opposition, g and b, respectively, gives us equation 8:

$$e = g(.5)A[v_D + 2(1 - t)(1 - 2d)v_R] - b(.5)A[v_D$$

$$- 2t(1 - 2d)v_R] + .5Av_R(2d - 1) + .5Pv_P + .5. \tag{8}$$

I have now defined both the probability of war and the probability of the government being reelected as linear combinations of the policy choices of the government and the opposition. To move to an understanding of the maximizing behavior of these two actors, we need to put these probabilities in the context of expected utilities.

The Utility Equations

In this model, I present the government and the opposition as players that receive utility both from being elected and from seeing their preferred results in the international system. Thus, both parties have mixed motives. They seek reelection and specific international outcomes. The politicians in this model are not the single-minded reelection maximizers that are common in many models of domestic politics alone. When the same actions maximize utility in both the international and domestic dimensions, the choice of policy will be relatively easy. The more difficult, and also more interesting, situations will arise when the same actions increase utility in one dimension while decreasing it in the other. The expected utility of the government and the opposition will be based on the utility they receive from war and election multiplied by the probabilities of these events. I will define a variable, W, to be the utility the government gets from war and $\bar{W}$ to be the utility from peace. Similarly, E will be the utility the government gets from being elected, while $\bar{E}$ will represent the utility from not being elected. For the opposition, I will use W° and E° for the utility of war and election, respectively.[8] The expected utility equations will be as presented in equations 9 and 10.

$$EU(\text{government}) = pW + (1 - p)\bar{W} + eE + (1 - e)\bar{E} \tag{9}$$

$$\text{EU(opposition)} = pW^\circ + (1 - p)\bar{W}^\circ + (1 - e)E^\circ + e\bar{E}^\circ. \tag{10}$$

Substituting p and e from equations 4 and 8 and rearranging terms gives us equations 11 and 12:

$$\text{EU(govt)} = g[(1 - t)(1 - 2d)(W - \bar{W}) + (Av_R(1 - t)(1 - 2d)$$

$$+ .5Av_D)(E - \bar{E})] + b[t(1 - 2d)(W - \bar{W}) + (Av_R t(1 - 2d)$$

$$+ .5Av_D)(E - \bar{E})] + d(W - \bar{W}) + (.5Av_R(2d - 1) + .5Pv_P$$

$$+ .5)(E - \bar{E}) + \bar{W} + \bar{E} \tag{11}$$

$$\text{EU(opp)} = g[(1 - t)(1 - 2d)(W^\circ - \bar{W}^\circ) + (Av_R(1 - t)(1 - 2d)$$

$$+ .5Av_D)(\bar{E}^\circ - E^\circ)] + b[t(1 - 2d)(W^\circ - \bar{W}^\circ) + (Av_R t(1 - 2d)$$

$$- .5Av_D)(\bar{E}^\circ - E^\circ)] + d(W^\circ - \bar{W}^\circ) + (.5Av_R(2d - 1) + .5Pv_P$$

$$+ .5)(\bar{E}^\circ - E^\circ) + \bar{W}^\circ + E^\circ. \tag{12}$$

Choosing a Foreign Policy

The utility equation for the government is linear in g. Thus, utility will be maximized when g is either 0 or 1.[9] For the purpose of this model, the choice of the government and the opposition will always be either complete belligerence or complete conciliation. Whether the government and the opposition choose belligerence or conciliation will be a function of the signs and magnitudes of the five remaining parameters (t, A, d, v_D, v_R), plus the relative utilities of war and of election.

    Equation 13 gives the change in the expected utility of the government for a change in belligerence. When the right side of this equation is positive, the government will pursue a belligerent policy. When the right side is negative, it will pursue a conciliatory policy. The critical point at which government policy will change from conciliatory to belligerent occurs when the right side of the equation is zero. This point is shown by equation 15. Equations 14 and 16 are the corresponding relationships for the opposition's choice of policy.

$$\delta\text{EU(govt)}/\delta g = (1 - t)(1 - 2d)(W - \bar{W}) + (.5Av_D$$

$$+ Av_R(1 - t)(1 - 2d))(E - \bar{E}) \tag{13}$$

$$\delta EU(opp)/\delta b = t(1 - 2d)(W° - \bar{W}°)$$

$$+ (.5Av_D - Av_R t(1 - 2d)) (E° - \bar{E}°) \tag{14}$$

Government:

$$(1 - t)(1 - 2d) / (.5Av_D + Av_R(1 - t)(1 - 2d)) = (E - \bar{E}) / (\bar{W} - W) \tag{15}$$

Opposition:

$$t(1 - 2d) / (.5Av_D - Av_R t(1 - 2d)) = (E° - \bar{E}°) / (\bar{W}° - W°). \tag{16}$$

The right side of equations 15 and 16 is simply the ratio of the relative utility of being elected over the relative utility of peace. I will call this the *utility ratio*. The left side looks more complicated, but it is also relatively straightforward to interpret. $(1 - t)$ is the relative importance of government policy for the behavior of state B. $(1 - 2d)$ is the probability that state B is deterrable mapped to the $[-1, 1]$ interval, so that it indicates both whether state B is deterrable or provokable (the sign) and the magnitude of that propensity (the absolute value of $(1 - 2d)$). Thus, the numerator tells us the likelihood that the government's actions will lead to war or peace. The denominator tells us the likelihood that the government's actions will lead to reelection. This has two components. The first component $(.5Av_D)$ shows the contribution of the government's policy to the difference between the policies of the government and the opposition weighted by the emphasis the voter puts on policy differences (v_D) and whether the voter has a strong attitude toward war or peace (A). The second component incorporates the likelihood of war expression we saw in the numerator, $(1 - t)(1 - 2d)$, with the weight the voter puts on results (v_R) and the voter's attitude toward war and peace (A). Thus, the left side of the equation is the ratio of the influence of government policy on war over the influence of government policy on reelection. I will call this the *effects ratio*. The effects ratio for the opposition is derived in the same manner, but it is conditioned by t, which is the attention state B pays to the opposition, rather than by $(1 - t)$, which reflects the relative attention paid to the government.

I have now derived a relatively straightforward single model that links the domestic and international incentives faced by government and opposition leaders. Both the government and the opposition attempt to balance the ratio of the effects of their policies with the ratio of utilities they get, respectively, from domestic and international outcomes. Some comparative statics will help to illuminate the kinds of behavior this model would predict with variation in the underlying components of the model at both the domestic and international levels.

Comparative Statics

Let us begin with a consideration of the effects of the perceived nature of state B. Suppose that the government values peace about three times as strongly as it values reelection. This will set the right side of the equation—the utility ratio—at 1/3. Let state B focus 80 percent of its attention on the actions of the government and 20 percent on the policy of the opposition ($t = .2$). Let the median voter be moderately antiwar ($A = -.5$). The median voter will put more emphasis on results than on policies but will also put some weight on a party bias ($v_R = .5$, $v_D = .3$, $v_P = .2$). Finally, we allow d, the probability that state B is deterrable, to vary. Figure 1 is a plot of the utility ratio and the effects ratio as a function of d. To the left of the asymptotic point for the effects ratio (where the effect of belligerence on the election is zero), the government will pursue a belligerent foreign policy whenever the effects ratio is above the utility ratio.[10] When the effects ratio is below the utilities ratio, the government will pursue a conciliatory foreign policy in accord with both the demands of the median voter and the international system. When the effects ratio line crosses the utilities ratio, which happens when $d \approx .52$, the government will switch from a conciliatory to a belligerent foreign policy. This suggests a very small zone between $d = .5$ and $d = .52$ when the government realizes that its policy is not optimal for avoiding war but pursues a conciliatory policy because of the perceived electoral benefits. Under these conditions it appears relatively unlikely that a government will be tempted to pursue a policy that compromises its sense of the national interest.

The incentives faced by the opposition in this case are a little more complex. In the first place, the opposition policy has much less impact on state B ($t = .2$). This increases the range in which the opposition will be tempted to pander to the public, since there is less of a down side in terms of the international effects. Likewise, good outcomes hurt the electoral prospects of the opposition in proportion to the degree that the public pays attention to outcomes. This means that the result and policy components of the electoral effect can cut in opposite directions (this can be seen in the minus sign in the denominator on the left side of eq. 16). If, like the government, the opposition is three times as concerned about peace as it is about getting elected, the opposition will be tempted to espouse a conciliatory foreign policy that increases the risk of war when the probability that state B requires deterrence is between .5 and .57. Unlike the case for the government, we can see in figure 2 that this temptation is highly elastic with respect to the utility ratio. If opposition politicians were to become twice as concerned about getting elected as they are about peace, they would pander to the public by espousing a conciliatory policy even if they were certain that such a policy would lead to war if it were to be enacted.

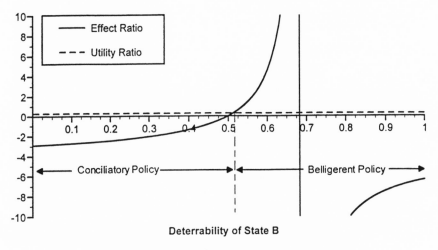

Fig. 1. Government incentives for a belligerent foreign policy

The Utility Ratio

The policy pursued by the government is considerably less sensitive to changes in the utility ratio. Going back to the government's incentives in figure 1 and thinking about the right side of the equation—the relative valuation of peace and reelection—we can see that the range for the treason temptation is quite stable as long as peace is preferred to war and elections are no more important than peace. In this case, holding the other parameters to the same values as in the previous example, the right side of equation 14 will fall within the [0, 1] range, and the temptation to pursue a conciliatory policy when there is a belief that state B is deterrable will be within the range $.5 \leq d \leq .54$. If reelection is more important to the government than peace, it is naturally more likely that policies that are suboptimal from the standpoint of international relations will be pursued. In this case, however, the government would have to have a *very* significant preference for reelection over peace to make much of a difference. If the government was 10 times more interested in reelection than in peace, it would pursue a conciliatory policy in accord with both its domestic and international interests as long as it was likely that state B was provokable. It would keep pursuing that policy—at odds with its sense of the national interest—if there was between a 50 and 60 percent probability that state B needed to be deterred. In that range, the electoral benefit of pandering to the public's desire for a conciliatory policy would outweigh the risk of war upsetting the results-oriented public. If the probability that belligerence will prevent war is above .6,

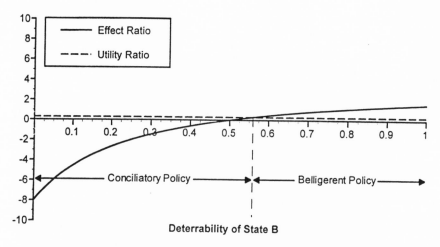

Fig. 2. Opposition incentives for a belligerent foreign policy

the results effect is sufficient to outweigh the policy effect. In this range, the concerns for reelection and peace will both work to make the government more belligerent.[11] Indeed, above the asymptotic point at about $d = .7$ there is no value for the utility ratio that will motivate a trade of the national interest for electoral interests.

There are, as we will see, ways to move the asymptotic point and thus to increase the range in which a greater relative concern with election will lead to policies that are perceived to compromise the national interest. But it is also important to emphasize that the utility ratio will be very much affected by the way in which the international results are framed. Foreign policy choices are rarely framed simply in terms of peace or war. If the war option is framed in a way that makes the costs of a given policy seem less, the utility ratio will get larger. One common way for this to happen is through time shifting. This analysis has been static. The choice of politicians, however, is often not a choice of war or no war but rather a risk of war now that may be repairable in the future. Thus, Roosevelt did not envision himself foregoing the possibility of deterring Hitler after the 1940 election just because before the election, while taking credit for the neutrality legislation he had consistently opposed, he assured the voters: "Your boys are not going to be sent into any foreign wars" (Divine 1974, 81–82). To put it in the most stark terms, his real choice was between deterring Hitler with some degree of effectiveness now (before the election) or deterring Hitler later (after the election) with some perhaps marginally diminished effectiveness. Even though the absolute costs of failing to deter Hitler were clearly very high, the marginal cost of delay may have been viewed as relatively low and thus could be traded off against the benefits of domestic electoral politics.

The utility ratio may also be affected to the degree that politicians blur the distinction between electoral and national interest gains. Politicians are often quite adept at what Alexander George (1980, 234) has labeled value extension—that is, the extension of values on one dimension onto another. To the degree that politicians see their own election as critical to the national interest, or concomitantly see grave threats to the national interest in the election of their adversaries, the importance of election will increase relative to the importance of a specific outcome on one particular issue. Politicians who conflate their election with the national interest are more likely to rationalize electorally expedient uses of force abroad.

Transparency

The transparency variable (t) indicates the degree to which state B pays attention to the policy statements of the opposition in state A. When $t = 0$ the opposition's policy statements are irrelevant to the actions of state B. In this case, the opposition will have no incentive to espouse responsible policies and will always pursue the policies that please the public. The larger t is the smaller will be the effect of government policies on the actions of state B and thus the larger will be the range in which the government will be willing to trade international risks for domestic electoral gains. If t were to rise above .5—indicating that state B pays more attention to the opposition's policy statements than to the government's policy actions—figures 1 and 2 would switch and the government would have consistently more liberty to pursue domestically popular policies with less concern about their international repercussions.

Retrospective and Prospective Voting

Increasing voter attention to results has opposite effects on the government and the opposition. The more results matter, the more the government has to pursue policies that it believes will ensure the optimal international outcomes, even at the expense of policy positions that alienate domestic constituencies. The opposition, on the other hand, will find its policies under less public scrutiny. There will be an increased temptation to seek electoral profits from working to sabotage the results achieved by the government's policies. Results-oriented voters will thus be able to place more trust in the sincerity of the governing party, but they will have to be more suspicious of the opposition.

Increasing voter attention to policies and decreasing their attention to results will flatten the relevant part of the curve and thus will increase the potential area of a treason temptation for both the government and the opposition. If we reverse the values we used in the earlier example, so that voter concern with policies is now .5 while concern with results is .3, the range for a government that is three times as concerned about peace as about reelection would only increase from about $.50 < d < .52$ to $.50 < d < .53$. The real change would come in the potential range. Where, in the case illustrated in figure 1, a government that is 10 times more concerned with reelection than peace would be tempted in the range $.50 < d < .57$, when we increase the voter's focus on policies the range becomes $.50 < d < .81$. The opposition case is even more dramatic. An opposition that values peace and reelection about *equally* would be induced to pander to public demands for any d in the range $.50 < d < .88$.

The importance of policy relative to results is particularly likely to be high when results are ambiguous or unknown. For the reasons given previously, this may be the case in international relations more often than we might want to admit. Except in truly dramatic times, voters will need to have a sense of the relationship between policies and outcomes in order to evaluate the difficult counterfactual question of whether things are going well or poorly.

An important implication of this model, then, is that for voters a little bit of intelligence is a most dangerous thing. A public that focuses solely on its party bias or on outcomes—that essentially ignores foreign policy—would create no treason temptation. Likewise, a public that recognizes the security dilemma and was as attuned to the intricacies of foreign policy as elites would leave no space between the demands of the international environment and the demands of the domestic environment. It is only when the public has strong policy preferences at odds with the preferences of the government and opposition parties that these actors will find it advantageous to sacrifice the national interest for their personal political needs.

The Attitude toward War

Finally, changing the public's attitude toward war changes the steepness of the curves in figures 1 and 2. Decreasing the public's antiwar attitude makes war a less critical electoral issue. This increases the steepness of the curves and thus decreases the range of the treason temptation for both the government and the opposition. Increasing the public's antiwar attitude makes war a more critical issue. This flattens the curves and makes the policy choice more sensitive to changes in the utility ratio. The irony, then, is that the more intensely the public feels about peace the more likely it is to get a government that will sacrifice peace for the electoral benefit of pursuing the popular policy.

Since in this model the danger and costs of war and exploitation are symmetric, making the public pro-war simply flips the figures around. A policy of belligerence will be in accord with both the national interest and the electoral interests of the parties as long as the probability that state B is deterrable is above .5. When it is clear that state B is provokable, both the government and the opposition are likely to pursue a conciliatory policy, despite public protestations. The government and especially the opposition will be most tempted to pander to the pro-war public with a belligerent foreign policy at the expense of the national interest when the probability that state B is deterrable (d) is just below .5.

The Probability of Election and the Probability of War

Thus far, I have focused on the temptation to pursue policies that are at odds with this formulation of the national interest. I turn back, now, to consider the relationship between these foreign policy choices and the probabilities of war and election. Figure 3 plots the probabilities of war and the government being elected under the parameters of the case presented earlier ($t = .2$, $A = -.5$, $v_R = .5$, $v_D = .3$). These parameters are sufficient for calculating the probability of war. For calculating the probability of the government being elected, I have added the assumption that there is no party bias ($P = 0$). The inclusion of a party bias would simply shift the curve up or down by the amount of the party bias multiplied by the weight on party bias (v_P).[12]

The Probability of War

There are several features to note in these plots. The most obvious characteristic is that the probability of war is inversely related to the extremeness of either the deterrability or the provokability of state B. The clearer the imperatives of the international system, the more likely state A is to choose the appropriate policy and the less likely war is. In this model, it is when there is the greatest ambiguity about the appropriate policy to pursue that the danger of war is the highest.[13]

It is also important to see the way that the probability of war interacts with the foreign policy choices of the government and the opposition. If the government and the opposition always pursue the optimal international result, the probability of war would be two straight lines in a single peak at $d = .5$ and $pr(\text{war}) = .5$. Compared with this baseline form, we see that in the small range between $d = .5$ and $d = .52$ the choice of the government to pursue a conciliatory policy, despite its sense that state B is marginally more likely to require deterrence, pushes the probability of war above the 50 percent mark. The probability of war then remains above its baseline as long as the opposition continues to argue for a conciliatory policy despite its awareness of the shortfalls of such a policy in the international realm. Thus, the temptation of the government and the opposition to focus on domestic political battles at the expense of the national interest is greatest precisely when the international system is the most dangerous. The international system, in turn, is made even more dangerous by this lack of attention.

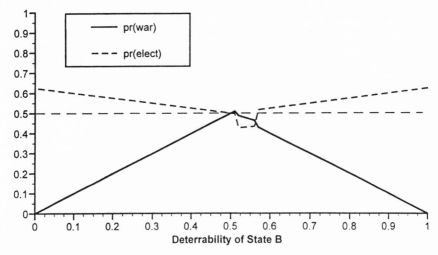

Fig. 3. The probabilities of war and election. ($t = .2$, $A = -.5$, $V_R = .5$, $V_D = .3$; the horizontal line at .5 is for reference.)

To look at this from another angle: when the policy implications of international dangers are clear, the opposing domestic political forces will have clear incentives to join together. Responsible political parties will have both national interest and electoral incentives to pursue the policies demanded by the international system, even when there is strong public pressure to follow another course. When the policy implications of international dangers are not clear, however, the two political parties will not respond with a united front. Ambiguities in the relationship between policies and outcomes will not only create more potential for policy differences because of this uncertainty, but they will also create a space in which there may be an electoral temptation to pursue a policy contrary to the national interest.

One can think here of the period leading up to World War II when the West (and Stalin as well, for that matter) vacillated between a policy of appeasement and a policy of belligerence toward Hitler. The inability to see clearly what the appropriate policy is leaves a political space for domestic political actors to pursue the electorally optimal policy. Stalin, admittedly, probably didn't have much of a problem with this, but in Britain, France, Canada, and the United States there were obvious dilemmas in trying to choose a foreign policy line that could optimize both the domestic and international outcomes. Isolationism flourished in the West, producing domestic demands for a conciliatory policy, while most government leaders recognized the need to restrain Hitler's ambitions. In Canada, MacKenzie King was able to pursue a belligerent policy in support of Britain only by limiting Canadian capabilities by promising not to send conscripts overseas.[14] The infamous prewar policy of the British Conservative Party was simultaneously "all sanctions short of war" and "peace at almost any price."[15] In the American presidential campaign of 1940, both Willkie and Roosevelt favored more involvement in the European war but felt electorally constrained to take a more neutral line. Willkie was pushed in that direction by his Republican backers. Roosevelt was pushed by the fear that Willkie would more vigorously take up the isolationist cause (Divine 1974).

The Probability of Election

The plot of the probability of the government's being reelected is also revealing. Because of the sensitivity of the electorate to international outcomes, the opposition party benefits from the increased probability of war, giving the electoral curve the inverse shape of the probability of war curve. As with the war curve, however, the opportunity to pander to public demands for a conciliatory policy when the international system marginally demands a deterrence policy distorts this baseline shape. In this case, the opposition can make a significant dent in the government's reelection prospects by pursuing a popular policy of conciliation when the government feels constrained by the demands of the international environment to pursue deterrence. Without the opportunity to pander to the public, the opposition would never be able to beat the government under the conditions described here.[16] It is only with the luxury of being out of power, and being relatively ignored by state B, that the opposition has any hope of gaining power. In the current example, the range from $d = .5$ to $d = .57$ puts the government in a difficult position: despite sharing the same relative preferences for peace and election and the same sense of the international system as the opposition, the responsibilities of power mean that the government will pursue a policy that, while maximizing its utility, also may cost it the election.

Limitations and Extensions

It is important to set out explicitly some of the limitations of this model both for the purpose of putting the results into perspective and because they are suggestive for ways in which the model might be improved in future iterations.

In the first place, some of the important results I have presented here are driven by the fact that I present the public as unsophisticated relative to elites. In particular, I have modeled the public as ignorant of the probability that state B is deterrable and unversed in the intricacies of the security dilemma. While there will be some controversy as to how far this assumption deviates from reality, it would clearly be preferable to be able to assess the role of different levels of public capabilities beyond the role of simple attentiveness to policies.

At the other end of the spectrum, this model may give voters too much credit by making their views independent of elite views. It is clear that there is a strong relationship between elite and mass opinion (see Zaller 1992). Since this model is not dynamic, I cannot use it to directly assess the role of rally effects or the creation of public attitudes by government and opposition leaders. Still, if Kennan (1951, 62) is right that demagogues will always be a problem because "the truth is sometimes a poor competitor in the market place of ideas," we could continue to think of the treason temptation being built on the relative manipulability of the public. In this case, the model would show when political leaders face a temptation to create public enthusiasms for policies that are at odds with the national interest.

The lack of a dynamic element also limits my ability to use this model to assess the interaction of government, opposition, and foreign actors. One obvious direction for future work would be to allow the choices of these actors to affect each other. In particular, it might make sense to force the government to choose a policy first and then give the opposition the opportunity to pick an optimal response. State B, in turn, might also be allowed to select a foreign policy in accordance with its expectations about domestic politics in state A. This would raise the important possibility of strategic behavior by all of the actors.

Finally, a more sophisticated model would allow more control over information conditions. In this model, the government and the opposition have the same perspective on the nature of state B. It is often the case, of course, that domestic actors cannot agree on the nature of state B. A more sophisticated model than the one I present here might assess the degree to which the government and the opposition deviate from their own individual perspectives on the national interest. This would be particularly useful in combination with the inclusion of interaction effects, since it would allow these actors to base their policy compromises more directly on political competition with their domestic adversaries.

Conclusions

The world is a complex place. There will always be occasions for conflict between popular and elite conceptions of the national interest. Unless our view of popular passion is so lofty that we always see in the public voice some best approximation of the national interest, we will have to be concerned about the temptation for elites to knowingly sacrifice their conception of the common good for their own political gains. In the model I have presented here, this temptation arises not from venality or short-sightedness but from rational utility maximization, from reason.

To the degree that this model accurately reflects the interaction of domestic and international incentives, there is both bad news and good news for those concerned with democracy and national security policy. The bad news is that there is a set of circumstances under which governments will sacrifice the national interest to their electoral needs. The intuition that there will be political actors who are willing to risk international crises and even wars to bolster their domestic standing is reproduced in this model. The good news is that there is only a small range of parameter values where that will happen. For the vast majority of possible parameter values, the government's international and national incentives are in accord.

Moreover, there is a plausibly large range in which the government will accept electoral defeat rather than pursue irresponsible policies. The fact that an irresponsible opposition is elected may be unfortunate, but this model should also be reassuring in that direction. The irresponsibility of the opposition arises precisely because it is not in power. Once in power it will face an incentive structure that emphasizes the international effects of its actions, and, in turn, it will behave as responsibly as did the previous government.

This model also suggests a number of interesting dynamics in the relationship between voters and the international system. Most significantly, increasing voters' concerns about foreign policy without increasing their ability to observe and understand the connection between policies and outcomes will increase the pressure on strategic politicians to act irresponsibly.

The challenge now, of course, is to discuss parameter values empirically. Is it the case that crises are characterized by high uncertainty about the deterrability of states and that political leaders are considerably more concerned about their electoral prospects than about almost anything else? If so, we will see the national interest compromised more frequently for domestic concerns. If, on the other hand, crises are distributed fairly evenly on the deterrability/ provokability continuum, and government leaders are, at worst, only two or three times more concerned with election than with war and peace, then, with moderate assumptions about the other parameters, it will be relatively unusual for government policy to reflect domestic rather than international concerns.

Whether pandering to public demands is a form of treason or a realization of the aspirations of representative democracy is a question that will continue to attract the attention of political philosophers. Since this dynamic affects the foundation of our conception of states as actors in the international system, it must also be of concern for students of international relations. The classical realists incorporated this concern into their analysis of international relations. My argument here has been that we need to understand the dynamics and prevalence of these trade-offs before we move too quickly with the structural realists to dismiss these concerns. My hope is that the model I have constructed will begin to provide a foundation for specifying more carefully the conditions under which the trade-off of domestic and international concerns will be more or less likely.

NOTES

1. On this debate, see Pitkin 1967. A more formal approach to this issue is provided by Riker 1982.

2. Bueno de Mesquita, Siverson, and Woller (1992) have also argued that in terms of war there is a strong connection between international incentives and domestic electoral incentives in that, historically, losing wars has proven a very bad electoral strategy.

3. Charles Fairbanks Jr. writes in *Commentary* in August 1989: "The Politburo, with tactical brilliance, has realized that the pause enforced by its internal crisis can be exploited in a peace offensive to weaken the West and lighten the pressures exerted by the international trend toward democracy. Lulled, we could well dismantle our military forces, and allow NATO to fall apart, thereby renouncing our ability to influence a complex and dangerous transition."

4. While these five variables are necessary for developing the model, most of the analysis will function with effectively just two variables: the attitude toward war and the relative weight of policies and outcomes.

5. Technically, this approach should not change the analysis as long as there is a gap between the voter's sense of the connection between policy and outcomes and the view of the government and opposition elites about this connection. Furthermore, while I use the war/peace issue to represent one kind of outcome, we could substitute less extreme categories such as conflict/cooperation.

6. In future models, this might be tied to the parties' anticipated electoral prospects. For now it is an independent variable.

7. The use of $(g - b)$ to represent policy difference is an important simplification. A more satisfactory function would be $|A - b| - |A - g|$ or the frequently used $(A - b)^2 - (A - g)^2$ with $A \in [0, 1]$. This has the disadvantage, however, of either making the math less tractable or requiring the subsequent analysis to be broken up into cases, depending on the relative values of A, b, and g. Because, as I will show, this model forces g and b to the values of 1 or 0, the use of $(g - b)$ and $A \in [-1, 1]$ maintains the appropriate coefficients for g and b for all of the cases. None of the following conclusions would change with the use of $|A - b| - |A - g|$ and $A \in [0, 1]$.

8. In this two-party model, the probability of the opposition being elected is the complement of the probability of the government being elected: $(1 - e)$.

9. This knife-edged situation is not surprising given the basic simplicity of this model. Increasing the interactive character of the terms is a direction of future development that would provide a more nuanced sense of the optimal degree of belligerence or conciliation.

10. Mathematically, whether the effects ratio being above or below the utility ratio produces a belligerent policy depends on the signs of the utility ratio and the domestic effects part of the effects ratio (through their effect on the direction of the inequality). Above the asymptotic point, at around .7 (where the denominator of the effects ratio approaches zero), the inequality shifts and belligerent policies will be pursued as long as the effects ratio is below the utility ratio.

11. Again, above .7 the inequality is reversed. Belligerence will be pursued when the effects line is *below* the utility line. The asymptotic effect occurs because as the election effect goes to zero, it will be irrelevant and the domestic costs of a belligerent foreign

policy will be completely ignored. As long as peace is preferred to war and election is preferred to not being elected the utility ratio will always be positive, so there is no treason temptation in the range where *d* is above .7.

12. The curve could also be shifted up or down by the use of a more sophisticated function for the distance between the voter's preferred policy and the policies of the government and the opposition. The dynamics of the model relative to *d* would remain the same. See note 7.

13. The stark shape of the probability of war curve in this case is a function of the knife-edged nature of the incentives to be belligerent or conciliatory. One could imagine a more sophisticated model that would allow state A to pursue a moderated policy that would be in accord with the more moderate probabilities that state B is either provokable or deterrable.

14. This restriction significantly hampered the Canadian war effort. It was overturned in 1942 after a national referendum freed King from his commitment. Even after that referendum passed by a substantial margin, King waited until 1944 to lift the restriction on overseas service for conscripts. He anticipated at the time that his course of action might well destroy the political viability of the Liberal Party (Stacey 1970).

15. This policy left the opposition Labour Party in a quandary. In the 1935 election, its opposition to Conservative Party foreign policy led it to advocate a more belligerent policy line, which was widely interpreted by the electorate as a policy of "sanctions, even if it means war" (Taylor 1961, 93).

16. This is under the assumption of no party bias. Party bias will shift the entire curve up or down.

REFERENCES

Aldrich, J., J. Sullivan, and E. Borgida. 1989. Foreign Affairs and Issue Voting: Do Presidential Candidates Waltz before a Blind Audience? *American Political Science Review* 83, no. 1:123–41.

Berelson, B., P. Lazarsfeld, and W. McPhee. 1954. *Voting: A Study of Opinion Formation in a Presidential Campaign*. Chicago: University of Chicago Press.

Beschloss, M., and S. Talbott. 1993. *At the Highest Levels: The Inside Story of the End of the Cold War*. Boston: Little, Brown.

Brace, P., and B. Hinckley. 1992. *Follow the Leader: Opinion Polls and the Modern Presidents*. New York: Basic Books.

Bueno de Mesquita, B. 1981. *The War Trap*. New Haven: Yale University Press.

Bueno de Mesquita, B., and D. Lalman. 1992. *War and Reason: Domestic and International Imperatives*. New Haven: Yale University Press.

Bueno de Mesquita, B., R. Siverson, and G. Woller. 1992. War and the Fate of Regimes: A Comparative Analysis. *American Political Science Review* 86, no. 3:638–46.

Divine, R. 1974. *Foreign Policy and U.S. Presidential Elections: 1940–1948*. Vol. 1. New York: New Viewpoints.

Fairbanks, C. 1989. Gorbachev's Cultural Revolution. *Commentary* 88, no. 2:23.

Fiorina, M. 1981. *Retrospective Voting in American National Elections*. New Haven: Yale University Press.

George, A. 1980. *Presidential Decisionmaking in Foreign Policy: The Effective Use of Information and Advice.* Boulder: Westview.

Jervis, R. 1971. *Perception and Misperception in International Politics.* Princeton: Princeton University Press.

Kennan, G. 1951. *American Diplomacy, 1900–1950.* Chicago: University of Chicago Press.

Levy, J. 1988. Domestic Politics and War. *Journal of Interdisciplinary History* 18, no. 4:653–73.

———. 1989. The Diversionary Theory of War: A Critique. In *Handbook of War Studies,* edited by M. I. Midlarsky, 259–88. Boston: Unwin Hyman.

Morgenthau, H. [1948] 1967. *Politics among Nations: The Struggle for Power and Peace.* 4th ed. New York: Knopf.

Page, B., and R. Shapiro. 1992. *The Rational Public: Fifty Years of Trends in American's Policy Preferences.* Chicago: University of Chicago Press.

Pitkin, H. 1967. *The Concept of Representation.* Berkeley: University of California Press.

Putnam, R. 1988. Diplomacy and Domestic Politics: The Logic of Two-level Games. *International Organization* 42, no. 3:427–60.

Riker, W. 1982. *Liberalism against Populism.* San Francisco: Freeman.

Stacey, C. P. 1970. *Arms, Men, and Governments: The War Policies of Canada, 1939–1945.* Ottawa: Queen's Printer.

Taylor, A. J. P. 1961. *The Origins of the Second World War.* 2d ed. New York: Fawcett.

Thucydides. [400 B.C.] 1951. *The Peloponnesian War.* Translated by R. Crawley. New York: Random House.

Zaller, J. 1992. *The Nature and Origins of Mass Opinion.* Cambridge: Cambridge University Press.

The Domestic and International Sources of Foreign Policy: Alliance Formation in the Middle East, 1948–78

Michael J. Gilligan and W. Ben Hunt

The dominant paradigm within the study of international security continues to be realism. Of the several varieties of realism, "structural neorealism," as described by Kenneth Waltz (1979), is the most developed and continues to be applied extensively (e.g., Grieco 1988; Mearsheimer 1990, 1994). Waltz argues that the international behavior of states is driven by the dictates of self-preservation within an anarchic system. A balance of power in which states group themselves in roughly equal constellations is the only logical outcome for such a system, else states risk dismemberment at the hands of some more powerful state or group of states. The mechanism is much like that of a perfectly competitive market in which firms must maximize profits or be driven out of business. Like Adam Smith's invisible hand, the balance of power forces states into certain behaviors. In this vision of international relations, the systemic constraints on state behavior bind so tightly that states have only two options: balance or be conquered.

This is a parsimonious and elegant theory, but we have two objections to its characterization of international politics. First, states don't make policies, people do, and these people may have objectives other than the welfare of the state as a whole. Second, while the neorealist characterization suggests that the threat of war is the primary constraint on international behavior, we believe that the prospect of war is rarely much of a threat at all and therefore rarely motivates policymakers' actions.

Our first objection really concerns the neorealist model's objective function of the state—the function of goods that the state maximizes or ills that it minimizes. For neorealists, this function contains one preeminent variable—survival of the state from foreign attack. We argue that this objective function should instead model the political survival of the politicians that make security policy. Such a revised objective function incorporates and extends the world suggested by neorealists, as politicians must worry about foreign military

143

threats to their regime's survival as well as internal threats from domestic rivals for power.[1] Second, we believe that in most cases external threats to regime survival are less constraining than domestic threats.[2] Examples of states being consumed by other states are extraordinarily rare. Examples of politicians being deposed, constitutionally or otherwise, are obviously much more common.

The Polity II (Gurr 1989) data set provides our information on polity change, both ordinary executive change where the basic polity remains intact and major change where the existing polity is replaced by another form of government. Although there is little difference in the relative distribution of sources of polity termination from the nineteenth century to the twentieth, there is a sharp decline in the relative number of polity changes due to external war in the post–World War II years. Major polity change looks rather different in the 1948–78 time period than for the entire Polity II time period of 1800–1985. In fact, according to the Polity II coding of events immediately preceding polity termination, there are no examples of major polity change imposed by victorious foreign forces.[3] Certainly governments fall during this time period as a result of losing a war, and occasionally the existing polity is overthrown, but this change comes primarily from within rather than outside the polity's borders. These are summarized in figure 1.

Simple tests (not reported here) to establish a correlation between likelihood of polity change and type of polity show a fairly clear relationship between highly factionalized polities and civil war, and between highly factionalized polities and ordinary executive change. Relatively little evidence exists, however, that the balance of civilian/military control over a policy—or any other broad polity characteristic—has any correlation with likelihood of change.

Given this distribution of threats, self-interested politicians seeking to preserve their regime are far more likely to be motivated by the next election or potential coups by domestic opposition groups than by the prospects of international conflict. We argue, then, that international anarchy and the constant threat of war such anarchy creates is a rather loose constraint on policymakers' behavior and that any theory that works exclusively from this systemic perspective is bound to miss a great deal. We suggest that the constraints of regime preservation are much more binding, and that such a combined perspective explains the behaviors accounted for by a systemic approach as well as those cases neorealism cannot explain.

We propose using the phenomenon of alliance formation to test our model. Balancing behavior—the heart of neorealist/balance-of-power theory—is generally considered to take place externally through the creation and shifting of alliances. Alliance formation is also more purely a matter of international security than are other policies. Defense spending may have other effects on domestic politics that would confound our analysis. For instance, it may be used to fund military forces for domestic repression.

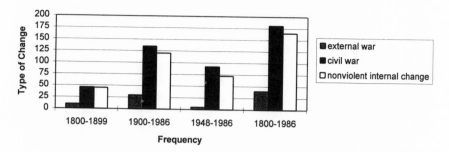

Fig. 1. Distribution of sources of major polity change by era

For initial tests of our model, we found it necessary to limit our observations to a few post–World War II instances of multilateral alliance formation. Not only does our model need economic and international event data that are simply unavailable before 1948, but we also wanted to look at regions where nations had fluid choices in the alliances potentially available to them, not alliances set in stone as a condition of the outcome of a war. For both sorts of reasons, the Middle East—broadly defined—provides an apt set of cases. Choosing a subset from the total universe of cases has additional benefits as well. It gives us the opportunity to describe the historical political conditions surrounding the formation of these alliances. We believe this descriptive information is as important as the evidence from the statistical results, since it can provide corroboration that the correlations are not spurious. The Arab League and Middle East Treaty Organization/Central Treaty Organization (METO/CENTO) provide a substantively appropriate set of cases for our project, as these alliances generate a puzzling array of allied and nonallied dyads among a broad range of states facing widely varying external and internal threats.

A System of Equations

The foundation of our project is a model of regime preservation through alliance formation. In the intuitive core of this model, politicians use alliance policy to maximize their security against *both* external and internal threats—to ensure that they have the proper defensive capability against potential foreign invaders, *and* to please domestic constituencies. Many scholars have argued that politicians use economic policy to please constituents and keep themselves in office.[4] We see no reason why security policy should be treated any differently. In short, our argument is that politicians use *international* security policy at least in part to please *domestic* constituencies (and therefore assuage internal security threats).[5]

Our hypothesis, then, is that, as realists would predict, alliance formation should be well predicted by the level of external threat a country faces (Cony-beare 1994 and Sorokin 1994 provide good examples of this type of analysis). However, we further argue that alliance formation should also be predicted by the *interactive* effect between the regime's domestic security and its external security. A relatively large literature on regime change (reviewed recently by Alt and King [1994]) provides estimates of the internal stability of a particular regime at a particular point in time. By using these estimates interactively with external security threats, we can establish whether or not regimes facing strong threats to internal security react differently to external threats than do regimes with weaker internal threats. If we are wrong, these interactive effects should not be significantly observable in the data.

We assume that policymakers do not know with certainty the utility they will derive from a particular external alliance, but they can form an expectation of that utility based on observable characteristics at the time the alliance is created. The utility from joining an alliance, then, is:

$$U_1 = \mu_1 + \varepsilon_1, \tag{1}$$

and the utility they derive from not joining an alliance is:

$$U_2 = \mu_2 + \varepsilon_2, \tag{2}$$

where μ_i is the systematic component of the policymaker's utility from choosing option i; in other words, the expected utility of choosing option i and ε_i is the stochastic component of the policymaker's utility from choosing option i, or the part of the policymaker's utility not predictable ex ante.

Policymakers will choose to join an alliance if $\mu_1 - \mu_2 > \varepsilon_2 - \varepsilon_1$. We will assume (as is typically done) that the difference of the systematic components is a linear function of various variables that we will describe more fully later. We assume that the difference in the stochastic components is distributed according to the standard normal. The parameters of $\mu_1 - \mu_2$ can be estimated easily with standard maximum likelihood techniques (probit). These assumptions imply that a particular policymaker will enter an alliance with probability $1 - F(\mu_1 - \mu_2)$.

We believe that policymakers join alliances as much to please constituents at home as to defend against potential attackers from abroad. Left to their own preferences, policymakers would join alliances according to a straightforward realist calculus, but constituents at home may have more domestically focused concerns.[6] Thus, the more a policymaker is worried about his chances of maintaining office, the more effect constituents' preferences will have on his decision. We can specify this formally as follows:

$$\mu_1 - \mu_2 = \alpha S + \beta E(P)S, \tag{3}$$

where S is the level of external security of the country in question and $E(P)$ is the expected probability of the policymaker being removed from office. The parameter estimates that make up α are expected to be such that a policymaker who sees his country's external security as threatened will derive more utility from an alliance ceteris paribus. This much is consistent with realism. Equation 3 also suggests that policymakers who face a greater threat from internal enemies—a higher $E(P)$—gain different utility from entering into an alliance. That is, the β parameters should be statistically significant from zero.

A policymaker's expected probability of being removed from office can itself be estimated by probit, and, indeed, it has been examined in a very large literature. For the time being we will specify this probability as:

$$E(P) = \gamma_1 S + \gamma_2 E + \gamma_3 D, \tag{4}$$

where S is the country's security as before, E is the state of the country's economy, and D consists of certain domestic political characteristics of the country that might make government change more or less likely. Many variables could be included in equation 4, and, in fact, many have been used by others. See Alt and King 1994 for a fuller survey of this literature.

One other point on this system of equations deserves discussion. As we have specified the system, there are no endogeneity or measurement error problems because the *expected* probability of removal from office enters the alliance equation—not the actual probability. Furthermore, whether or not a country joins a particular alliance (the dependent variable in eq. 3) does not enter directly on the right side of equation 4. We recognize that the dependent variable in equation 3 may be correlated with some of the security variables on the right side of equation 4, but we have not found endogeneity to be a problem in our empirical tests thus far.

Historical Background: Multilateral Alliances in the Middle East

Two multilateral alliances took root in this region following World War II, the Arab League and CENTO (see table 1). Although formally created in March 1945, the Arab League did not become a mutual defense alliance until 1950, following the Israeli War of Independence.[7] Since then, it has expanded from its original seven members to 22 and continues to be an influential actor in regional events. CENTO,[8] on the other hand, collapsed in 1979 following Iran's Islamic Revolution and subsequent withdrawal from the alliance. For a good span of years, however, particularly in the mid-1950s, CENTO was perceived as a viable alliance that offered a meaningful alternative or addition to the Arab League. One question our efforts should help answer, then, is whether the relative success of the Arab League and the relative failure of CENTO can be explained by a model that combines domestic and foreign political considerations.

It would be a mistake to consider either the Arab League or CENTO to be as cohesive a collective security arrangement as the more familiar post–World War II alliances of NATO and the Warsaw Pact. Even though the treaty implementing the 1950 Arab League reforms is usually referred to as the Arab Collective Security Pact, it seems clear that the alliance is designed more for collective defense against the common enemy of Israel than for collective security against an aggressive fellow Arab League member (Zacher 1979). Likewise, the Baghdad Pact implementing METO and its successor CENTO was clearly aimed at containing one particular enemy, in this case the Soviet Union.

Little military utility has been attached to either CENTO or the Arab League by its members. CENTO oversaw a fair number of joint planning and training exercises, but there was never a permanent central command structure or even specific military commitments by its members. Arab League bylaws re-

TABLE 1.   CENTO and Arab League Membership Dates

CENTO (1955–79)	Arab League (1950)
Turkey	Iraq
Pakistan	Jordan
Iran	Lebanon
United Kingdom	Saudi Arabia
Iraq (1955–58)	Yemen
	Egypt/UAR (1950–79)
	Syria (1950–58, 1961)
	Libya (1953)
	Sudan (1956)
	Tunisia (1958)
	Morocco (1958)
	Kuwait (1961)
	Algeria (1962)
	South Yemen (1968)
	Bahrain (1971)
	Oman (1971)
	Qatar (1971)
	United Arab Emirates (1972)
	Mauritania (1973)
	Somalia (1975)
	Djibouti (1977)

quire a unanimous vote (except for the aggressor) before the League may intervene militarily, and only two examples exist of the creation of such a force. An Arab League Force was sent to Kuwait in 1961 to protect the new regime against Iraqi threats and to obviate the need for British troops requested by the Kuwaiti emir, but this group contained only slightly more than 3,000 soldiers. The 1976 Arab Deterrent Force in Lebanon massed 10 times this number of troops, but even this group was originally named the "Symbolic Arab Security Force" (Pogany 1987). The formation of the Arab League has certainly not prevented member states from fighting each other directly (most notably the Saudi-Egyptian conflict over the Yemeni civil war between 1962 and 1967). Still, as Zacher (1979) points out, given the high levels of political hostility between various "camps" in the Arab world between 1946 and 1977, the surprising fact is how few militarized disputes broke out between Arab states during this period.

Despite the lack of concrete military applications, however, Middle Eastern nations have invested a great deal of political significance in these alliances. The implications of membership in one or the other alliance have toppled governments, even though the alliances themselves have been neither militarily active nor even opposed to each other. Particularly within Arab nations, the question of whether or not to join an alliance with real or perceived ties to the West has concrete domestic political repercussions.

From its inception, Arab League policy explicitly forbade alliances with Western nations because of the West's support of Israel. In 1953, however, Libya signed a bilateral pact with the United Kingdom to allow British use of Libyan ports (the same year Libya joined the Arab League). The League offered to compensate Libya for British payments if Libya would back out, but Libya stuck to the treaty. Libya was a tangential member of the League, both geographically and economically, but important symbolically as the first new addition to the League, and complaints over the alliance decision were soon dropped. The precedent, however, would prove to be very troublesome to the League in subsequent years.

In the spring of 1954, Turkey and Pakistan signed a security pact; although invited, the members of the Arab League (Iraq, Syria, Egypt, Saudi Arabia, Yemen, Libya, Jordan, and Lebanon) declined the offer, noting that a mutual defense relationship already existed between their nations. But, in early 1955, Iraq broke with League policy and signed a mutual defense treaty with Turkey, referred to as the Baghdad Pact. A few months later, Britain officially joined the Baghdad Pact, soon joined by Pakistan and then Iran, creating the Middle East Treaty Organization (METO), headquartered in Iraq. The Soviet Union, of course, was strongly opposed to the formation of the new security alignment; the United States was just as vigorously in favor.

METO's ties to the West were obvious in the form of Britain's membership, but equally important were these implied ties to the United States. In fact, Secretary of State John Foster Dulles took credit for the whole concept, saying that he had conceived the idea of the Baghdad Pact during a visit to the Middle East in 1953. Still, the United States took great pains to prevent its ties with METO from ever becoming official, recognizing that no Arab state would join an alliance that contained Israel's primary benefactor, much less Israel itself (Israel wanted to join the METO alliance from the outset).

As the most powerful member of the Arab League, Egypt had the most to lose from a competing multilateral alliance and took steps to prevent further defections. However, its initial efforts to pass a League resolution banning pacts with nations outside the League was blocked by Syria, Jordan, and Lebanon, clear evidence that these other nations were considering a move similar to Iraq's. Egypt dropped its efforts to control the League as a whole, moved to a bilateral strategy, and was successful in convincing Syria and Saudi Arabia to join in a semiformal mutual defense bloc separate from the League. Egypt half-heartedly offered to merge the Egyptian-Saudi-Syrian bloc with METO (on the condition that Israel cede the Negev), but primarily it worked from within this new bloc to destabilize the Iraqi government as well as other Arab governments considering METO membership. The United States countered these efforts with the Eisenhower Doctrine in 1957, a military aid program ostensibly aimed at containing Soviet influence in the Middle East but more concretely aimed at limiting Egyptian influence. Iraq, Lebanon, Libya, Jordan, and Saudi Arabia accepted U.S. aid under this program, which, like METO, did not require these Arab states to join in an official alliance with the United States to receive concrete benefits.

Domestic politics in each of these regimes was strongly affected by these alliance machinations. In Jordan, the government fell in 1955 as public pressure against joining the pact reached a crescendo. In Lebanon, the country virtually fell apart in 1958 over these debates; in fact, the United States sent troops to both Lebanon and Jordan that year to prevent pro-Nasser factions from seizing control. Syria's 1958 decision to merge with Egypt to form the United Arab Republic (UAR) was heavily influenced by Iraq's decision to distance itself from the Arab League, as was Saudi Arabia's decision to move closer to Egypt despite their clear ideological differences. And in Iraq the success of General Qassem's 1958 coup overthrowing the pro-Western government would not have been possible without support from Egypt and Syria.

Following Iraq's withdrawal from METO, the alliance name was changed to the Central Treaty Organization (CENTO), and its headquarters was moved to Turkey. Recognizing that its efforts to establish a multilateral alliance system containing Arab states was effectively quashed, the United States signed identical bilateral pacts with Turkey, Iran, and Pakistan in 1959, just before the official Iraqi withdrawal from the alliance. The United States never officially joined CENTO (or allowed Israel to join), as the dream to recruit Arab states into the pact never completely died, but CENTO quickly became largely irrelevant to the politics of the Arab world. It continued to play a role in the domestic and international politics of Iran and Pakistan, however. Both Yahya Khan in Pakistan and Reza Pahlavi in Iran used CENTO (particularly its unofficial ties to the United States) as a conduit for military aid from the West.

As for the Arab League from 1959 to 1979, Egypt's dream of reasserting leadership of the Arab world through the League never reached fruition, although the League remained perhaps the most prominent arena for this political competition. Iraq under Qassem proved to be a competitor for Arab leadership rather than a follower, as did Syria and Iraq under the Ba'ath regimes that took power in 1963. Saudi Arabia and Egypt resorted to a shooting war over the Yemeni civil conflict, Jordan fought to kick the Syrian-supported Palestine Liberation Organization (PLO) out of its territory and into Lebanon, and the wars with Israel in 1967 and 1973 obviously failed to achieve the goals of the Arab states. But, while individual Arab states made bilateral arms sale agreements with Western nations throughout this time period (e.g., Morocco and Mauritania asked for and received substantial military aid from France to fight the Polisario insurgency in the western Sahara), no Arab League member reprised the Iraqi experience of 1955–59 by joining a multilateral alliance connected with the West. In this respect, the Arab League and CENTO shared a unique political relationship that provides an appropriate backdrop for our models of alliance policy and domestic politics.

Empirical Tests

Operationalization

The first set of variables that we place in the government change equation can be classified as security variables. Other researchers have added security considerations to a government change equation, and they relied on a series of dummy variables as proxies for performance in war (Bueno de Mesquita, Siverson, and Woller 1992; Bueno de Mesquita and Siverson 1995). We agree with the conclusion of these essays that constituents are worried about their nation's performance in an armed international conflict and that they keep or remove their government from office accordingly. However, if constituents sanction their governments based on their nation's performance in war we believe that they should similarly reward or punish their government for their country's preparations for war. In other words, we argue that constituents can keep track of their country's security even before a war erupts.

Our proposed security variable is the military expenditure of the country in question as a share of the total military expenditures of the other countries in the region plus the global powers (operationalized as the five permanent members of the United Nations Security Council). The variable is called *military expenditure* in the tables that follow. We also use the military expenditures of the country's allies normalized in the same way, called *alliance military expenditure* in the results presented later.

The expected sign of the coefficient of a country's own military expenditure is ambiguous a priori in the government change equation. We argue that constituents like the security that large military expenditures produce but that they do not like the large tax bill that they also require. Governments that spend too much on the military may actually have higher probabilities of removal from office because of the economic burden those expenditures place on their societies. To further complicate the effects of this measure, governments can also use a strong military to repress opposition within their countries and reduce the probability of government change. Because of all of these conflicting effects we do not make a claim as to the sign or significance of a country's own military expenditure in the government change equation. The effect of alliance military expenditure should be quite clear, though. Higher alliance military expenditures improve the national security at very little economic cost to constituents in the country. Governments in countries with militarily strong alliances, then, should unambiguously be safer from internal deposition than governments that are not.

In addition to military expenditures we include measures of the threat posed by external enemies of the country and its allies, termed *external threat* and *alliance external threat* in the tables below. We measure these variables by the sum of threatening events directed against the country as recorded by the Conflict and Peace Data Bank (COPDAB). We created a similar variable for the country's allies.[9] Once again, an ex ante prediction on the effects of this variable is difficult. On the one hand, we might expect that countries that are more threatened by outside foes, or whose allies are, should have less stable governments if constituents do indeed punish policymakers for weak national security. On the other hand, it has often been said that governments sometimes look for enemies abroad in order to shore up support at home, and, of course, Mueller's (1970) "rally 'round the flag" effect is well documented in the United States and other countries.

That said, one clear effect of the severity of outside threat should be that security, as measured by our other variables, is more important the more threatened the country is by outside foes. In other words, *interactive* effects between these COPDAB measures and the other security measures should be strong. Military expenditures of and threats facing allies should have stronger respective negative and positive effects on the probability of government change for countries that face severe outside threats because the constituents in such countries out of necessity hold their governments more accountable for security than do constituents in relatively unthreatened countries.

Economic variables have been included in several studies of government change. Robertson (1983) takes into account the role of inflation in causing government change. O'Kane's (1981) study of coups tested for the effects of a country's trade specialization in primary products, trade dependence on a small number of goods, and national poverty levels. Some of the more sophisticated studies of this type have taken into account the potential simultaneity between executive change and economic variables, as poor economic performance may cause high government turnover and high government turnover may also lead to poor economic performance. Using growth of real GDP per capita as their economic variable, Londregan and Poole (1990) and Alesina et al. (1991) estimated simultaneous equation systems of this sort, but none found simultaneity. Londregan and Poole found that the economy affected government change but not vice versa, while Alesina et al. found the opposite, that high government turnover produced low economic growth but not vice versa. In light of these past findings, we control for the effects of two economic variables in our estimates, *real GDP per capita* and *inflation,* but we do not control for the potential endogeneity of these variables. We also include government spending as a share of GDP in an attempt to control for any purely fiscal effects of military expenditure.

A rich range of variables has been collected by researchers to characterize the domestic political environment a regime must cope with to keep itself in office. For instance, Jackman (1978) found that coups in his sample of African nations were positively related to social mobilization and multipartyism and negatively related to cultural pluralism and political participation—all features of the domestic political environment. Other studies control for the characteristics of the leaders themselves, such as whether they were military or civilian leaders or how long the government had been in power (Bienen and van de Walle 1989, 1991).

We check the robustness of our results in the government change equation against a large number of political institutional variables taken from Gurr's Polity II data set. Since the performance of these variables is not the main concern of this essay, we present only the statistically significant findings here. The variables that we include are: a measure of the competitiveness of political participation (*participation competitiveness*), a measure of the level of autocratic rule (*autocracy*), and a similar measure of *democracy.* According to Gurr's coding, democracy is not the opposite of autocracy, making it meaningful to use both measures.

We also test for interactive affects between autocracy and military expenditure in the government change equation. Recall that the expected sign of military expenditure is ambiguous in equation 4. High military expenditure should have positive effects on the probability of government change because it increases the tax burden on the citizenry. However, it also may reduce the probability of turnover because constituents like the security it offers, and in autocracies the government can use the military to quash domestic rivals. For this reason, we believe that military expenditure should be more clearly negatively related to government change in autocracies because those governments are relieved somewhat from the constraint of an overtaxed populace and because such governments can use their military to crush domestic opposition.

For roughly the same reasons in reverse, we expect *alliance* military expenditure to be more negatively related to probability of government change in a democracy. A democratic government will be rewarded by its citizens for easing their tax burden by finding help to shore up national security, while an autocratic government would not face as severe a budget constraint in the first place. Also, alliance military expenditure is not helpful in crushing domestic opposition, a fact that bears less on a democratic government's chances of staying in office than on an autocracy's. These interactive effects, to the extent that they are present in the data, should confirm our intuitions about why military expenditures may not be significant in the first place.

Finally, we operationalize the dependent variable in the government change equation with a dummy variable equal to one if a government change occurred in the country in the year in question and zero otherwise. The data can be found in Banks's coding of government change as found in Polity II. In it, any kind of government change is coded as one, whether due to a coup, a revolution, or a constitutional transfer of power. The dependent variable in the alliance membership equation is a dummy variable equal to one if the country in question is a member of the alliance in question in a particular year. This data may be found in Singer and Small 1984, Zacher 1979, and Hadley 1971. Descriptive statistics of all of the variables described in this section are offered in table 2.

Effects of Security on Government Change

The first step in finding the parameters of this system of equations is to estimate equation 4. The vast majority of previous studies on this topic have attempted to explain either coups or legal transfers of government. Only a handful have actually combined the two types of government change to get a general model of government change (Alesina et al. 1991; Bueno de Mesquita, Siverson, and Woller 1992). Although our ultimate concern is the effect of political instability on alliance formation, we must first estimate the parameters of government change with such a general model.

Table 3 provides the estimates of various specifications of the government change model. In these results, two points are very clear: (1) domestic military expenditure has an ambiguous effect on the probability of government change, as anticipated, and (2) alliance military expenditure has a strong negative impact on the probability of government change. Two other results support our argument for why military expenditure is not significant and alliance military expenditure is significant: autocracies seem to benefit from military expenditure more than nonautocratic governments do, and democracies seem to benefit more from the military expenditure of allies than less democratic governments do. However, these latter two results are not as robust across specifications as the first two were.

The results in the first column show (as do all of the results in table 3) that alliance military expenditure significantly reduces the probability of government change. It also shows that a country's own military expenditure does not. The threat variables do not perform well in this specification, having virtually no effect on turnover. As with military expenditure, this is not surprising given that the variable may make citizens feel both less secure and more nationalistic. The economic variables do not perform well at all. Among them, only real GDP per capita has a coefficient that is larger than its standard error. Finally, the two domestic political variables that we include are very good predictors. Autocratic governments experience significantly less turnover, and countries with highly competitive participation experience more. Needless to say, the re-

TABLE 2.   Description of Variables

	Mean	Minimum	Maximum	Standard Deviation	Obs
Predicted and dependent variables					
Expected probability of government change	0.16262	5.97940e–12	0.67835	0.16436	554
Alliance	0.44765	0.00000	1.00000	0.49770	554
Executive change	0.15613	0.00000	1.00000	0.36366	269
Economic variables					
Real GDP per capita	5,200.51	480.000	77,835.0	12,038.3	269
Inflation	−3.34077e–03	−0.66779	0.24667	0.10410	269
Government share of GDP	18.61981	2.88000	47.64000	10.70659	269
Security variables					
Military expenditure	2.71023e–03	8.51005e–05	2.98429e–02	4.59309e–03	277
Alliance military expenditure	2.00737e–02	1.46617e–03	7.24796e–02	2.02521e–02	277
External threat	1,346.63	0.00000	21,309.0	2,630.10	277
Alliance external threat	9,881.58	1,302.00	20,120.0	5,355.16	277
Domestic political variables					
Autocracy	5.75093	0.00000	10.00000	3.39683	269
Participation competitiveness	0.30483	0.00000	1.00000	0.46119	269
Democracy	2.02974	0.00000	10.00000	3.09053	269

sults for alliance military expenditure become even stronger once the insignificant economic and threat variables are removed as shown in column 2 of table 3.

The third specification in table 3 includes an interaction between the security variables and external threat. The logic behind this specification is that

TABLE 3.   Estimates of Government Change Model

	1	2	3	4	5
Constant	−0.42	−0.74*	−0.82*	−0.66*	−0.60*
	0.56	0.26	0.26	0.27	0.24
Economic variables					
Real GDP	-2×10^{-5}	-6×10^{-6}	-8×10^{-6}	-9×10^{-6}	-1×10^{-5}
per capita	-2×10^{-5}	5×10^{-6}	6×10^{-6}	6×10^{-6}	8×10^{-6}
Inflation	0.39	—	—	—	—
	1.17				
Government	-7×10^{-3}	—	—	—	—
share of GDP	−0.02				
Security variables					
Military	−31.70	13.27	—	—	—
expenditure	49.92	26.83			
Alliance military	−10.30*	−10.55*	—	—	—
expenditure	5.78	4.82			
External	3×10^{-5}	—	—	—	—
threat	4×10^{-5}				
Alliance external	5×10^{-6}	—	—	—	—
threat	2×10^{-5}				
Variables interactive with external threat					
Military	—	—	2×10^{-3}	1×10^{-3}	—
expenditure			4×10^{-3}	4×10^{-3}	
Alliance mili-	—	—	$-7 \times 10^{-5*}$	$-6 \times 10^{-5*}$	—
tary expenditure			3×10^{-5}	3×10^{-5}	
Alliance external	—	—	$8 \times 10^{-9*}$	$9 \times 10^{-9*}$	5×10^{-9}
threat			4×10^{-9}	4×10^{-9}	4×10^{-9}
Domestic political variables					
Autocracy scale	−0.13*	−0.09*	−0.10*	−0.11*	−0.12*
	0.05	0.03	0.04	0.04	0.04
Participation	0.86*	0.89*	0.87*	0.93*	0.87*
competitiveness	0.26	0.21	0.23	0.23	0.22
Autocracy scale ×	—	—	—	−10.20	−16.21
military expenditure				10.69	10.76
Democracy scale ×	—	—	—	−2.85	−3.13*
alliance military				1.67	1.74
expenditure					
N	269	286	277	277	277
Log likelihood	−89.35	−102.21	−95.65	−93.14	−95.40
Correctly predicted	85.87%	84.96%	84.84%	85.20%	85.20%

*Significant at better than the 5 percent level

security issues should be more salient in countries facing high external threats and therefore should be better predictors of government change. These results are borne out to a certain extent. A country's own military expenditure is still not a significant predictor of government change. The effects of alliance military expenditure remain significant. However, the impact of external threat to alliance increases considerably, suggesting that countries with alliances with highly threatened countries experience more government turnover than do countries with alliances with less threatened countries. It would seem that a government is punished for making alliances with highly threatened countries when its own country's national security is already at risk. The domestic political variables remain highly significant in this specification, while the economic variables remain insignificant.

The specification in column 4 tests some of our arguments about why a nation's military expenditure is not significant and alliance military expenditure is significant by separating out the effects of military expenditures in autocratic governments and the effects of alliance military expenditures in democratic governments. While the results are not terribly strong, they do show that high military expenditures tend to reduce government turnover in autocracies. Recall that they had no effect among governments in general. This evidence supports our earlier argument that autocracies can gain from military expenditure because they can use the military against domestic rivals for power and because citizens who are unhappy with the high costs of a large military cannot remove such governments as easily.

Furthermore, the results in column 3 show that alliance military expenditure reduces the probability of government change to a greater extent in highly democratic governments. This is consistent with our argument that democracies with strong allies reap the rewards of supplying national security cheaply whereas less democratic governments do not because they do not face as serious a threat of removal from office by overtaxed constituents. The other variables perform similarly to earlier specifications.

While the results in the fourth column hinted that these arguments might be correct, they were not significant at standard significance levels. The specification in column 4 attempts to improve these results by removing the noninteractive military expenditure variables. Doing so increases the magnitude of the coefficient on the military expenditure autocracy interaction but not to standard levels of significance. The effects of the alliance military expenditure and democracy interaction do improve to standard levels of significance. However, the impact of a country's own military expenditure was always quite weak and that of alliance military expenditure was always quite strong—a fact that may be driving these results.

We should be cautious about reading too much into the results of these last two specifications, then, because they are not particularly strong. Also, they were even weaker in a specification (not shown here) in which military expenditure and alliance military expenditure were not interactive with external threat. In short, these latter results are substantively important but are not particularly strong or robust across specifications. One point is clear from table 3—a country's own military expenditure has weak and contradictory effects on the probability of government change (at least in the full sample of countries) while alliance military expenditure has a strong negative effect on the probability of government change (especially in democracies). In this latter conclusion, we can enjoy a fair amount of statistical confidence, borne out by cursory process tracing of the historical record. For example, although the Iraqi regime fell in 1958, many observers attribute its survival to that point to the influx of support from its strong Western allies.

Empirical Tests

Determinants of Alliance Formation:
International and Otherwise

In this section, we use our estimates of the probability of government change to estimate the alliance formation model, equation 3. In our original formulation of the domestic foundations of alliance formation, we argued that governments may use security policy to shore up domestic support for their regimes just as they might use economic policy, as has been argued by so many others (Nordhaus 1975 is the seminal work in this area). We chose to examine alliance policy rather than military expenditure because of the unclear effects of military spending. What quickly became apparent from our empirical results, though, was that our characterization of this problem was naive. Whereas governments have a fair degree of autonomy over their economic policies at home (governments choose fiscal or monetary policies as they please), they do not have nearly that degree of autonomy in choosing alliances. They must find another country willing to ally with them.

    In the back of our minds was a "market" for alliances that was perfectly competitive and atomistic (Conybeare [1992, 1994] seems to have a similar conception of the government's alliance problem). A country that wanted an alliance could find one simply by entering the market. We found instead that procuring an ally is much more like finding a spouse than buying a commodity. If a market analogy is appropriate, the market for allies is much more of a dual monopoly than a perfectly competitive atomistic market. More specifically, every country is at the same time a demander of allies and a supplier of an ally (itself). Furthermore, those countries that are likely to be high demanders of alliance are also likely to be particularly poor suppliers. Countries are likely to want allies when they are militarily weak and faced with severe external threats. Unfortunately, those are precisely the types of countries with which other countries do not like to ally themselves. On the other hand, strong, relatively threat-free countries do not particularly need allies, but other countries would very much like to ally with them.

This relationship is summarized in table 4. The first column of table 4 gives results for a "realist" version (i.e., a version without any domestic political elements) of our original characterization of the alliance formation problem. Our expectation was that countries with low military expenditures and high external threats would be more likely to join alliances, and that they would be more likely to join the higher the military expenditure and the lower the external threats of the alliance they were considering joining.[10] Clearly, these expectations were not fulfilled by the results in column 1. Strong and relatively unthreatened countries were *more* likely to join alliances, and countries were *less* likely to join strong and relatively threat-free alliances. The seemingly paradoxical results are explained when one considers both the jointness of the alliance decision and the degree of control over that decision that the larger party—the alliance considering a new member—is likely to have. Consider the coefficients of table 4, column 1, in this light: as a country becomes stronger (whether through greater military spending or reduced external threat), a potential alliance makes greater efforts to recruit that country; likewise, as an alliance becomes weaker (whether through reduced military spending by its

TABLE 4. Estimates of Basic Alliance Formation Model

	Realist Model	Realist/Domestic Model
Constant	6.5×10^{-2}	0.27
	0.13	0.16
Military expenditure	4.86	-0.93
	13.05	13.11
External threat	-1.4×10^{-4}*	-1.3×10^{-4}*
	2.9×10^{-5}	3.0×10^{-5}
Alliance military expenditure	-14.85*	-16.13*
	2.52	2.64
Alliance external threat	7.7×10^{-5}*	7.4×10^{-5}*
	1.2×10^{-5}	1.2×10^{-5}
Probability of government change	—	-0.89*
		0.37
N	554	554
Log likelihood	-314.15	-311.31
Correctly predicted	73.10%	75.99%

*Significant at better than the 5 percent level.

members or increased external threat), it makes a greater effort to recruit a new member.

We think this process has some significant bearing on the other essays in this volume. At least six other authors represented in this book—Smith, Ishida, McGillivray, Gaubatz, and Morgan and Palmer—postulate a strategic relationship between some domestic nation D and foreign nation F. While D is modeled as a strategic environment in its own right, F is treated (more or less) as a black box. It would obviously be nice to model F's behavior with the same specificity as that of D, and we think that we are taking a significant step in that direction by looking at the *joint* parameters of alliance decisions. To be sure, we are not estimating these joint parameters explicitly, but we have identified what we think are the first-order relationships at work.

Given this interpretation of the joint alliance decision, what impact should we expect from the domestic stability of potential alliance recruits? The greater the likelihood of government change, the less attractive an alliance partner that country should be. We form this expectation on the assumption that alliances worry about new regimes keeping the promises (and alliance commitments) of the old regime. Especially in our sample of cases, where the Arab League is actively supporting the opposition in several instances, we expect alliances to shy away from domestically threatened governments. Our expectations are confirmed in table 4, column 2, where the likelihood of government change (from column 5, table 3) is included in the estimation. As likelihood of regime deposition increases, the likelihood of that country joining an alliance decreases. Note that the only parameter lacking statistical significance in these estimations is a country's military spending; this is not too surprising given the potentially confounding and contradictory effects of military spending on domestic stability suggested earlier.

As noted, the results in table 4 are confounded to some degree by the jointness of decision between an alliance and its potential members. The first column of table 5 separates out the decisions of the existing alliance and the potential ally with the following logic. The main cost of extending (or accepting) an alliance offer is the increased probability of being drawn into a war by an ally or of becoming the enemy of the enemy of allies. Unthreatened countries are in a relatively powerful bargaining position vis-à-vis a potential alliance decision, while severely threatened countries do not have the option to choose allies because other countries make that choice for them (and usually the choice is no alliance). In other words, unthreatened countries should behave according to our original prediction.

We show this by making the original variables interactive with a measure of how *unthreatened* a country or alliance is (the negative of the threat variable).[11] Unthreatened countries have more latitude for choice than other countries do, so these countries should be less likely to make alliances the stronger they are, the stronger the alliance under consideration is, and the less threatened that alliance is. These predictions are borne out to some extent in the first column of table 5. Less threatened countries (and therefore countries with some measure of choice in their alliance commitments) are less likely to enter into alliances as domestic military spending increases, as alliance spending decreases, and as the external threat faced by the alliance increases.

The realist characterization of countries' alliance decisions does fairly well, then, once we take into account the flexibility of choice (or lack thereof) of the country in question. Nor should this come as any great surprise. To paraphrase Mark Antony, we have come neither to praise nor to bury structural neo-

TABLE 5. Estimates of Alliance Formation Model Controlling for Attractiveness as Alliance Partner

	Realist Model with Interaction	Domestic Model with Interaction
Constant	-0.12	-2.0×10^{-2}
	7.4×10^{-2}	8.4×10^{-2}
Interactive with $(-1 \times$ external threat$)$		
Military expenditure	-8.0×10^{-4}	-6.3×10^{-3}
	8.9×10^{-3}	7.8×10^{-3}
Alliance military expenditure	7.4×10^{-3}*	4.6×10^{-3}*
	2.4×10^{-3}	2.1×10^{-3}
Alliance external threat	-7.8×10^{-9}	-2.2×10^{-9}
	4.1×10^{-9}	4.7×10^{-9}
Interactive with $(-1 \times$ alliance external threat$)$		
Military expenditure	5.9×10^{-4}	8.3×10^{-4}
	1.6×10^{-3}	1.5×10^{-3}
Alliance military expenditure	1.0×10^{-3}*	-7.6×10^{-4}*
	2.8×10^{-4}	2.8×10^{-4}
Interactive with (probability of government change)		
Military expenditure	—	$-4.8 \times 10^{+2}$*
		$1.5 \times 10^{+2}$
External threat	—	-6.9×10^{-5}
		2.7×10^{-4}
Alliance military expenditure	—	-44.03*
		10.73
Alliance external threat	—	2.4×10^{-4}*
		5.4×10^{-5}
N	554	554
Log likelihood	-345.19	-323.12
Correctly predicted	60.65%	70.94%

*Significant at better than the 5 percent level.

realism. Rather, by including neorealist insights into a theory of individual utility maximization, we are attempting to develop a more accurate (yet still parsimonious) representation of international behavior. Evidence for the usefulness of such a model—with its central claim that governments choose alliances in part to shore up domestic support for their regimes—is presented in column 2 of table 5. There, in addition to the interactive variables of column 1, the security variables are multiplied by the expected probability of government turnover. The expected probability was calculated from the specification in column 5 of table 3.

Once we controlled for a nation's degree of choice in making alliances, we found that there are significant domestic political objectives in policymakers' decisions to join alliances. Although the results are not shown here, the relationships shown in the second column of table 5 are robust to different values of the expected probability of government (those calculated by other specifications of the government change equation), and the same relationships hold when probability of government change is included explicitly as an independent variable. These results, then, support our contention that policymakers join alliances at least in part with an eye on their domestic political environment.

Conclusion

In this essay, we have made the simple claim that policymakers set security policy, as they do economic or any other policy, with an eye on keeping themselves in office. Put another way, we have questioned the assumption that policymakers are single-minded seekers of *external* security because their chances of being removed from office through foreign invasion are much smaller than their chances of losing power at the hands of domestic opposition groups. To provide evidence for this claim, we chose to examine alliance policy, in part because the other major security policy—military expenditure—has such varied, complex, and even contradictory causes and effects. We specified a model in which policymakers chose alliances for all the familiar national security reasons but also in which these choices are affected by the stability of the regime domestically. Governments with higher probabilities of being removed from office must take into account the wishes of constituents to a greater extent than do "safer" regimes.

To test our model of alliance formation, we first had to determine regimes' probabilities of deposition. We showed that military expenditure was not a good predictor of government turnover (as we had anticipated due to the complex and contradictory effects of military spending) but that alliance military expenditure was consistently a strong force in reducing government turnover. Constituents seemed to reward their governments for creating alliances. There was some weak evidence that this latter relationship was stronger in democracies, where, of course, constituents would presumably have a larger voice in government. There was also some weak evidence that military expenditure decreased the probability of government change in autocracies.

Finally, we used our estimated probabilities of government change to determine the extent of domestic political constraints on alliance formation. First, however, we had to develop a basic realist model (with no domestic political elements). Interestingly, simply including the security variables produced results that were exactly the opposite of what we had anticipated. We concluded that these results were due to the fact that countries cannot choose their allies at will—allies also have to choose them. Furthermore, those features that make a country a high demander of an alliance make it a poor supplier of one. Since relatively threat-free countries have more choice of allies than threatened countries do, we tested the realist version of the model, taking into account the differential latitude of choice countries may have. Estimated in this fashion, the results were precisely as we had anticipated. Armed with a satisfactory "realist" version of the alliance equation, we tested our proposition that governments in trouble at home will have different alliance policies abroad. Our results suggested that this was indeed the case, that regimes with high probabilities of deposition had different alliance commitments than did countries that were stronger at home.

What is perhaps most important about this work is how it changes our usual perceptions of alliance formation in general and Middle Eastern multilateral alliances in particular. Overall, the ordinary conception of alliance formation has focused on external security dimensions and has been conceived in terms of a nation simply choosing its allies in the same way that an investor chooses a portfolio of investments. We present empirical evidence that domestic security plays a considerable role in alliance policy and that nations are better thought of as alliance "suitors" than "investors."

Government leaders appear to have approached the question of membership in CENTO or the Arab League with precisely these parameters in mind. Nascent countries in the Middle East, from Kuwait to South Yemen to Djibouti, have immediately sought membership in the Arab League, not so much for military protection from invading enemies but for political protection from contending domestic factions. It is difficult to believe that a temporary 3,000 man force provided a real deterrent against an Iraqi invasion of Kuwait in 1961, but it is very conceivable that such a force provided a strong deterrent among domestic factions hostile to the emir.

And in those nations where CENTO membership or consideration of CENTO membership contributed to government change, recall that these were highly factionalized polities in the first place. One can make a strong case that the only reason these governments lasted as long as they did was because of Western support channeled through CENTO (and its shadow, the Eisenhower

Doctrine). The U.S. and British troops sent to Lebanon and Jordan in 1959 to preserve those polities from revolutionary change after the coup in Iraq were only the most visible manifestations of this support.

Given U.S. willingness to provide the regime with strengthening benefits of alliance (arms sales, economic aid) without requiring regime-damaging comembership in a multilateral alliance, it makes perfect sense that the Arab League grew and CENTO declined in the Middle East over time. By joining the Arab League, nations could have their cake and eat it, too. By joining CENTO, they might realize slightly greater "strong ally" benefits (from Britain, Turkey, Pakistan, and Iran), but they would incur far greater regime-weakening costs in the form of the enmity of other regionally powerful states such as Egypt.

In sum, then, our work has attempted to show that policymakers use security policy to shore up political support at home as well as abroad. At least for this set of cases from the Middle East, it would appear that domestic factors influence, but do not determine, alliance choice.

NOTES

1. The domestic or microfoundations of international state behavior are rapidly becoming a central issue for many research programs in political science. See, for example, Evans, Jacobson, and Putnam 1993, Morrow 1988, and Rosecrance and Stein 1993. In fact, our previous research—Gilligan on tariff policy (1997) and Hunt on mass media (1997)—suggested precisely the kind of theory we are attempting to formalize and test systematically here.

2. A possible neorealist response would be that this fact simply shows that states are very good balancers—so good, in fact, that wars that threaten polity survival rarely break out. Our evidence suggests that this is not the case—that nations often alter security policy away from the realist ideal when faced with strong *domestic* political threats.

3. Gurr is generous to domestic groups in the coding of polity termination. Essentially, if a polity collapses under the pressure of both foreign and internal forces, the latter gets the nod.

4. With regard to the macroeconomy, see Nordhaus 1975, McCrae 1977, and Alesina and Rosenthal 1995, not to mention the entire "rent-seeking" literature (e.g., Magee, Brock, and Young 1989) and sources cited therein.

5. See other essays within this volume for possible formal models of such a process.

6. Other essays in this volume (Ishida's, for example) develop the concept of differential utility functions between leaders and electorate over government functions more fully.

7. Alliances take on many shapes and degrees of constraint, ranging from mild ententes to credible mutual defense agreements. And, too, the formal arrangement of an alliance does not always correspond with reality. During the time span of our investigation—1948 to 1978—we concluded that the Arab League from 1950 onward was reasonably close in conception and scope to CENTO from its 1955 inception onward. We

did not include the other two multilateral alliances that claim some of these countries as members—NATO, with Turkey, and the Organization of African Unity (OAU) and North African Arab League members—in our investigation because of their sharp differences in scope and region.

8. By CENTO, we mean the Central Treaty Organization and its precursors, the Baghdad Pact and the Middle Eastern Treaty Organization (METO).

9. Each threatening event is weighted for its severity with weights given by COPDAB.

10. The alliance military expenditure and threat variables in the specifications in tables 4 and 5 are different from those in table 3. The estimations in table 3 used the military expenditures and external threats of *all* the country's allies, while those in tables 4 and 5 use the military expenditure and external threat only of the alliance that the country is considering joining.

11. That is, we multiplied the variables used in table 4 by an index consisting of $(-1 \times$ external threat) and $(-1 \times$ alliance external threat), respectively. High values of this index should correspond with more choice to join or not join an alliance than lower values of this index should.

12. Egypt was dismissed from the Arab League following the Camp David agreement with Israel in 1979, and the organization's headquarters was moved from Cairo to Tunis. In 1987, however, League members were allowed to restore diplomatic relations with Egypt, and the League headquarters was moved back to Cairo in 1990.

13. Syria merged with Egypt to form the United Arab Republic in 1958 and dropped out of the UAR in 1961. Syrian attributes are combined with Egypt's for the years 1959 and 1960 and are listed in our data set under Egypt.

REFERENCES

Alesina, Alberto, Sule Ozler, Nouriel Roubini, and Phillip Swagel. 1991. Political Instability and Economic Growth. Paper presented at the National Bureau of Economic Research conference, Political Economics, Cambridge, MA.

Alesina, Alberto, and Howard Rosenthal. 1995. *Partisan Politics, Divided Government, and the Economy.* New York: Cambridge University Press.

Alt, James E., and Gary King. 1994. Transfers of Governmental Power: The Meaning of Time Dependence. *Comparative Political Studies* 27:190–210.

Azar, Edward E. 1993. *Conflict and Peace Data Bank (COPDAB).* ICPSR 07767. Ann Arbor, MI: Inter-university Consortium for Political and Social Research.

Bienen, Henry, and Nicolas van de Walle. 1989. Time and Power in Africa. *American Political Science Review* 83:19–34.

———. 1991. *Of Time and Power.* Stanford: Stanford University Press.

Bueno de Mesquita, Bruce, and David Lalman. 1988. Empirical Support for Systemic and Dyadic Explanations of International Conflict. *World Politics* 41:1–20.

———. 1992. *War and Reason: Domestic and International Imperatives.* New Haven: Yale University Press.

Bueno de Mesquita, Bruce, and Randolph Siverson. 1995. War and the Survival of Po-
    litical Leaders: A Comparative Study of Regime Types and Political Accountabil-
    ity. *American Political Science Review* 89:841–55.
Bueno de Mesquita, Bruce, Randolph Siverson, and Gary Woller. 1992. War and the Fate
    of Regimes: A Comparative Analysis. *American Political Science Review* 86:
    638–46.
Christensen, Thomas J., and Jack Snyder. 1990. Chain Gangs and Passed Bucks: Pre-
    dicting Alliance Patterns in Multipolarity. *International Organization* 44, no. 2
    (Spring): 137–68.
Conybeare, John. 1992. A Portfolio Diversification Model of Alliances. *Journal of Con-
    flict Resolution* 36:52–85.
———. 1994. The Portfolio Benefits of Free Riding in Military Alliances. *International
    Studies Quarterly* 38:405–20.
David, Steven R. 1991. *Choosing Sides: Alignment and Realignment in the Third World.*
    Baltimore: Johns Hopkins University Press.
Donovan, John, ed. 1972. *U.S. and Soviet Policy in the Middle East, 1945–56.* New
    York: Facts on File.
Doyle, Michael. 1986. Liberalism and World Politics. *American Political Science Re-
    view* 80, no. 4: 1151–69.
Evans, Peter B., Harold Jacobson, and Robert Putnam, eds. 1993. *Double-Edged Diplo-
    macy: International Bargaining and Domestic Politics.* Berkeley: University of
    California Press.
Fearon, James D. 1994. Domestic Political Audiences and the Escalation of International
    Disputes. *American Political Science Review* 88:577–92.
Gilligan, Michael J. 1997. *Empowering Exporters: Reciprocity, Delegation, and Col-
    lective Action in American Trade Policy.* Ann Arbor: University of Michigan
    Press.
Gilligan, Michael J., and W. Ben Hunt. 1995. Linking Domestic and International
    Sources of Foreign Policy: The Microfoundations of Alliance Formation. New
    York University. Mimeo.
Grieco, Joseph. 1988. Anarchy and the Limits of Cooperation: A Realist Critique of the
    Newest Liberal Institutionalism. *International Organization* 4, no. 3 (Summer):
    485–507.
Gurr, Ted Robert. 1990. *Polity II: Political Structures and Regime Change, 1800–1986.*
    ICPSR 09263. Ann Arbor, MI: Inter-university Consortium for Political and Social
    Research.
Haas, Michael. 1971. *International Subsystems, 1649–1963.* ICPSR 05011. Ann Arbor,
    MI: Inter-university Consortium for Political and Social Research.
Hadley, Guy. 1971. *CENTO: The Forgotten Alliance.* Sussex: Institute for the Study of
    International Organization.
Hunt, W. Ben. 1997. *Getting to War.* Ann Arbor: University of Michigan Press.
Jackman, Robert. 1978. The Predictability of Coups d'Etat: A Model with African Data.
    American Political Science Review 72:1262–75.
Keohane, Robert, ed. 1986. *Neorealism and Its Critics.* New York: Columbia Univer-
    sity Press.

Leng, Russell J. 1995. *Behavioral Correlates of War, 1816–1975.* ICPSR 08606. Ann Arbor, MI: Inter-university Consortium for Political and Social Research.

Londregan, John, Henry Bienen, and Nicolas Van de Walle. 1995. Ethnicity and Leadership Succession in Africa. *International Studies Quarterly* 39:1–26.

Londregan, John, and Keith Poole. 1990. Poverty, the Coup Trap, and the Seizure of Executive Power. *World Politics* 42:151–83.

Magee, Stephen, William Brock, and Leslie Young. 1989. *Black Hole Tariffs and Endogenous Policy Theory.* New York: Cambridge University Press.

Maoz, Zeev, and Bruce Russett. 1993. Normative and Structural Causes of Democratic Peace, 1946–1986. *American Political Science Review* 87, no. 3:624–38.

McClelland, Charles. 1978. *World Event/Interaction Survey (WEIS) Project, 1966–1978.* ICPSR 05211. Ann Arbor, MI: Inter-university Consortium for Political and Social Research.

McCrae, Duncan. 1977. A Political Model of the Business Cycle. *Journal of Political Economy* 85:239–64.

Mearsheimer, John J. 1990. Back to the Future: Instability in Europe after the Cold War. *International Security* 15, no. 1: 5–56.

———. 1994. The False Promise of International Institutions. *International Security* 19, no. 3: 5–49.

Merritt, Richard L., Robert Muncaster, Dina Zinnes, eds. 1993. *International Event-Data Developments.* Ann Arbor: University of Michigan Press.

Morgenthau, Hans. 1948. *Politics among Nations.* New York: Knopf.

Morrow, James. 1987. On the Theoretical Basis of a Measure of National Risk Attitudes. *International Studies Quarterly* 31:423–38.

———. 1988. Social Choice and System Structure in World Politics. *World Politics* 41:75–97.

———. 1991. Alliances and Asymmetry. *American Journal of Political Science* 35:904–33.

Mueller, John. 1970. Presidential Popularity from Truman to Johnson. *American Political Science Review* 64:18–34.

Nordhaus, William. 1975. The Political Business Cycle. *Review of Economic Studies* 42:169–90.

O'Kane, Rosemary. 1981. A Probabilistic Approach to the Causes of Coups d'Etat. *British Journal of Political Science* 11:287–308.

Pogany, Istvan. 1987. *The Arab League and Peacekeeping in the Lebanon.* New York: St. Martin's.

Robertson, John. 1983. Inflation, Unemployment, and Government Collapse. *Comparative Political Studies* 15:425–44.

Rosecrance, Richard, and Arthur Stein. 1993. *The Domestic Bases of Grand Strategy.* Ithaca: Cornell University Press.

Roth, Alvin, and Marilda Sotomayor. 1990. *Two Sided Matching: A Study in Game-Theoretic Modeling and Analysis.* Cambridge: Cambridge University Press.

Singer, J. David, Stuart Bremer, and John Stuckey. 1972. Capability Distribution, Uncertainty, and Major Power War, 1820–1965. In *Peace, War, and Numbers,* edited by Bruce Russett. Beverly Hills, CA: Sage.

Singer, J. David, and Paul Diehl, eds. 1990. *Measuring the Correlates of War.* Ann Arbor: University of Michigan Press.

Singer, J. David, and Melvin Small. 1984. *Wages of War, 1816–1980.* ICPSR 09044. Ann Arbor, MI: Inter-university Consortium for Political and Social Research.

Snyder, Jack. 1991. *Myths of Empire: Domestic Politics and International Ambition.* Ithaca: Cornell University Press.

Sorokin, Gerald. Arms, Alliances, and Security Tradeoffs in Enduring Rivalries. *International Studies Quarterly* 38:421–46.

Walt, Stephen. 1987. *The Origins of Alliances.* Ithaca: Cornell University Press.

Waltz, Kenneth. 1979. *Theory of International Politics.* New York: McGraw-Hill.

Zacher, Mark W. 1979. *International Conflicts and Collective Security, 1946–77.* New York: Praeger.

Zakaria, Fareed. 1992. Realism and Domestic Politics. *International Security* 17, no. 1: 177–98.

Electoral Incentives and the Political Economy of National Defense Spending Decisions

Atsushi Ishida

This essay presents a two-level game model of national defense spending decisions of a democracy, which interacts with its foreign rival in a bilateral international military rivalry. By specifying the economic roles of a democratic government and the institutional features of its domestic decision-making process, I identify and analyze the domestic and international origins of the demand for defense spending. In particular, this essay offers a two-level game model to explain a variety of aspects of the political economy of defense spending such as the microlevel decisions of individual voters, the electoral strategies of competing political parties, and the macrolevel public choice of military expenditures, which have been noted in the previous empirical research. This wide range of empirical questions cannot be coherently addressed by the alternative—the unitary rational actor model, which ignores domestic politics.

Previous empirical quantitative studies have examined not only the international sources of defense spending (the spending of an adversary, the spending of allies, threat perception, technological progress, and so on) but also domestic origins such as income distribution (Seiglie 1991) and an electoral competition. The primary goal of this essay is to provide a conceptual framework that coherently accounts for these various findings. More specifically, the model shares some basic assumptions with existing second- and third-image models and derives implications not only on the domestic microlevel but on the international macrolevel.

The structure of this essay is the following. In the first section, I discuss the theoretical motivation behind this research project. In the second section, I specify a two-level game model of defense spending decisions in which two parties play *a majoritarian income redistribution game* to finance national defense. Then, I identify and analyze Nash equilibrium levels of defense spending. In the third section, I relax the assumptions about the policy motivations of competing political parties and the information about the policy preferences of the voters during a campaign and explore the logical implications of these new assumptions. I examine the effects of their partisan preferences on their electoral behavior. In the fourth section, I summarize the theoretical results. The final section provides a conclusion.

Motivation

To give the reader a brief sketch of the nature and background of my modeling strategy, in this section, first, I discuss my understanding of the essence of a two-level game model compared with the unitary rational actor model. Second, I preview the theoretical issues I address in my two-level model analysis of national defense spending decisions. Third, I emphasize the significance of developing an empirically falsifiable two-level game model of foreign policy choice to demonstrate its empirical relevance. Aside from these considerations, the final part of this section discusses two additional strengths of this theoretical perspective.

In the model developed in the following section, the central government of neither of the two strategically interacting countries has any incentive to change its defense spending decision either for domestic electoral or international security reasons. Generally, no government has any incentive to deviate unilaterally from its foreign policy decision for either domestic or international reasons in a two-level game model (Ishida and Wolinsky 1995). In this sense, the model synthesizes the domestic and international levels of analysis in international relations. Adopting this analytical perspective, it is necessary to be fully aware of an obvious trade-off: whereas a two-level game model will be able to introduce *methodological individualism* to the analysis of foreign policy choice, the synthesis of the two levels will require a precise specification of the institutional features of domestic politics and as a consequence will limit the scope of applicability of the model (Achen 1995, 1).[1]

Admittedly, the unitary rational actor assumption is useful in analyzing complex international interactions such as multilateral, not bilateral, interactions and interactions over more than one issue. However, as this essay endeavors to show, these benefits of *analytical tractability* of the unitary rational actor model must be weighed against the potential for an *analytical bias* it brings to our understanding of international relations.

More specifically, my two-level game model shows that it is necessary to know not only the aggregate national income but also its distribution in order to correctly predict a national defense spending decision. This is the case because politics is sensitive not only to the mean but also to the variance of the individual income within a country. Existing unitary rational actor models, however, attempt to deduce the foreign policy choice of a nation-state from its aggregate resource size. In the field of the political economy of defense spending, for instance, aggregate parameters like Gross National Products (GNP) are frequently hypothesized to have impacts on a defense-spending decision in a variety of models such as burden sharing within an alliance and arms races between adversaries (Sandler 1993). Yet, what would make one believe that the mean income or the aggregate income provides adequate information to predict national defense spending decisions if more specific information about decision-making institutions, such as a specific electoral system, were available?

Moreover, my two-level game model not only links domestic and international levels of analysis but also addresses the question of issue linkage. In particular, I analyze the link between the issue of national security and the issue of domestic welfare spending generated by the budget constraint that the central government of an internationally competing country faces.

The two-level game model in this essay is designed to address the following questions: (1) what are the effects of internal socioeconomic characteristics—income distribution, in particular—of a country on its external behavior—especially the level of its defense spending? (2) what is the origin of the partisan preferences over the provision of national security? and (3) who supports an increase in defense spending? In addition, the model simultaneously examines the international strategic interdependence between adversaries.

In addition to this set of theoretical motivations, I would stress the empirical relevance of the theory. The existing formal models of two-level games generate comparative statics based on *unobservable* theoretical concepts such as discount factors (Iida 1993; Mo 1994). As a consequence, their theoretical claims are hard to falsify empirically. It is true that the two-level game models have achieved the important goals of introducing the domestic political foundation of foreign policy decisions and of deriving precise causal implications, which are not accounted for by the alternative unitary rational actor model. But, in order to demonstrate fully that the two-level game approach makes contributions to our understanding of the reality of international relations, the models should be tested, or at least be intrinsically testable, against the unitary rational actor model, which ignores domestic politics.[2]

Aside from these considerations, the model presented in this essay has two additional strengths. First, although its analytical results are interpreted in the context of national defense as public goods provided by the central government, this model is applicable across several issue areas of interest in international relations as long as they share the common strategic problem. Second, the model helps to clarify the analytical distinction between certain issue areas since those issue areas are associated with different strategic problems.

The two-level game model developed here is a general model of the public finance of domestic public goods, which have either positive- or negative-externality effects internationally. In the model, national defense is assumed to be public goods on the domestic level, but the same spending is considered to have *security-reducing* negative-externality effects simultaneously on its adversaries on the international level.

Although I interpret the implications of the model in the specific context of national defense, this model can be alternatively applied to some other policy questions, including but not limited to the international politics of environmental protection. This versatility of the model is one of its attractive features. National environmental protection can be modeled as a public good domestically, but it can be reasonably argued to have positive-externality effects internationally, in contrast to the assumed negative-externality effects of national defense spending on its adversary in this essay. For instance, if the central government of one country adopts a policy to regulate air pollution, then the policy not only cleans the air in that specific country but simultaneously ameliorates an acid rain problem in its neighboring country. In this way, this two-level game is applicable across issue areas in international relations as long as the core strategic problem is identical.

On the other hand, the two-level game approach helps to shed light on the analytical distinction between issue areas. In general, foreign policy has some welfare effects on the population.[3] National security policy tends to have *homogeneous* welfare effects on the population as a whole, whereas foreign economic policy tends to have *heterogeneous* effects on various social groups such as interest groups, classes, and regions. The nature of these domestic welfare effects thus distinguishes national security problems from international political economic problems.

It is intuitively obvious that, if foreign policy has heterogeneous effects on various domestic groups, then domestic politics will have nontrivial effects on its foreign policy decisions. The logic behind this claim is as simple as the following: domestic politics shapes the objectives of a policymaker and also defines the link between the policymaker and other political actors who are subject to the welfare effects of foreign policy. If a certain foreign policy has heterogeneous welfare effects on the population, then the subsequent choice of foreign policy by the policymaker depends on the preferences of those political actors who exert influence on him. And this channel of influence is characterized by the institutional feature of domestic politics. But what if foreign policy has homogeneous welfare effects? In this essay, I demonstrate that even if foreign policy has homogeneous welfare effects across boundaries of societal groups, domestic politics still matters.

The Model

The Outline

Previous studies of U.S. defense spending have presented a long list of factors that affect levels of military expenditure (Schneider 1988; Looney and Mehey

1990). International events, changing administrations, public opinion, Congress, domestic economy, perceptions of the Soviet threat, arms control agreements, elections, interservice rivalry, and intra-alliance burden sharing, among others, have been shown or have been claimed to have impacts on U.S. defense spending. Obviously, it would not be a manageable task to model all these aspects of defense spending simultaneously.[4] Rather, the model in this essay concentrates on the public finance of national defense, which has been considered to be a quintessential public good, and explains *the demand for defense spending* by examining the social bases of prodefense policies. The primary modeling task is to identify the individual demand for military expenditures and examine the way in which politics shapes the process of aggregating microlevel individual demand into macrolevel national public policy. In the end, the model generates implications on different analytical levels and contributes to narrowing gaps between domestic and international political analyses of defense spending.

In the following, first, I outline the model. Second, I introduce the basic assumptions. The players, their strategies, their preferences, the structure of the game, and the solution concept of the game are discussed. Third, I specify the economic roles of a democratic government. Fourth, I model the effect of governmental policy choice on the welfare of individual voters. Then I define two alternative forms of domestic political competition. Assuming that the electorate votes prospectively, an electoral competition between two parties determines the levels of defense spending either by choosing the income tax rate to generate the governmental revenues that finance defense and welfare spending or by choosing how to allocate the revenues between defense and welfare spending. Fifth, on the issue of taxation, I derive the induced preferences of the voters about taxation. Since the voters can perfectly anticipate the individual welfare effects of the tax policy, they are induced to have ex ante preferences about the income tax rate. Perfectly anticipating how the electorate would rationally vote over the issue of the income tax rate, strategic political parties choose vote-maximizing strategies; they announce the ideal income tax rate of the median voter as their campaign promise. Thus, I identify the optimal level of defense spending to win an election. Up to this point, I assume that the defense spending of an adversary is exogenously given. In other words, the optimal defense spending is indeed conceptualized as a best reply to the assumed adversarial defense spending. Further relaxing this exogeneity, I identify and analyze the Nash equilibrium levels of defense spending of both the home and the foreign countries. I compare the implications derived from this two-level game model with those of the alternative unitary rational actor model. Sixth, alternatively assuming that an election takes place over the defense-welfare trade-off, I derive and examine the Nash equilibrium levels of defense spending of the strategically interacting countries. The last part of this section discusses some features of this two-level game model.

Basic Assumptions

The strategic players in the following game are two parties in the home country (party L and party R) and the foreign country. For the sake of analytical simplicity, I initially assume that the foreign country is a unitary actor.[5] In this bilateral international military rivalry, the defense spending of one country has security-reducing negative-externality effects on the welfare of the citizens of the other country. The two parties in the home country—which is assumed to be a democracy—choose their strategies—the ways to finance national defense—in anticipation of the adversary's rational reply. And their strategies determine the levels of defense spending over the set of which voters have preferences. Each party is interested only in winning office, and its strategy takes a form of campaign promise. Each player announces its policy platform without the knowledge of the other player's strategy. The solution concept in this game is a Nash equilibrium. In a Nash equilibrium, neither party has incentives to unilaterally alter its campaign promise, which determines the level of defense spending. Nor does the foreign country have incentives to deviate unilaterally from its defense-spending decision. In this sense, defense spending is in Nash equilibrium both domestically and internationally. The model is designed to analyze a majoritarian income redistribution game to finance national defense in the context of bilateral international military rivalry. Furthermore, it aims at empirically distinguishing between the two-level game and the unitary rational actor models, as is accomplished by Murdoch et al. (1993) in a different context.

The model is based on the following set of simplifying assumptions. First, the roles of the central government are not only to provide national defense as public goods but also to redistribute wealth among the citizens through welfare spending.[6] Second, the spending of the government is financed by its income tax revenues. Third, the levels of spending—both defense and welfare spending—are determined as a consequence of a majoritarian income-redistribution game (Romer 1975, 1977). Two parties compete over votes, and their electoral incentives shape their choices of campaign promises. In contrast to Putnam's (1988) conceptualization of a two-level game, the *unobservable* preferences of the central government of the home country are not *exogenously* assumed but *endogenously* derived and linked with an *observable* parameter so that the empirical investigation of theoretical implications is to a lesser degree subject to multiple subjective interpretations by the researcher. Fourth, voters are rational in that when they vote prospectively, they vote for one party whose policy platform is preferable to that of the other.

The Economic Roles of a Democratic Government

In a democracy, political rights are distributed more equally than in the market, and citizens can reallocate resources that they do not own through some political processes (Przeworski 1990). In order to capture this redistributive aspect of democracy, I assume that a central government taxes the resources of the population not only to provide public goods but also to redistribute them and that the rate of income tax, t, where $0 \leq t \leq 1$, is proportionate.[7] In other words, a voter with income y_i pays her income tax, ty_i. The total revenue of the government, G, is

$$G = \sum_{i=1}^{n} ty_i = tY,$$ (1)

where Y is defined as the GNP and n is the population of this economy. Income is assumed to be distributed in a skewed manner so that mean income is greater than median income.[8] I assume that a part, w, where $0 \leq w \leq 1$, of this governmental revenue is spent on welfare. Total welfare spending, W, is determined by

$$W = wG.$$ (2)

Welfare spending is redistributed equally among the population. More specifically, each individual in this economy receives identical welfare benefits, W/n. Mean income, Y/n, is denoted hereafter as $\bar{y}$. Based on the assumption that the budget is balanced, the total military expenditure of the home country, M_h, is determined by

$$M_h = G - W = (1 - w)G = (1 - w)tn\bar{y}.$$ (3)

As a first cut, I initially assume that national defense is a pure public good.

The Welfare Effects of Governmental Policy on the Electorate

Public policy has welfare effects on the population. I assume that an individual voter has a utility function, which is defined with respect to the level of post-fisc private consumption and the level of national security.[9] The level of post-fisc private consumption, C_i, for an individual, i, is

$$C_i = (1 - t)y_i + wt\bar{y}.$$ (4)

As was mentioned in the beginning of this section, the defense spending of the foreign country has security-reducing negative-externality effects on the level of national security in the home country.[10] Specifically, the level of national security, S_h, given the adversarial defense spending of the foreign country, M_f, is modeled to be

$$S_h(M_f) = M_h - kM_f = (1 - w)tn\bar{y} - kM_f, \tag{5}$$

where k is a constant, which captures the negative-externality effects of the foreign country's defense spending. A plausible interpretation of k is that k increases as the military technology of the foreign country improves relative to that of the home country. Alternatively, k can be interpreted as the perceived threats of the foreign country. In the latter case, I assume that k is shared among the population.[11] Given these preliminary definitions, the utility function of a typical voter is defined by

$$U_i(C_i, S_h) = C_i^\alpha S_h^\beta, \tag{6}$$

where

$$0 < \alpha + \beta < 1 \tag{7}$$

(α and β are positive real numbers here).

It should be parenthetically noted that in this economy each individual has an identical utility function. This assumption is crucial. Although this restrictive assumption can be relaxed to some extent, it enables us to analyze the logical connection among (1) the induced policy preferences of an individual voter on the microdecision level, (2) the income distribution in the economy or the socioeconomic characteristics of the polity, and (3) the public choice of national defense spending on the macropolicy level. In the following, I show that this assumed homogeneity of utility function, or the assumed identical taste, induces members of this economy to have heterogeneous preferences over the taxation and appropriation policies of the government due to the variance in individual income.

Politics—Taxation

Politics in a democracy is assumed to take the form of a two-party electoral competition. Two parties, L and R, compete for votes in an election. The issue can be either the taxation or the appropriation. In this economy, the level of income taxation, t, fully determines the size of the government, as was discussed earlier. The tax revenues of the central government are then appropriated either for defense, M_h, or for welfare, W. In the following, I first assume that they compete over the rate of income taxes while the relative allocation of the revenues between defense and welfare spending is exogenously given. In the next subsection, I examine the electoral competition over the spending trade-off while fixing the income tax rate.

In this polity, politics takes place over a one-dimensional issue space while voters are concerned about two issues in this model. Also, politics is one dimensional whereas the government provides two distinct services. In other words, the one-dimensionality of politics does not require awkwardly simplistic assumptions about the dimension of voter preferences and the economic roles of the government in this model.[12]

The voters are rational in that they can perfectly anticipate the welfare effects of the policy of the central government. Specifically, they can anticipate the ex post effects of a specific income tax policy both on their post-fisc private consumption levels and on the national security. Therefore, they are induced to have ex ante policy preferences.

What are the induced preferences of a typical voter with income y_i over the issue space of income tax rate t? It is assumed that w is fixed at w_{sq}. The first-order condition of the optimal income tax rate, t^*, is the following:

$$\frac{dU[C_i(t), S_h(t)]}{dt} = \frac{\partial U}{\partial C_i} \frac{dC_i}{dt} + \frac{\partial U}{\partial S_h} \frac{dS_h}{dt} = 0. \tag{8}$$

When equation 8 is satisfied, the following inequality should hold.[13]

$$\frac{dC_i}{dt} = -y_i + w_{sq}\bar{y} < 0, \tag{9}$$

since the other terms of equation 8 are all positive by assumptions 4, 5, and 6.

Note that

$$\frac{d^2U}{dt^2} < 0, \tag{10}$$

due to equations 6 and 9. Inequality 10 indicates that every voter in this economy has a globally concave utility function over the issue space, t, or all the voters are induced to have well-behaved, *single-peaked* preferences. At t^*, which satisfies equation 8, the voter's utility will be certainly maximized.

Equations 4, 5, 6, and 8 combine to yield the optimal income tax rate, t^*, to finance the spending programs:

$$t^*(M_f) = \frac{\alpha}{(\alpha + \beta)} \frac{kM_f}{(1 - w_{sq})n\bar{y}} + \frac{\beta}{(\alpha + \beta)} \frac{y_i}{(y_i - w_{sq}\bar{y})} .$$ (11)

Note that, within a given income distribution,

$$\frac{dt^*(M_f)}{dy_i} = \frac{\beta}{(\alpha + \beta)} \frac{(-w_{sq}\bar{y})}{(y_i - w_{sq}\bar{y})^2} < 0.$$ (12)

Inequality 12 establishes the following result: *the higher the level of initial individual income is, the lower the level of income tax rate the voter prefers.* It follows that, as the level of pre-fisc individual income increases, her ideal size of the government will decrease.

More intuitively, the income tax rate affects the welfare of a voter in that an increase in income tax improves national security at the cost of decreasing the level of private consumption. Since the fixed portion, w_{sq}, of the revenue is redistributed among the population, whereas the income tax is proportionate, the effective tax rate is progressive. In other words, the effective tax rate increases as income increases. The ratio of the individual burden of national defense, $y_i - C_i$, to individual income, or the effective tax rate, $\tau(y_i)$, is

$$\tau(y_i) = \frac{y_i - C_i}{y_i} = t\left(1 - w_{sq}\frac{\bar{y}}{y_i}\right).$$ (13)

Clearly, as y_i increases, $\tau(y_i)$ increases. This is why the wealthier the voter is, the smaller size of government she prefers.

Similarly, one can deduce the following comparative statics:

$$\frac{dt^*(M_f)}{dM_f} = \frac{\alpha}{(\alpha + \beta)} \frac{k}{(1 - w_{sq})n\bar{y}} > 0.$$ (14)

In other words, given the status quo, w_{sq}, *the higher the level of defense spending of the foreign country is, the higher level of income taxation the voter prefers.*

In order to connect these microlevel policy preferences of voters with a macrolevel policy outcome, it is necessary to specify the collective decision-making institutional environment. This domestic institutional structure aggregates individual demand into national defense policy. As was briefly mentioned earlier, the level of income taxation is determined as a consequence of two-party electoral competition. In this model, voters are assumed to vote prospectively. And it is assumed that the parties can commit themselves to implementing an announced policy after winning an election. The voters expect the winning party to implement its campaign promise. To be precise, the strategy space of party L is $\Sigma_L = [0, 1]$. Party R's strategy space is similarly defined. The utility function of party L is $U_L : \Sigma_L \times \Sigma_R \to \Re$, such that its only goal is winning an office. They announce their campaign promises simultaneously or do so without the knowledge of the strategy of each other. For instance, party L chooses $\sigma_L \in \Sigma_L$ and party R chooses $\sigma_R \in \Sigma_R$, and (σ_L, σ_R) determines which party wins the election and which level of the income tax rate is chosen as a result. Since all the voters in this economy have single-peaked preferences over the issue space, t, the policy platforms of the two parties will converge in a Nash equilibrium to the ideal point of the median voter, as long as there is no uncertainty about the location of the median voter's ideal point. In this game, it has been deduced that the voter's ideal point over t is a monotonically decreasing function of her income. The *median voter theorem* establishes that the unique Nash equilibrium of this is (t_m^*, t_m^*) and the policy outcome is of course t_m^*, the ideal tax level of the voter whose income is in the median position among the population.

Defense spending in the home country in equilibrium is

$$M_h^*(M_f) = (1 - w_{sq}) t_m^* n \bar{y}. \tag{15}$$

Equations 11 and 15 combine to determine

$$M_h^*(M_f) = \frac{\alpha}{(\alpha + \beta)} k M_f + \frac{\beta}{(\alpha + \beta)} I_h, \tag{16}$$

where

$$I_h = \frac{(1 - w_{sq}) n \bar{y}}{\left[1 - w_{sq} \left(\dfrac{\bar{y}}{y_m} \right) \right]}, \tag{17}$$

where y_m is the median income in this economy.[14] I_h is the term that is shaped by the income distribution of the home country. It should be noted that, with mean income, $\bar{y}$, fixed, the lower the median income is, the greater I_h is. And the greater I_h is, the greater the optimal defense spending is (given adversarial defense spending). Therefore, the lower median income is, the greater optimal defense spending in the home country is.

Note that $M_h^*(M_f)$, computed earlier, is the best reply of M_h to M_f. Now, what is the best reply of M_f to M_h? The foreign country is assumed to be a unitary actor. Therefore, its resource allocation is not shaped by its domestic income redistribution. The utility of the foreign country is defined as follows:

$$U = (Y' - M_f)^{\alpha'}(M_f - k'M_h)^{\beta'}. \tag{18}$$

Y', k', α', and β' are the parameters of the foreign country. These parameters are defined as in the previous definitions. Then, the optimal level of defense spending for the foreign country is deduced to be

$$M_f^*(M_h) = \frac{\alpha'}{(\alpha' + \beta')}\, k'M_h + \frac{\beta'}{(\alpha' + \beta')}\, Y'. \tag{19}$$

This is the best reply of M_f to M_h. Obviously, income distribution has no impact on the military expenditure of the foreign country.

The Nash equilibrium levels of M_h^{ne} and M_f^{ne} are identified as the intersection of the two best reply functions, based on the assumption that each strategic player—the foreign country and the two parties in the home country—makes its defense-spending decision without the knowledge of the strategic decisions of the other players. In other words, I assume that national defense spending decisions are made under imperfect information. Solving the set of simultaneous equations 16 and 19, I obtain the Nash equilibrium levels of defense spending of these two countries in the two-level game model:

$$\begin{bmatrix} M_h^{ne} \\ M_f^{ne} \end{bmatrix} = \begin{bmatrix} \gamma_{11}\gamma_{12} \\ \gamma_{21}\gamma_{22} \end{bmatrix} \begin{bmatrix} I_h \\ Y' \end{bmatrix}, \tag{20}$$

where

$$\gamma_{11} = \frac{(\alpha' + \beta')\beta}{[(\alpha + \beta)(\alpha' + \beta') - \alpha\alpha'kk']} \tag{21}$$

$$\gamma_{12} = \frac{\alpha\beta'k}{[(\alpha + \beta)(\alpha' + \beta') - \alpha\alpha'kk']} \tag{22}$$

$$\gamma_{21} = \frac{\alpha'\beta k'}{[(\alpha + \beta)(\alpha' + \beta') - \alpha\alpha'kk']} \tag{23}$$

and

$$\gamma_{22} = \frac{(\alpha + \beta)\beta'}{[(\alpha + \beta)(\alpha' + \beta') - \alpha\alpha'kk']}. \tag{24}$$

The superscript *ne* indicates the Nash equilibrium levels of defense spending in this political-economic system.

Parenthetically, it should be noted that unlike some other two-level game models this two-level game model is so simple that it does not require the foreign country to be a unitary actor. This is another attractive feature of this model. Suppose that the foreign country also has a two-party system and that its national defense spending decision is made as a consequence of two-party electoral competition over the income tax rate. Then, the Nash equilibrium levels of defense spending are determined by

$$
\begin{bmatrix} M_h^{ne} \\ M_f^{ne} \end{bmatrix} = \begin{bmatrix} \gamma_{11}\gamma_{12} \\ \gamma_{21}\gamma_{22} \end{bmatrix} \begin{bmatrix} I_h \\ I_f \end{bmatrix},
\tag{25}
$$

where γ_{11}, γ_{12}, γ_{21}, and γ_{22} are the same as they are defined above and

$$
I_f = \frac{(1 - w_{sq}')n'\bar{y}'}{\left[1 - w_{sq}' \left(\dfrac{\bar{y}'}{y_m'} \right) \right]},
\tag{26}
$$

where w_{sq}', n', $\bar{y}'$, and y_m' denote the status quo spending trade-off between defense and welfare, the population, mean income, and the median income of the foreign country, respectively.

How different are the Nash equilibrium levels of defense spending in the two-level game, identified in equation 20, from the Nash equilibrium levels of defense spending in the alternative unitary rational actor model? Suppose that not only the foreign but also the home country are unitary actors. Then, the Nash equilibrium levels of defense spending in this unitary rational actor model would be

$$
\begin{bmatrix} M_h^{ura} \\ M_f^{ura} \end{bmatrix} = \begin{bmatrix} \gamma_{11}\gamma_{12} \\ \gamma_{21}\gamma_{22} \end{bmatrix} \begin{bmatrix} Y \\ Y' \end{bmatrix}.
\tag{27}
$$

The superscript *ura* indicates the Nash equilibrium levels of defense spending in the unitary rational actor model. The comparison of equations 20 and 27 reveals that unless GNP, Y, is the same as I_h, or unless $w_{sq} = 0$, the Nash equilibrium levels of defense spending in the two-level game will diverge from the ones in the alternative unitary rational actor model. The way in which I_h diverges from Y depends on the domestic income distribution. Thus, this two-level game model generates implications that are *observationally* different from those of the unitary rational actor model.

Equations 20 and 27 produce the following set of implications.[15] First, as the negative externality of defense spending, k, increases, the defense spending of not only the home but also the foreign countries will increase. Second, as the aggregate size of the home country's economy, Y or $n\bar{y}$, increases, the defense spending of both of the countries will increase. As the income distribution in the home country becomes more unequal, in that its median income goes down with its mean income fixed, the defense spending of both of the countries will increase. In a Nash equilibrium, a change in a parameter that would raise the defense spending of one country will simultaneously increase that of its adversary because their budget-increasing effects are fully anticipated by the adversary.

The two-level game model produces all three implications, whereas the unitary rational actor model generates only the first two. In this sense, the two-level game model is more encompassing than the unitary rational actor model is.

Politics—Appropriation

Political redistribution in a democracy is achieved not only through progressive taxation but also through the redistributive spending of the central government. The tax revenues of the government can be appropriated either for the provision of public goods, such as national defense, or for more directly income-redistributing spending, typically welfare spending. Either assuming that the total revenues of the government are determined as in the process discussed in the preceding section or assuming simply that they are exogenously given, I examine the effects of redistributive fiscal activities on the trade-off between welfare and warfare.

In the following, I assume that the campaign issue is the proportion of the total revenues spent on welfare, w. I assume that the income tax rate, t_{sq}, is exogenously given in this section. In other words, I introduce an alternative assumption about the economic roles of a democratic government. What would be the expected welfare effects of governmental policy on the electorate? The voters perfectly anticipate the welfare impact of governmental policy, and they are induced to have the policy preferences over w. The first-order condition of the optimal w^* is the following:

$$\frac{dU[C_i(w), S_h(w)]}{dw} = 0. \tag{28}$$

Since

$$\frac{d^2U}{dw^2} < 0, \tag{29}$$

each voter in the home country has single-peaked preferences over the one-dimensional issue space of w. From the first-order condition, I obtain the optimal level of w for an individual whose income is y_i, given the adversary's military expenditure:

$$w^*(M_f) = \frac{\alpha t_{sq} n\bar{y} - \alpha k M_f - \beta(1 - t_{sq})n y_i}{t_{sq}ny(\alpha + \beta)}. \tag{30}$$

Since

$$\frac{\partial w^*(M_f)}{\partial y_i} < 0, \tag{31}$$

the optimal proportion of welfare spending in the governmental revenue is monotonically decreasing with respect to the individual income level. In other words, the wealthier the voter is, the lower level of welfare spending she prefers. Since the ideal proportion of defense spending is $1 - w^*$, inequality 31 implies that *the wealthier the voter is, the higher level of defense spending she prefers.*

More intuitively, as was discussed in the preceding section, the effective tax rate in this polity is progressive. In other words, the tax system redistributes resources from the rich to the poor. Between welfare and defense spending, defense spending is less redistributive from the rich to the poor. This is why the wealthier the voter is, the higher level of defense spending she prefers.

I assume that the electorate votes prospectively in a two-party competition over the proportion of welfare spending. The game between the two strategic parties is defined similarly to the one in the previous section. Then the median voter theorem holds. The campaign promises of the two parties will converge to the ideal point of the voter whose income is in the median position.

Since

$$M_h^*(M_f) = (1 - w_m^*)t_{sq}n\bar{y}, \tag{32}$$

where w_m^* is the ideal proportion of welfare spending for the voter whose income is in the median position, the optimal level of defense spending, given the adversarial spending, is

$$M_h^*(M_f) = \frac{\alpha}{(\alpha + \beta)} kM_f + \frac{\beta}{(\alpha + \beta)} \tilde{I}_h, \tag{33}$$

where

$$\tilde{I}_h = n[(1 - t_{sq})y_m + t_{sq}\bar{y}]. \tag{34}$$

In equation 34, $(1 - t_{sq})y_m + t_{sq}\bar{y}$ is a convex division of the distance between y_m and $\bar{y}$. Given t_{sq}, $\tilde{I}_h$ will decrease as the distance between median and mean income increases. In other words, the military expenditure of the home country increases as income distribution becomes more equal, with mean income fixed.

Equation 33 identifies the home country's best reply to the level of defense spending of the foreign country. The Nash equilibrium levels of the defense spending of the two countries are located at the intersection of the two best reply functions. They are identified as follows:

$$\begin{bmatrix} M_h^{ne} \\ M_f^{ne} \end{bmatrix} = \begin{bmatrix} \gamma_{11}\gamma_{12} \\ \gamma_{21}\gamma_{22} \end{bmatrix} \begin{bmatrix} \tilde{I}_h \\ Y' \end{bmatrix}. \tag{35}$$

In the unique Nash equilibrium, the negative externality of defense spending and the aggregate size of the economy have the same effects[16] on the levels of defense spending of the two countries, as was derived in the preceding section. Income distribution, however, has the opposite effect here. To reiterate, since defense spending is less redistributive from the rich to the poor than welfare spending is, the wealthier the voter is, the higher level of defense spending she prefers. This implies that, the more equal the income distribution is, the greater the level of defense spending is. In the Nash equilibrium, again, a domestic parametric shift that will raise defense spending in one country will simultaneously increase the level of its adversary's military expenditure.

Discussion

For practical purposes, it seems reasonable to assume that an electoral competition takes place over either one of the two issues. The analysis of the model has shown the following: on the size of the government, the wealthier the voter is, the smaller size of government the voter prefers. This relationship seems to hold in a survey, since the voter evaluates her individual tax burden when asked about her preferred size of government. However, since the income tax rate changes less often than the proportion of welfare spending, I argue that a majoritarian income redistribution game over the spending trade-off characterizes the political economy of defense spending decisions. Therefore, the wealthier the voter is, the higher level of defense spending she prefers. Moreover, the more equal the income distribution is, the higher the level of national defense spending is.

From the perspective of two-level game analysis, the set of implications derived so far are important for two reasons. First, the equilibrium analysis has established that not only the aggregate size of national resources but also their distribution among the population shape national defense spending decisions.

The distribution of income crucially affects the way in which a majoritarian income redistribution game is played domestically. This result derives from the specific *institutional* characterization of domestic politics in which the political process is sensitive not only to the aggregate size of the economy but also to the distribution of income. This might explain why aggregate parameters like GNP do not produce good predictions about foreign policy decisions of nation-states.

Second, these theoretical claims are empirically falsifiable. In the two-level game conceptualized by Putnam (1988), the policy preferences of the chief negotiator are crucial to understanding his bargaining behavior. Yet, his preferences are unobservable. The model in this essay, on the contrary, connects the unobservable policy preferences of the central government with the observable income level of the median voter by assuming that each member of society shares the same taste and by connecting her policy preferences with her income level.

Yet, a theoretical problem remains. The theoretical challenge in this essay is to establish a causal link among the optimal voting decisions of rational individuals, the domestic income distribution, and the subsequent national defense spending decision in an equilibrium. To achieve this goal, I have introduced three rather restrictive assumptions: (1) the income tax is proportionate; (2) the negative externality effects of the adversary's defense spending are linear; and (3) a typical voter's utility function is of the Cobb-Douglas form. I conjecture that I can relax some of these assumptions without substantively altering the theoretical implications of the model. Yet, the extent to which these assumptions can be relaxed remains to be explored in my future work.

Electoral Uncertainty and Redistribution through National Defense

So far, I have assumed that the two political parties in the home country pursue a single goal of winning an office. In addition, I have assumed that these two parties have complete information about the location of the ideal point of the median voter over the issue space—whether it is the level of taxation or the allocation of total revenues. To put it differently, I have assumed that the parties know exactly which campaign promise will allow them to gain power. The implications derived earlier are contingent on these restrictive assumptions—the assumption about the electoral motivations of the strategic parties and the assumption about the information available to them. Specifically, given these assumptions, the model has predicted that the party in power would not affect the levels of defense spending. In this brief section, I argue that the partisan preferences of the party in power affect the equilibrium levels of defense spending.[17]

I assume that the two political parties represent two distinct segments of the national constituency and therefore that they have their own policy preferences. In addition, I assume that the parties have incomplete information about the preferences of the voters, as in Alesina 1988.[18]

Suppose that one party (party L) represents the lower income population, whereas the other (party R) represents the higher income population. This assumption implies that party L has higher ideal points than party R does on either the issue of taxation (t) or the issue of the allocation of tax revenues (w).

As Alesina (1988) shows, in an equilibrium, the policy platforms of the parties diverge, though they do not diverge as far away from each other as their ideal points are, due to an electoral centripetal force. Therefore, the level of defense spending of the home country partially depends on the party in power. Specifically, if the parties compete over the proportion of welfare spending (w), then the level of defense spending of the home country will be higher when party R is in power than it will be when party L is in power. This partial divergence creates more policy fluctuation over time than the variation of the parameters such as the GNP or the domestic income distribution alone would under complete information.

Theoretical Results

In this section, I summarize the theoretical results of this essay on three aspects of the political economy of defense-spending decisions: first, the microlevel decisions of individual voters; second, the electoral strategies of political parties; and, third, the macrolevel public choice of military expenditures.

As was briefly mentioned, the ratio of welfare to total governmental spending (w) varies more dramatically than does the rate of income taxes (t). For instance, the U.S. data (U.S. Office of Management and Budget 1994) show that the ratio of defense to the total governmental spending, the empirical indicator for $1 - w$, fluctuated more than the ratio of total governmental expenditure to the GDP, the empirical indicator for t, during the Cold War years. In addition, the data of the allies of the United States (U.S. Arms Control and Disarmament Agency 1995) show that the variation of the defense burden is explained by the variation of the ratio of defense to total governmental spending among 15 countries in 1991 (Ishida 1995). This seems to justify the assumption that an electoral competition takes place over the allocation of governmental revenues between defense and welfare.

From the preceding formal analyses, I have derived the following empirical hypotheses on three levels. On the microlevel decisions of individual voters, I have hypothesized that: (1a) the greater the level of individual income is, the lower level of governmental services (t) the individual voter prefers; and (1b) the greater the level of individual income is, the higher level of national defense spending $(1 - w)$ the individual voter prefers. On the strategies of political parties, I have hypothesized that (2) the party, which represents the lower (higher) income population, is less (more) prodefense than the party, which represents the higher income population. Finally, on the macrolevel of defense-spending decisions, I have hypothesized that (3a) the "more threatening" the foreign country is, the higher the levels of defense spending of not only the home country but also the foreign country are; (3b) the greater the aggregate size of the home (foreign) country's economy, the higher the levels of defense spending of the two countries are; and (3c) the more equal the income distribution is, the higher the level of national defense spending is.[19]

Conclusion

This essay has developed a two-level game model of national defense spending decisions in which no central government has any incentive to alter its level of defense spending unilaterally either for domestic or international reasons. Domestic politics in a democracy has been modeled to be a majoritarian income redistribution game that determines how to finance national defense. Given this assumed institutional setup, I have *endogenously* explained the way in which the electoral incentives of the competing parties in a democracy shape the preferences of the central government—or the winning party—and derived implications about various aspects of the political economy of defense spending.

I have examined two public finance mechanisms to provide national defense: taxation and appropriations. The income-contingent preferences of the voters over the way to finance national defense have been shown to govern the majoritarian income redistribution game in this essay.

The implications hinge on the specific assumption that a domestic decision-making institution is a two-party system.[20] When certain conditions about the issue space, the voters' preferences, the number of candidates, and so on are satisfied, a two-party electoral competition with prospective voting generates a median voter result. This specificity of the assumed institutional characteristics limits the scope of empirical application of the model. Yet, as long as one believes that the preferences of a majority shape a political outcome in a democracy, the median voter theorem might be a way to operationalize this mechanism (Alesina and Rodrik 1992, 31).

I conclude by emphasizing the following three features of my analysis in this essay. First, I have constructed a methodologically individualistic model of defense-spending decisions. In particular, I have specified domestic decision-making institutions, endogenously deduced the electoral actions of the strategic parties, and identified and analyzed the Nash equilibrium levels of defense spending of interacting countries. Second, I have derived empirically falsifiable hypotheses, which can be tested against the alternative unitary rational actor model. Third, I have derived the empirical implications not only on the macrolevel of national defense spending decisions but also on the microlevel of individual voters' electoral decisions. In this sense, I have demonstrated the encompassing nature of my model.

NOTES

I gratefully acknowledge the helpful comments on earlier versions of this essay from Daniel Carpenter, Xinyuan Dai, James D. Fearon, Henk Goemans, Andrew Kydd, Walter Mattli, Sara McLaughlin, James D. Morrow, Ido Oren, Adam Przeworski, Carlos Seiglie, Duncan Snidal, Gerald Sorokin, Daniel Verdier, R. Harrison Wagner, Suzanne Werner, Yael Wolinsky, and the participants of the Conference on Strategic Politicians, Institutions, and Foreign Policy, University of California, Davis, April 28–29, 1995.

1. For instance, I assume in the following that a two-party competition determines the level of national defense spending. However, the two-party system is only one of the many possible institutional setups we observe in the world.

2. This is exactly Dennis C. Mueller's criticism of some public choice models (1989, 193).

3. Public policy in general is expected to have some welfare effects on the population, and these expected effects motivate political actors to choose their actions to induce the central government to adopt their preferred policy. For a comprehensive discussion on this topic, see Page 1983.

4. Nevertheless, the model in this essay can be used to address the defense-spending-increasing effects of parties, public opinion, domestic economy, perceptions of Soviet threats, and elections in a single coherent framework (Ishida 1995).

5. I make this assumption to avoid notational clutter, but this is not an assumption necessary to derive a unique Nash equilibrium in this game. Indeed, I relax this assumption and explore its logical implication later in this essay.

6. Meltzer and Richard (1991) concentrate exclusively on the demand for redistribution. They neglect public goods such as national defense provided by the government. Romer and Rosenthal (1979) discuss the literature on the public finance of public education in a local community. The specific choice of an assumption about the role of the government affects the implications derived from the model. I will discuss the implications in a later section.

7. According to Meltzer and Richard (1991, 26), "reliance on a linear tax follows a well-established tradition" in the public finance literature. Indeed, "this assumption is not unrealistic when the total incidence of the tax system is taken into account." (Dudley and Montmarquette 1981).

8. Consequently, in the model, a revenue-neutral tax reform is not considered.

9. See also Dudley and Montmarquette 1981, 9, for a similar specification of the utility function. My model differs from their model with regard to the assumed redistributive role of the government and to the negative-externality effects of the adversarial military expenditure. More specifically, they assume that the government provides only

national security, which they admit is problematic. Also, they focus on the positive-externality effects of the allies, but not the negative-externality effects of the adversaries, on the security of the home country.

10. See also Bruce 1990. Bruce introduces the negative-externality effects of defense spending between adversaries into the well-understood public good model of alliance, first analyzed by Olson and Zeckhauser (1966). Bruce shows that intra-alliance cooperation in setting military expenditures is not necessarily welfare improving for those cooperating allies.

11. Arguably, k might correlate with the individual income level. For instance, during the Cold War years, the supporters of labor, socialist, or social-democratic parties among the United States' allies tended to underrate the threat of the Soviet Union compared with their wealthier counterparts such as the supporters of conservative parties.

12. The assumed budgetary trade-off of the model links the domestic redistributive issue with the international security issue. As a consequence, the voting decisions of the population do not need to be based exclusively on their evaluation of the foreign policy of the central government, as is often assumed in a similar two-level game model.

13. This inequality means that the net contribution of any individual voter to national defense is positive. The reason is the following. The individual contribution is the difference between post-fisc consumption and initial income: $y_i - C_i = t(y_i - w_{sq}\bar{y})$. The inequality $-y_i + w_{sq}\bar{y} < 0$ is equivalent to the inequality $y_i - C_i > 0$. What if this condition is violated? Then, for those who satisfy $-y_i + w_{sq}\bar{y} \geq 0$, the optimal income tax rate will be one ($t^* = 1$). The violation of condition 9 does not affect the substantive implications of this model.

14. Inequality 9 assures that the denominator of I_h is always positive.

15. These comparative statics are based on the signs of the relevant partial derivatives of the Nash equilibrium levels of defense spending with respect to a respective parameter.

16. They have the same effects in terms of the signs of respective partial derivatives.

17. See Ishida 1995 for an extensive discussion of the partisan politics of defense spending summarized in this brief section.

18. See also Alesina 1989; Alesina and Rosenthal 1994, 19–29; and Roemer 1993, 1995).

19. For an analysis of the time-series data of the US defense spending during the Cold War, see Ishida (1995).

20. Gonzalez and Mehey (1990) develop a bureaucratic decision-making model in the tradition of William Niskanen.

REFERENCES

Achen, C. H. 1995. How Can We Tell a Unitary Rational Actor When We See One? Paper presented at the annual meeting of the Midwest Political Science Association, Chicago, April 6–8.
Alesina, A. 1988. Credibility and Policy Convergence in a Two-Party System with Rational Voters. *American Economic Review* 78:796–806.

———. 1989. Macroeconomics and Politics. In *NBER Macroeconomic Annual, 1988,* edited by S. Fisher. Cambridge: MIT Press.

Alesina, A., and D. Rodrik. 1992. Distribution, Political Conflict, and Economic Growth: A Simple Theory and Some Empirical Evidence. In *Political Economy, Growth, and Business Cycles,* edited by A. Cukierman, Z. Hercowitz, and L. Leiderman. Cambridge: MIT Press.

Alesina, A., and H. Rosenthal. 1994. *Partisan Politics, Divided Government, and the Economy.* New York: Cambridge University Press.

Bruce, N. 1990. Defense Spending by Countries in Allied and Adversarial Relationships. *Defence Economics* 1:179–95.

Dudley, L., and C. Montmarquette. 1981. The Demand for Military Expenditures: An International Comparison. *Public Choice* 37:5–31.

Gonzalez, R. A., and S. L. Mehey. 1990. Publicness, Scale, and Spillover Effects in Defense Spending. *Public Finance Quarterly* 18:273–90.

Hartley, K., and T. Sandler, eds. 1990. *The Economics of Defense Spending: An International Survey.* London: Routledge.

Iida, K. 1993. When and How Do Domestic Constraints Matter? Two-Level Games with Uncertainty. *Journal of Conflict Resolution* 37:403–26.

Ishida, A. 1995. The Political Economy of National Defense Spending Decisions. Ph.D. diss., University of Chicago.

Ishida, A., and Y. Wolinsky. 1995. Double-Edged Theories: Rationality, Institutions, and Foreign Policy. University of Chicago. Manuscript.

Looney, R. E., and S. L. Mehey. 1990. United States Defense Expenditures: Trends and Analysis. In *The Economics of Defense Spending: An International Survey,* edited by K. Hartley and T. Sandler. London: Routledge.

Meltzer, A. H., and S. F. Richard. 1991. A Rational Theory of the Size of the Government. In *Political Economy,* edited by A. H. Meltzer, A. Cukierman, and S. F. Richard. New York: Oxford University Press.

Mo, J. 1994. The Logic of Two-Level Games with Endogenous Domestic Coalitions. *Journal of Conflict Resolution* 38:402–22.

Mueller, D. C. 1989. *Public Choice II.* New York: Cambridge University Press.

Murdoch, J. C., T. Sandler, and L. Hansen. 1993. An Econometric Technique for Comparing Median Voter and Oligarchy Choice Models of Collective Action. *Review of Economics and Statistics* 87:115–32.

Olson, M., Jr., and R. Zeckhauser. 1966. An Economic Theory of Alliance. *Review of Economics and Statistics* 48:266–79.

Page, B. I. 1983. *Who Gets What from Government.* Berkeley: University of California Press.

Przeworski, A. 1990. *The State and the Economy under Capitalism.* Chur, Switz.: Harwood Academic.

Putnam, R. D. 1988. Diplomacy and Domestic Politics: The Logic of Two-Level Games. *International Organization* 42:427–60.

Roemer, J. E. 1993. Political-Economic Equilibrium When Parties Represent Constituents: The Unidimensional Case. Working Paper Series, no. 93–19. Department of Economics, University of California, Davis. Manuscript.

———. 1995. Political Cycles. *Economics and Politics* 7:1–20.

Romer, T. 1975. Individual Welfare, Majority Voting, and the Properties of a Linear Income Tax. *Journal of Public Finance* 4:143–70.

———. 1977. Majority Voting on Tax Parameters: Some Further Results. *Journal of Public Economics* 7:127–33.

Romer, T., and H. Rosenthal. 1979. The Elusive Median Voter. *Journal of Public Economics* 12:143–70.

Sandler, T. 1993. The Economic Theory of Alliances: A Survey. *Journal of Conflict Resolution* 37:446–83.

Sandler, T., and K. Hartley. 1995. *The Economics of Defense.* New York: Cambridge University Press.

Schneider, E. 1988. Causal Factors in Variations in U.S. Postwar Defense Spending. *Defense Analysis* 4:53–79.

Seiglie, C. 1991. Determinants of Military Expenditures. Ph.D. diss., University of Chicago.

U.S. Arms Control and Disarmament Agency. 1995. *World Military Expenditures and Arms Transfers.* Washington, DC: GPO.

U.S. Office of Management and Budget. 1994. *Historical Tables: Budget of the United States Government.* Washington, DC: GPO.

Room to Move: Security, Proaction, and Institutions in Foreign Policy Decision Making

T. Clifton Morgan and Glenn Palmer

Students of international politics have devoted a great deal of attention recently to examining the relationship between domestic politics and foreign policy. Many, in breaking with traditional realist thought, have argued that domestic political factors are important determinants of state behavior in the international realm. Evidence has been offered for the contention that democracies exhibit patterns of conflict and alliance behavior that differ from those followed by other types of states (Rummel 1985; Doyle 1986; Maoz and Abdolali 1989; Russett 1993; Morgan and Campbell 1991; Morgan and Schwebach 1992; Bremer 1993; Ray 1993; Dixon 1993, 1994; Siverson and Emmons 1991), and there is growing evidence that domestic political considerations influence decisions by state leaders regarding the use of force (Morgan and Bickers 1992; Levy and Vakili 1992; Richards et al. 1993; Ostrom and Job 1986; James and Oneal 1991; Morgan and Anderson 1995). Numerous (though certainly not all) scholars have been persuaded by this evidence to abandon the realist contention that state behavior is dictated almost entirely by the constraints imposed by the international system. Explanations for the observed regularities abound, but none has been accepted by a sizable portion of the scholarly community. Research continues to produce additional empirical findings as well as arguments attempting to explain these findings. There is little to indicate, however, that we are moving closer to a consensus regarding why, when, and how domestic politics influences foreign policy.

Perhaps the greatest impediment to advancing our understanding lies in the way in which we have sought to explain our empirical results. Generally, explanations have been offered for particular findings, but these explanations have not been embedded in, or drawn from, broader theories of international politics (exceptions can be found in Rummel 1975–81; and Bueno de Mesquita and Lalman 1992).

For example, most explanations for the democratic peace phenomenon suggest that the observed results are a product of either the cultural norms that are developed within democracies or the institutional structures that shape decisions within democracies. Both explanations account for the finding that democracies seldom, if ever, fight one another, but neither explains much more—at least as they are currently constructed.

Realism has appeal precisely because it offers a parsimonious account of so much in international relations. It may omit key variables, it may be based on ambiguous concepts, and its logical basis may be suspect. But it does provide a perspective from which many draw a general understanding of most aspects of world politics and foreign policy. Proponents of realism can accept the evidence associating domestic political factors with state behavior and still argue that, relative to system-level variables, domestic factors account for little of the variance in state behavior. Given the evidence, this argument is hard to refute. We find statistically significant relationships between domestic factors and international behavior, but it is true that relatively little of the variance in behavior is a product of these factors.

Scholars focusing on the domestic politics/foreign policy relationship thus face a two-edged problem: they cannot account for the observed relationships in the context of a general theory showing how domestic factors interact with the international environment to produce foreign policies, and the explanations they offer for the observed relationships account for little of the variance in the dependent variables. The purpose of our research, a portion of which is reported in this essay, is to develop and test a general theory of foreign policy that incorporates both environmental and domestic variables as explanatory factors to explain a broad range of state behaviors. Although we adopt a set of assumptions that are clearly distinct from those realists accept, the theory offers explanations for how the international system affects state behavior. We incorporate domestic factors into this theory, however, so we can show that the broad explanations are refined and improved through this extension.

In this essay, we explore how two aspects of domestic political structures, the institutional procedures for making foreign policy decisions and the method of leadership selection, affect the relationship between environmental variables and state dispute behavior. We begin by summarizing the unitary actor variant of our general model and some of the hypotheses derived from this variant. We then show how the domestic factors influence the way states react to changes (or the absence of changes) in the international environment. Our theoretical results suggest that the degree to which decision makers are constrained by the environment depends on domestic institutions. Finally, tests of our hypotheses against the patterns of initiation in the context of militarized interstate disputes lend support to our theory.

A General Theory of Foreign Policy:
The Unitary Actor Variant

Our general theory is based on a number of assumptions regarding what states seek through their foreign policies, how the international system affects their abilities to pursue these interests, and how domestic political factors come into play. The unitary actor variant of the theory (i.e., excluding the domestic factors), which has been presented elsewhere (Morgan and Palmer 1997), serves as a baseline version of the model. Here we summarize this variant of the model.

Our first assumption is that states pursue two general types of goals through their foreign policies—security and proaction. By a state's security, we mean its ability to inhibit change in those elements of the status quo that conform to its preferences. The higher a state's security, the greater is its ability to resist attempts by other states to bring about changes it opposes. These changes can involve territorial issues, economic issues, or issues of foreign or domestic policies. By a state's proaction, we mean its ability to bring about desired changes in the status quo. We assume that every foreign policy action in which a state engages is intended to be either security enhancing or proaction enhancing and that the entire portfolio of policies adopted by a state is designed to provide its preferred mix of security and proaction. Note that any particular action, such as an alliance formation or a conflict initiation, can be either security or proaction seeking, depending on circumstances. For instance, a conflict initiated for the purpose of seizing territory would be proaction seeking while one initiated against a strong state to keep vital sea lanes open would be security seeking. With this assumption, we are following closely Morrow's (1991) argument that alliances can be formed to enhance either states' security or their proaction, though we hold that all of a state's foreign policies, not just alliance behaviors, are security or proaction seeking.[1]

Our second assumption is that the foreign policy environment sets limits on a state's ability to provide security and proaction. A state's capabilities, relative to that of others, and the policies adopted by other states affect its ability to provide security and proaction, as do such diverse factors as the level of technology and the weather. Given a state's capabilities and the foreign policies of other actors, there is a limit to what it can accomplish. Some states are better able to provide security and proaction than are other states. Furthermore, resources are limited, and those expended in the pursuit of one goal cannot be used in the pursuit of another. The environment thus determines the maximum amounts of security and proaction that can be produced as well as the trade-offs that must be made across the two goods. Although our broader theoretical perspective incorporates a wide range of environmental factors, here we focus primarily on the capabilities of states. Relative capabilities are probably the single most important environmental factor, and, since they are seen as a critical variable in almost all theories of international politics, it is worthwhile to focus initially on the effects of capabilities on foreign policies.

The argument to this point is captured in figure 1. In this figure, we represent a state's foreign policy portfolio by a point in two-dimensional space. The coordinate of the horizontal axis depicts the amount of proaction sought by the foreign policy portfolio, and the coordinate of the vertical axis depicts the amount of security sought. The northwest to southeast curve represents the production possibility frontier, or the maximum amount of security and proaction that can be provided, given the foreign policy environment. If the state's foreign policy portfolio provides levels of security and proaction beneath this frontier, it can increase both. On the other hand, if its policy portfolio provides a balance of security and proaction that is on this frontier, the state could increase one only at the expense of the other. This frontier reflects the trade-offs across the two goods that the state must make, and the slope and intercept of the frontier vary according to the state's situation.

The other curves in the figure represent the indifference contours for an actor. For the moment, we treat the state as a unitary actor. We shall introduce multiple domestic actors shortly. The state is indifferent between any combination of security and proaction that falls on a given contour, and it prefers those combinations on contours farther to the northeast to those on contours closer to the origin. This model provides an equilibrium "prediction" regarding the specific security/proaction combination the state will select. This occurs at the point at which the production possibility frontier is tangent to an indifference contour—this puts the actor on the most desirable indifference contour.

Note that the state in this figure values security and proaction about equally. We can also represent states that value one over the other. A security-seeking state's indifference contours would be nearly (or, at the limit, totally) horizontal. Such a state would be unwilling to trade any security for even a large amount of proaction and would correspond to the type of state assumed in traditional realist theory. Note also that the equilibrium specifies a particular combination of security- and proaction-seeking policies. It does not identify the specific policies adopted. In fact, we assume that a wide range of policy portfolios can produce a specific mix of proaction and security; that is, to some extent, different policies are substitutable (Most and Starr 1984). For example, a state seeking to enhance its proaction could achieve this either by forming an alliance with a smaller state or by initiating a conflict aimed at altering the status quo in its favor. Thus, at this stage, our expectations are probabilistic. We identify factors that should increase the probability of certain types of actions rather than attempting to specify determinant hypotheses.

At this point, it is necessary to specify more fully the assumptions we make regarding the trade-offs between security and proaction. A traditional axiom in

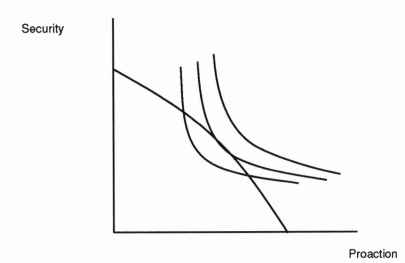

Fig. 1. Security and proaction: the goals of foreign policy

international relations is that a primary purpose of state power is to provide security for the state. The presumption is that great powers are better able to provide for their security than are minor powers. It is also presumed, however, that more powerful states are able to take what they want from the weaker—the strong do what they will, the weak do what they must. We capture the essence of this conventional wisdom with a set of assumptions characterizing the relationship between state power and the ability to produce security and proaction. First, we—not surprisingly—assume that the ability of a state to pursue security and proaction increases with the power of the state. The general form of these relationships, which is of greater interest, is depicted in figure 2.

Figure 2(a) represents the amount of security a state can provide as a function of the state's power. The vertical scale shows the range of power the state can have, and the horizontal shows the amount of security that can be "purchased." The curve shows the amount of security that could be provided at each level of power if all available capabilities were devoted to producing security. Similarly, figure 2(b) depicts the relationship between a state's power and its ability to provide proaction. Notice that both curves are increasing, which indicates that the strong can produce more security and/or more proaction. The rate of change is quite different, however. Each additional unit of power obtained by the state can provide a smaller increment of security, but a larger increment of proaction, than could each preceding unit.

The general forms of these relationships are intended to capture the notion that it is easier to maintain the status quo than it is to change it and that there

2a) Power and Security

Amount of
Security that
Can Be
Purchased

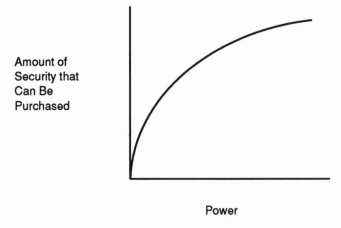

Power

2b) Power and Proaction

Amount of
Proaction that
Can Be
Purchased

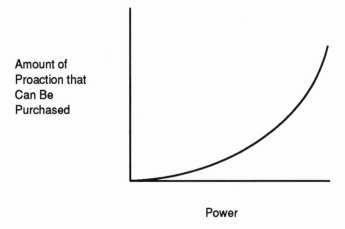

Power

Fig. 2. Provision of security and proaction as a function of power

are more weak states than strong ones. This implies that there is a "production advantage" in security for weak states and in proaction for strong states. That is, an additional increment of power can provide a greater amount of security than proaction for a weak state but a greater amount of proaction than security for a strong state. Thus, we expect, ceteris paribus, that weak states will be predominantly security seeking (in the sense that gains in power will be primarily devoted to providing additional security) and that strong states will be predominantly proaction seeking.

This assumption seems to capture a great deal of the conventional wisdom regarding the effect of power on states' views of security and proaction, but two words of caution are in order. First, the ceteris paribus condition cannot be overstressed. This assumption reflects the ability of states to translate their power into security and proaction; it does not take into account the preferences (as reflected in the indifference contours) of the actors. It is possible for a weak state to be relatively proaction seeking (perhaps Libya under Khaddafi) and for a strong state to be security seeking (perhaps the United States prior to World War II).

Second, the shape of the curve for proaction indicates that additional increments of power provide an increasing ability to produce proaction over the entire range of power. We would actually expect this curve to flatten out at some point. Consider an extreme case in which one state possesses a substantial majority of the capabilities in the system. Additional increments of power would probably add little to such a state's ability to provide proaction. If this is the case, the curve spanning the full range of state power should be S-shaped. We have chosen to ignore the upper end of this curve because we believe that the second inflection point lies far beyond the range of capabilities that has been observed in the international system. For example, it is hard to imagine a more dominant state, in terms of capabilities, than the United States immediately after World War II; yet the United States found its ability to structure the world to its liking to be quite limited. Thus, we believe little damage is done to the generality of our model by focusing only on the portion of the curve that is increasing at an increasing rate.

The assumptions specified to this point constitute the external variant of the model. States are treated as unitary actors, and no domestic political factors are incorporated. These assumptions are sufficient for the derivation of a number of general hypotheses regarding the impact of environmental factors on foreign policies, however (see Morgan and Palmer 1997). These hypotheses provide a means of associating our theory with much of the conventional wisdom in international relations as well as a baseline with which to compare our later results.[2] Not surprisingly, the model leads us to expect that the strong will be more active in foreign policy than will the weak and that the strong should devote relatively more of their resources to proaction-seeking behavior than should the weak. In addition, however, the model produces hypotheses regarding how states should alter their foreign policies in response to changes in their relative capabilities. Increases in power are expected to produce more security-seeking behavior and more proaction-seeking behavior for all states. The proportion of any increase in power that is devoted to proaction-seeking behavior is positively associated with the level of capabilities of the state. Conversely, the proportion of any increase in power that is devoted to security-seeking behavior is inversely associated with the level of capabilities of the state.

In an earlier essay (Morgan and Palmer 1997), these hypotheses were tested in the context of militarized interstate disputes (MIDs). We argued that dispute initiation is generally associated with proaction-seeking behavior and dispute reciprocation is generally associated with security-seeking behavior. The hypotheses were tested by determining if the probability that a state would initiate or reciprocate a dispute is associated with the power, and change in power, of the state in the manner predicted by the theory. The results generally supported the theoretical expectations in the sense that virtually all of the relationships were in the predicted direction. The relationships, though statistically significant, were relatively weak, suggesting that power and changes in power alone do not account for a great deal of the variance in states' dispute initiation and reciprocation. The results did suggest that the theory is on the right track but that the unitary actor variant leaves a great deal unexplained.

We suspect that domestic political factors may account for a great deal of the weakness in the prior results. Domestic political structures may affect the manner in which state policies react to changes in the environment. Leaders of some states may have greater leeway in altering their foreign policies in response to environmental change than do other leaders. The domestic institutions within which they work may enable them to deviate significantly from what the unitary actor variant of the model would lead us to expect. We now turn to the domestic politics variant of the model, which is designed to account for these factors. Here we do not develop this variant of the model fully. We focus on two particular aspects of domestic political structures and show how these can account for some of the weakness in our earlier empirical results. We also derive some additional hypotheses regarding these variables, however, so that our explanation can be subjected to some initial testing.

A General Theory of Foreign Policy:
The Domestic Politics Variant

The model just outlined is based on the assumption that states are unitary actors that can be characterized by a single set of indifference contours over security and proaction. The domestic politics variant of the model is based on the idea that states are actually made up of a number of individuals, each with his or her own preferences regarding the appropriate mix of the two goods that should be pursued. Domestic politics is the process by which a state determines which specific set of indifference contours will guide its foreign policy. Domestic political institutions specify the rules by which individual preferences are aggregated into societal choices. Thus, the pattern of preferences within a state and the institutional structures through which these preferences are aggregated can affect the specific policies adopted for dealing with the external environment. Whereas some states may behave almost exactly as the unitary actor variant of the model would predict, domestic political arrangements can provide the leaders of other states with a great deal of leeway regarding foreign policy. The domestic politics variant of the model is a generalization of the unitary actor variant—not a fundamentally different model. It tells us when states should behave as unitary actors and when they should not.

Figure 3 provides a representation of this conceptualization. In this figure, we depict two production possibility frontiers, labeled f and f', the latter representing an increase in capabilities over the former. We also depict three sets of indifference contours representing three groups of domestic actors. Note that these groups can contain any number of individuals and they may or may not be of equal size. Furthermore, nothing in the model restricts us to three actors; we adopt this number in the figure solely for visual clarity.

From this alone, it is clear that the specific foreign policy portfolio adopted by the state will depend not only on the environmental factors but on which domestic actor's preferences are adopted. How institutional structures influence the aggregation of individual preferences into social choices is the focus of what follows. For the purposes of this essay, we assume that there are two features of the structure of states' political systems that affect the aggregation of preferences: the method by which state leaders are selected and the institutional procedures allocating responsibility for making foreign policy decisions.

The first variable, method of leadership selection, distinguishes states on the basis of how many members of society must support a leader's rise to power. At one end of the spectrum are states whose leaders are determined by heredity; at the other end are those states whose leaders are elected by universal suffrage. States whose leaders owe their positions to some smaller set of the population (e.g., those who achieve power through a military coup or those who are selected by the members of a single party) are located in the middle of the scale.

The second variable characterizes states on the basis of how foreign policy decisions are made. States at one extreme have their policies determined by the wishes of a single individual. The chief executive has sole responsibility for setting policy. States at the other extreme have their policies determined by referendum. All members of society can propose changes in policy, and the outcome is determined by majority rule. In the middle are states where the chief executive has a large measure of responsibility over policy, but there are (to a greater or lesser extent) constraints placed on this authority.

We conceive of these variables as continua, but to facilitate discussion we

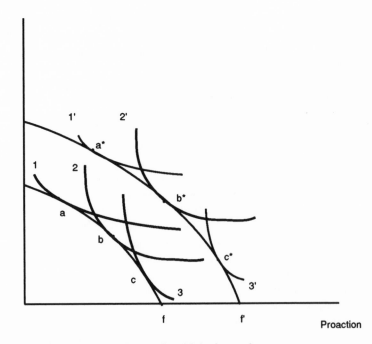

Fig. 3. Security, proaction, and multiple domestic actors

can think of three ideal-type states. The first, which we refer to as pure democracies, have their leaders selected by universal suffrage and select their policies by referenda. The second, which we refer to as dictatorships, are characterized by leaders who achieved power with the help of relatively few members of society and who have nearly full control over the setting of policy. Finally, there are divided democracies whose leaders are selected by universal suffrage and have a predominate role in setting foreign policy subject to the constraint that any changes in policy must be approved by some other set of political actors.

The unitary actor variant of the model leads to expectations regarding how states unconstrained by domestic politics adjust their foreign policies in reaction to changes in the international environment. The task at hand is to determine how a state's position on each of the domestic structure variables affects this relationship. To begin the discussion, consider our first ideal-type state—a pure democracy in which all members of society are involved in the selection of leaders and all are equally responsible for determining foreign policy. The process would be one in which any individual could propose changes in foreign policy and these proposals would be voted upon by all members. In such a state, the leader is irrelevant, so we can focus on the impact of the decision-making process. Our expectations for the foreign policy behavior of such a state would be determined by the median voter theorem (Downs 1957; Abrams 1980; Enelow and Hinich 1984). At any production possibility frontier, the precise mix of security and proaction will be determined by the indifference contours of the median member of society (e.g., if all groups in fig. 3 were equal in size, the median voter would be a member of group 2).[3] To illustrate this result with figure 3, suppose that the groups are equal in size and notice that the foreign policy portfolio determined by the median actor's indifference contours and the production possibility frontier can defeat any other possible portfolio by majority vote. Clearly, any proposed portfolio not on the frontier would be less preferred by at least two groups of actors. In addition, any other proposal that is on the frontier would be less preferred by two groups. Moving from the point determined by group 2's indifference contours toward that determined by group 1's contours would be less preferred (and thus defeated) by 2 and 3. Similarly, any proposal toward the point determined by 3's contours would be defeated by 1 and 2.

Such a state should react to changes in the international environment exactly as would a state controlled by a unitary actor. As we move from f to f' in figure 3, the changes in foreign policy portfolios would follow the path defined by the median voter's indifference contours. At each frontier, the median voter's indifference contour would hold sway.[4] Somewhat surprisingly, this result suggests that the foreign policy of a pure democracy should be quite stable, changing only in response to changes in the international environment and in a fairly predictable manner.

Next, let us consider our second ideal-type state—a pure dictatorship in which virtually none of the members of society have any input into the selection of a leader and in which the leader is solely responsible for the determination of foreign policy. In this type of state, we also expect foreign policy to change in response to changes in the environment exactly as in the unitary actor variant of the model. Whichever actor is dictator will determine the specific mix of security- and proaction-seeking policies, and changes in policy resulting from changes in the environment will follow the dictator's indifference contours. Thus, we expect the foreign policies of dictatorships, like those of pure democracies, to respond to changes in the environment exactly as the unitary actor version of the model would lead us to expect.

Note, however, that, unlike pure democracies, there are conditions under which the foreign policies of dictatorships can be highly volatile. The possibility for drastic changes in policies occurs whenever there is a change in leadership. When one dictator is replaced by another, the new dictator's preferences will define a new set of indifference contours for the state. If the new and old dictators have identical, or nearly identical, preferences, policy would change little. On the other hand, if the new dictator has significantly different preferences from the old, the policy portfolio could change dramatically, even without a change in the environment. Consider the changes that would result from a change in leader from a member of group 1 to a member of group 3 in figure 3, for example. Thus, we expect that foreign policy in a state led by a pure dictatorship would be more volatile than would be the foreign policy of a pure democracy (controlling for changes in the environment). The times at which a dictatorship's policy is volatile are fairly predictable, however, and will occur only in conjunction with leadership changes.

Our task now is to show how variations in domestic political structures between these ideal types affect the stability of foreign policy portfolios. Consider first the leadership selection variable. We expect that as an increasingly large proportion of the members of society have input into the selection of the chief decision maker foreign policy would become increasingly stable in the face of changes in leadership. We have seen that a pure dictatorship can experience large shifts in portfolios as a result of leadership change and that the specific identity of the leader in a pure democracy matters little (in that any leader chosen should represent the preferences of the median voter). For any size group having responsibility for selecting the leader, we expect the leader's preferences over security and proaction to reflect those of the median of the group. As the size of this group increases, the likelihood that the median of the group corresponds with the median of society increases, and the impact produced by changes in the selecting group lessens. That is, replacing a few members of the leadership selection group is less likely to shift the median position of the group noticeably in a large group than in a small group. In general, then, we expect that states with highly inclusive procedures for selecting leaders will have more stable foreign policies.

Next consider the institutional structure assigning foreign-policy-making responsibility. We have seen that both dictatorships and pure democracies should have stable policies, in that the policy portfolios selected in response to changes in the environment should be identical to those expected in the unitary actor variant of the model. This result does not hold across the entire range of the continuum, however. States with decision-making processes that grant substantial authority to a single individual (or very few) while also constraining that individual by giving approval power to another institution can have policies that are quite unstable in the face of environmental changes.

To illustrate the argument, consider the United States as an example of such a state. The president has substantial foreign-policy-making powers, but many of his decisions are subject to the approval of Congress. Essentially, the president is an agenda setter who has the ability to propose changes in the status quo policy portfolio. While these changes must be approved by another body, the fact that changes can only be proposed by the president grants him substantial powers. Suppose, for the moment, that the status quo portfolio is located at point b in figure 3. Since this is the position favored by the median voter, any proposal to shift the portfolio would be defeated. If the environment changes such that f' becomes the production possibility frontier, however, the agenda setter has a great deal of leeway. If a leader with preferences like those of group 1 is the agenda setter, for example, she could propose a change in policy portfolios to point a* and have it accepted. Both 1 and 2 prefer a* to b, the old status quo. A leader of a state with this form of institutional structure can thus use environmental changes to shape foreign policy more to her liking than would be possible in other polities.[5]

Note, too, that this type of structure can result in some volatility in policy as a result of leadership changes. If one leader has used environmental change to shift policy away from what is preferred by the median voter, a subsequent leader may have the ability to shift policy without waiting for an environmental change—provided the new leader prefers policies more in line with those desired by the median voter. We do not expect policy to be as volatile, on average, in regard to leadership changes as is the case for dictatorships, however. If the leader is elected by a fairly large proportion of the members of society, it is likely that her preferences would be close to those of the median voter.

At this point, we can see how these results account for the weakness of the empirical findings in our earlier essay (Morgan and Palmer 1997). These arguments suggest that the expectations of the unitary actor model should hold at all times only for pure democracies. The results for dictatorships can deviate from the unitary actor variant's expectations following leadership changes. States with institutional structures that divide foreign policy responsibility across institutions can deviate from the expectations of the unitary actor variant when changes in the external environment occur. We do not expect these latter types of states to deviate from expectations at all times, but the volatility should be noticeable. This can explain why our earlier empirical results were generally supportive of the hypotheses but failed to account for a great deal of the variance in dispute initiation and reciprocation.

If this explanation is correct and if our domestic variant of the model is on the right track, we should be able to observe a number of empirical regularities. If we track the patterns of dispute initiation and dispute reciprocation of states over time, we should be able to specify when states would experience high levels of foreign policy volatility on the basis of identifying their domestic institutional structures. If we control for changes in the environment, states with smaller proportions of the members of society involved in selecting leaders should experience greater volatility in their rates of dispute initiation after leadership changes than will states whose leaders are selected by a large proportion of society. Similarly, states whose leaders have agenda control over foreign policy but whose decisions are subject to constraint should have more volatility in their rates of dispute initiation and reciprocation in response to environmental changes (e.g., changes in their relative power) than will states located on either end of the continuum.

It is important to note that at this point the model produces no hypotheses suggesting that states characterized by any particular domestic structure should have higher or lower rates of initiation or escalation than any other type of state. The average rates of dispute behaviors may or may not vary across state type and should be determined more by the level of relative capabilities of the state. These hypotheses suggest that there should be significant differences in the variation around the central tendencies, depending on state type. Our empirical analyses focus on differences in variation.

Operationalizing the Variables

The domestic variant of our model centers on the effects of two aspects of the political structure of states: the manner in which leaders are selected and how responsibilities for making foreign policy decisions are distributed. We believe that each of those aspects will affect the degree to which the indifference contours of the state will be determined by the leader, at one extreme, or be reflective of the preferences of the median voter, at the other. To render our expectations more precise, we first define the central concepts involved in our model.

Our initial task is to operationalize these two domestic political dimensions. We have chosen to use Ted Gurr's Polity II to operationalize our two central concepts. The first dimension of interest is the method by which leaders are selected. Theoretically, this dimension is continuous, extending from selection by heredity to selection by a small set of individuals (such as a central committee) to selection by universal suffrage. At this stage of the analysis, we felt it was sufficient to dichotomize this dimension, and we have chosen to call the resulting categories democratic and nondemocratic. The categories are constructed by using three variables in the Polity II data set: regulation of chief executive recruitment, competitiveness of executive recruitment, and openness of executive recruitment.

The second domestic-political dimension regards the institutional procedures for allocating responsibility for making foreign policy decisions. Again, this dimension is, theoretically, continuous. To make our analysis clearer, we chose to trichotomize the dimension. We used two variables from Polity II to construct this variable: monocratism and executive constraints, variables 2.4 and 2.5, respectively. We refer to the resulting three categories of states as "dictatorships," "divided democracies," and "pure democracies." (For a discussion of our coding methods for our two dimensions, please refer to the appendix.)

We need, third, to operationalize "leadership change." For our purposes, the leadership of a state is considered to have changed any time one head of state is replaced with another. The list of such changes can be found in the data set compiled by Bienen and van de Walle (1991; see also Bueno de Mesquita, Siverson, and Woller 1992; and Bueno de Mesquita, and Siverson 1994).

A fourth definitional task is to describe the behavior to which our expectations will be subjected to testing. Our model allows a wide range of behavior to be used by a state to increase its security or proaction. Trade agreements, alliance formation, and arms transfers can each serve to transfer proaction from one state to another in exchange for security. We have chosen to center our analysis here on conflict behavior, particularly on the initiation of militarized interstate disputes, and we have chosen to use the data set Militarized Interstate Disputes, 1816–1992, currently being updated by the Correlates of War Project. Militarized interstate disputes are "a set of interactions between or among states involving threats to use military force, displays of military force, or actual uses of military force" (Gochman and Maoz 1984, 586).

In our past work (Morgan and Palmer 1997), we used the initiation and reciprocation of MIDs as indications of proaction- and security-seeking behavior, respectively. We believe this is justified because conflicts are initiated largely by those seeking to change the status quo. While proaction seekers have a range of other policy options available, our emphasis on conflict initiation is consistent with our model's implications. For the analysis, we excluded MIDs that occurred during the world wars, as many (perhaps most) of these were outgrowths of the wars and did not represent attempts to alter an established status quo. Security seekers attempt to protect what they have, and thus a state following a security-enhancing policy is more likely to respond forcefully to a challenge issued by another.[6] In this essay we restrict our analysis to the initiation of disputes, that is, to proaction-seeking actions. We made this decision to facilitate presentation of the analysis and in the interests of space.[7]

Our hypotheses are aimed at discerning how decisions in different political structures are affected by environmental factors, primarily a state's relative capability. To measure relative capability, or power, we use the Correlates of War Composite Index of National Capability (CINC), as described by Bremer (1980).

Our hypotheses and subsequent analyses require that we adopt units of analysis in which (1) states initiate disputes, (2) we can evaluate the effect of environmental factors and different political structures, and (3) there are changes in regime leadership. No one set of cases can simultaneously accomplish this. The units of analysis therefore vary. When we analyze whether states initiate disputes or not, for instance, we use nation-years as the units of analysis. But much of the analysis concerns *changes* in leadership and *changes* in foreign policy orientation. When we want to investigate these relationships, the year is too short a time period for analysis, particularly given that dispute initiation is the foreign policy dimension we have chosen to study. We wanted a time period that afforded sufficient time for some (but not too many) leadership changes to occur while simultaneously allowing for discernible and meaningful changes in foreign policy to be observed. In other words, we want time periods in which some leadership changes occur and which show nonrandom changes in the rate of dispute initiation. After investigating various time periods, we settled on three-year periods as the most appropriate; in much of the following, therefore, the nation-triennium is the unit of analysis.

Our model does not differentiate between political structures in major and minor powers, and we include both types of countries. Our analysis includes all countries for which the data that we require exist.

Operational Hypotheses

The basic direction our hypotheses take is to distinguish the manner in which states of different domestic political structures react to changes in environmental factors. Our model also implies that, since the ability of leaders to impose their preferences on the policy of the state varies by institutional arrangement, the effect of changes in leadership will vary accordingly.

Our model's theoretical implications are modified somewhat when subjected to empirical testing. This is usually the case in theory-driven quantitative research; in this instance, however, some of the operationalizations that we require do less justice to the conceptualizations than is desirable.

Our expectations can be divided along three dimensions, regarding the effects of the international political environment, the effects of how leaders are selected, and the effects of how authority in foreign policy issues are distributed. We first present the hypotheses regarding the expected effects of the environment.

Our model implies that stronger states, better able to purchase proaction, are more likely to initiate disputes than weaker states are. Additionally, since the ability to acquire proaction increases faster than a state's power, our theory posits that *changes* in power should have an increasingly strong effect on the rate of dispute initiation as states become more powerful.

> Hypothesis 1: There should be a positive relationship between a state's power and its probability of initiating a dispute.

> Hypothesis 2: The relationship between changes in power and the probability of dispute initiation should become more strongly positive as the state's power increases.

Our next hypotheses deal with the effect of domestic political structures on the relationship between international environmental factors and state behavior. The unitary actor version of our model specifies that more powerful states devote proportionately more of their resources to proaction-seeking behavior than do less powerful states. These unitary actor expectations are modified by the domestic political structure of the states.

Hypothesis 3: The effect of state power should have the least effect on the dispute behavior of divided democracies; the effect of power on dictatorships and pure democracies should be greater and equal to each other.

Environmental factors that our model says will be modified by domestic political institutions include changes in power. The model implies that divided democracies and dictatorships should behave largely in accordance with the expectations of the unitary actor variant of the theory, while divided democracies should show little systematic response to power changes.

Hypothesis 4: The effect of changes in state power should have the greatest effect on the dispute behavior of divided democracies; the effect of such changes on dictatorships and pure democracies should be weaker.

Our model addresses the effects of leadership selection. In dictatorships, a relatively small number of individuals choose the leader. This implies that the leader in such states has great latitude in altering the policy preferences of her state and may (but need not) use that latitude. Within pure democracies, on the other hand, large numbers of actors are involved in the selection of the leader. The model implies that the preferences of the median voter will hold sway regardless of the individual leader: changes in leadership should have no effect in such states. Within divided democracies, finally, the leader is seen as the agenda setter. While, as with the pure democracy, the selection of the leader is a function of the preferences of the median voter, the leader's ability to determine state preferences is stronger than in pure democracies. The institutional arrangements allow the agenda setter to suggest policy changes that she prefers to the status quo and that are acceptable to the median voter. Thus, leadership changes in divided democracies may have some effect on foreign policy, greater than can be the case with pure democracies, but less than is possible in dictatorships.

These expectations hold if we control for the effect of changes in the environment; if there are environmental changes, our model allows new leaders, even within democracies, to propose new foreign policy orientations that may achieve the support of a majority of the politically important public. Operationally, we define environmental changes to be changes in the power of the state.

Hypothesis 5: Controlling for changes in power, changes in leadership in dictatorships may show the greatest effect on dispute involvement, changes in leadership within pure democracies should show the least effect on dispute involvement, and the effect of leadership changes among divided democracies should be moderate in comparison.

This hypothesis has no directional expectations. Dictators, for instance, may alter their states' portfolios, but the model does not say whether the foreign policies will become more security or proaction seeking. We can only expect that there will be some change in policy without being able to specify its precise nature. Therefore, the dependent variable we use in our tests of this hypothesis is the absolute change in the rate of dispute initiation. That change is measured by the absolute difference between the rate in one triennium and the next.

Last, our model predicts that dictatorships will demonstrate greater responses to power during leadership changes than will other types of states. This is so because the new dictator may have a set of preferences that varies dramatically from the old leader's, and thus changes in foreign policy can be anticipated. Additionally, the greater the state's power, the greater the latitude the leader has in altering the foreign policy orientation of her country: new leaders in stronger states have more options available than do leaders of weaker states. If our model is right, this greater latitude should manifest itself in more significant changes in policy.

Hypothesis 6: During periods of leadership change, a state's power should have a greater effect on the behavior of dictatorships than on the behavior of democratic states.

We turn now to a description of the tests of our model.

Data Analysis

The first set of analyses we present tests whether there is a relationship between state power and the likelihood of dispute initiation, as hypothesis 1 maintains. The analysis of initiation was undertaken using LOGIT regression, and the results are presented in table 1. Here, the dependent variable is dichotomous and measures whether a state initiated a dispute in a given year or not. The independent variable is the power (as measured by the CINC value) of the state in a given year. Additionally, to test hypothesis 3 we categorized the nation-years in the analysis as dictatorships, divided democracies, or pure democracies and ran three equations that investigated the relationship between power and dispute initiation in these types of states. As table 1 shows, there is a very strong positive association between a state's power and the likelihood of dispute initiation. Further, the relationship is similar in the three types of states, which is contrary to hypothesis 3. The predictive capacity of power varies across the types of states, however: as the tau-b's indicate, it is greatest in divided democracies and weakest in dictatorships. The reason for this latter result is that the power of even the strongest dictatorship is not sufficiently high for the statistical model to generate predicted initiations. (We will revisit this fact again.)[8]

Table 2 shows the results of our tests of the hypothesis regarding changes in power and initiation. The unit of analysis here is the nation-triennium. The dependent variable, as before, is whether a state initiated a dispute in the period and is dichotomous. The independent variable is the change in the state's mean CINC value from the previous triennium to the current one.

For this analysis, we divided the states into three categories, weak, middle, and strong states. We operationalized these categories as follows. To control for changes in the number of countries in the system, we investigated the distribution of CINC scores among all the states in five periods separately: 1816–50, 1851–1900, 1901–38, 1946–60, and 1961–84. For each of the five periods, states in the lower two-thirds of the distribution were defined as weak;[9] states stronger than the weak but with CINC values less than 5 were defined as "middle" powers; and states with CINC values greater than 5 were defined as "strong." All major powers, regardless of CINC value, were defined as "strong." Again, LOGIT regression was used. The results are shown in Table 2.

The table shows that changes in power are positively associated with the initiation of disputes in weak and middle states but not in the strong states. Further, the effect of changes in power is substantially more pronounced in the middle states than in the weaker ones. This is at slight variance with our expectations and hypothesis 2, and we think there are two reasonable explanations for this. First, while we believe that the production curve for proaction increases over the range of power observed (as illustrated in fig. 2b), it must eventually flatten out: once a state has remade the world according to its pref-

TABLE 1.   Effect of Environmental Factors and State Structure on Dispute Initiation (unit of analysis: nation-years)

	All States	Dictatorships	Divided Democracies	Pure Democracies
Intercept	−2.41***	−2.18***	−2.63***	−2.54***
(S.E.)	(.04)	(.06)	(.18)	(.08)
Log (power)	.74***	.62***	.99***	.78***
(S.E.)	(.03)	(.05)	(.09)	(.06)
N	9,081	4,513	611	3,027
Percentage correctly predicted	66.8	63.6	80.0	67.0
−2 log likelihood	6,659.7	3,485.7	466.0	2,216.2
Tau-b	.069	—	.419	.095
Chi-square (1)	598.4	164.7	150.5	210.0
Significance	.0001	.0001	.0001	.0001

Note: Dependent variable: dispute initiation (1 = yes, 0 = no)
***Significant at the .01 level

erence, further increases in power are not effective. Perhaps this flattening occurs at an earlier point than we have assumed, however. The results suggest that the translation of increases in power into proaction becomes more pronounced as a state moves from the "weak" to the "middle" range, and this is consistent with the increasing slope of our proaction production curve. That the conflict behavior of powerful states appears not to be altered by changes in power may imply that the marginal value of greater power declines earlier than we originally assumed.

The second explanation for this finding rests on the notion that strong states have a variety of foreign policy devices available to them. The ability to achieve proaction proceeds the way we have assumed, but the methods that strong states use to acquire proaction proliferate as they become increasingly powerful. Very strong states may, for instance, establish international regimes, which makes the initiation of disputes counterproductive. Our investigation here of one method of achieving proaction should not cloud the fact that there are multiple means to that end. In future work, we intend to pursue this issue.

Table 3 presents our test of the fourth hypothesis, regarding the differential impact of changes in power on the three types of states. Here we simply observed whether a state had decreased in power from one triennium to the next, on the one hand, or had increased or maintained its power on the other. We used the mean CINC values from each triennium to determine this. After dividing the states into the three categories, we determined whether the states had or had not initiated a dispute within the period. The results indicate that there are positive relationships of marginal statistical significance in each of the three types

TABLE 2.   Changes in Power and Dispute Initiation
(unit of analysis: nation-triennium)

	Weak States	Middle States	Strong States
Intercept	−1.53***	−.56***	.45***
(S.E.)	(.06)	(.08)	(.13)
Change in power	.49**	1.47***	.22
(S.E.)	(.23)	(.51)	(.94)
N1,731	661		267
Percentage correctly predicted	59.8	57.3	50.8
−2 log likelihood	1,634.1	863.1	356.9
Tau-b	−.001	.128	−.111
Chi-square (1)	6.26	9.38	.056
Significance	.0124	.0022	.8134

Note: Dependent variable: dispute initiation (1 = yes, 0 = no)
**Significant at the .05 level   ***Significant at the .01 level

TABLE 3. Increasing Power, State Structure, and Initiation of Disputes (unit of analysis: nation-triennium)

a. Dictatorships

	Not increasing power	Increasing power	
Not initiate	540 (84%)	621 (80%)	1,161 (82%)
Initiate	104 (16%)	158 (20%)	262 (18%)
	644 (100%)	779 (100%)	

Tau-b = .053, chi-square = 4.01, probability = .045.

b. Divided democracies

	Not increasing power	Increasing power	
Not initiate	80 (86%)	76 (76%)	156 (81%)
Initiate	13 (14%)	24 (24%)	37 (19%)
	93 (100%)	100 (100%)	

Tau-b = .127, chi-square = 3.12, probability = .077.

c. Pure Democracies

	Not increasing power	Increasing power	
Not initiate	445 (86%)	363 (82%)	808 (84%)
Initiate	72 (14%)	79 (18%)	151 (16%)
	517 (100%)	442 (100%)	

Tau-b = .054, chi-square = 2.80, probability = .094.

of countries. The hypothesis predicts that divided democracies will show the strongest effect, and, while the tau-b demonstrates the strongest relationship within these states, the significance is not overwhelming. Two factors, however, lead us not to reject the hypothesis. First, the weak statistical significance of the relationship for divided democracies is largely a function of the relatively small number of cases: there are only 193 for these states, compared with more than 1,400 for the dictatorships. Second, divided democracies are the most powerful states in our analysis: while less than 10 percent of the entire sample consists of "strong states," 24 percent of the divided democracies are in that category. Also, recall from table 2 that strong states are the only ones not to show an effect of changes in power on the frequency of dispute initiation. Thus, because divided democracies are disproportionately powerful and because there is a relatively small number of cases, we have reason to find support for hypothesis 4. Divided democracies seem to be more affected by changes in the environment than other types of political systems are.

Table 4 shows the test of hypothesis 5, which predicted that leadership change in dictatorships may have the greatest effect on changes in foreign policy behavior. Here the dependent variable is created by comparing the number of initiations per year in one triennium and the subsequent one; the resulting absolute change in the rate of initiation serves as our indicator of change in foreign policy for this test. We use an interactive variable consisting of a state's absolute change in power multiplied by its power to control for the effects of

TABLE 4. Leadership Change and Change in Rate of Dispute Initiation (unit of analysis: nation-triennium)

Independent Variable		
Intercept		.166***
		(.008)
(Absolute power change $\times$ power)		.062***
		(.008)
Leadership change, dictatorship		.006
		(.018)
Leadership change, divided democracy		.012
		(.035)
Leadership change, pure democracy		.020
		(.021)
N	2,395	
R^2		.022
Adjusted R^2		.021
Significance		.00001

Note: Dependent variable: absolute change in the rate of dispute initiation
***Significant at the .01 level

environmental change, as our model demands and as the hypothesis specifies. As there was significant autocorrelation involved in this equation, we used generalized least squares to run the analysis.

The results indicate that, when controlling for changes in power, changes in leadership do not significantly affect a state's dispute behavior, at least as far as initiation is concerned. Our hypothesis, following from our model, does not *require* dictatorships to show the largest effect, but merely *allows* them to do so; in that manner, the results do not contradict the model. Nonetheless, the findings provide little support for the hypothesis.

Our final test is about the effect of environmental factors during periods of leadership change. Our hypothesis predicted that power would have the greatest effect during leadership transitions in dictatorships. LOGIT regression was used. The results, which are shown in table 5, very strongly support that hypothesis. Aside from "power," the three independent variables are interactive ones formed by multiplying leadership change dummy variables for each of the three types of states by "power." As the table shows, the effect of a state's power is not affected by leadership changes in divided democracies, and during leadership changes in pure democracies power has a more significant and positive effect. But during leadership changes in new dictatorships the effect of power is almost twice as large as when there is no leadership change. This is fully consistent with our hypothesis.

TABLE 5. Leadership Change, Power, and Dispute Initiation

Independent Variable		
Intercept		-1.44***
		(.062)
Power		.700***
		(.059)
Leadership change, dictatorship $\times$ power		.647**
		(.320)
Leadership change, divided democracy $\times$ power		.287
		(.240)
Leadership change, pure democracy $\times$ power		.218*
		(.127)
N	2,876	
Percentage correctly predicted	64.9	
-2 log likelihood	2,801.8	
Tau-b	.275	
Chi-square (1)	208.4	
Significance	.0001	

Note: Dependent variable: dispute initiation (1 = yes, 0 = no)
***Significant at the .01 level   **Significant at the .05 level   *Significant at the .10 level

Conclusion

In this essay, we have continued to develop the general theory of foreign policy begun in Morgan and Palmer 1997. Our previous results suggested that a state's external environment does shape its foreign policy in predictable ways but that these factors alone do not explain fully all of the variance in states' foreign policies. The argument advanced in this essay holds that the form of domestic political structure (in particular, the methods of executive selection and the allocation of authority over foreign policy decisions) determines the leeway that decision makers have in responding to changes in the environment. Our argument led to a number of hypotheses associating state power and domestic structures to foreign policy behavior. We have tested some of these hypotheses in the context of militarized interstate disputes. By and large, the results of these tests tend to support the theory. While some of the empirical relationships were not as expected, the majority were consistent with the theory and many of the results were quite strong.

We are encouraged by these results, though the lesson we draw from this exercise is that our research is on the right track, not that it is concluded. We have examined only two aspects of domestic political structures, we have tested only some of the hypotheses that follow from the theory, and we have tested the hypotheses in the context of only one type of behavior. The model is intended to account for a broad range of behaviors and to identify the conditions under which various policies are substitutable for one another. Furthermore, we recognize that no state acts in a vacuum. The foreign policies of each are affected by the policies of others. Capturing the interactive nature of foreign policy making requires moving from the monadic level of analysis to the dyadic. The tests of the unitary actor variant of the model support the theory while suggesting that a great deal is left unexplained. The results presented here indicate that we have improved on the earlier version of the model while suggesting that room for improvement remains. Further work developing and testing this theory is clearly warranted.

APPENDIX

In this appendix, we discuss in detail how we operationalized our variables of interest that measure domestic political structure. We are interested in operationalizing the method of leadership selection and the locale of foreign policy decision-making authority. We first discuss the leadership selection measure.

The leadership indicator was constructed from three variables in the Polity II data set (Gurr et al. 1989): "regulation of chief executive recruitment," "competitiveness of executive recruitment," and "openness of executive recruitment," variables 2.1 through 2.3, respectively. The first two of these variables have three categories each, while the "openness" variable consists of four categories. We defined any state that had values of 1 or 2 on the "regulation" variable as *nondemocratic,* regardless of the values those states were assigned on the other two variables. States to which Polity II gave values of 3 (regulated) on the "regulation" variable required that we attend to the "competitiveness" and "openness" variables. We coded any state that had a value of 3 (election) on "competitiveness" as *democratic.* Additionally, states that a 2 on "competitiveness" (dual/transitional) were coded democratic if they received scores of 3 (dual/election) or 4 (open) on the "openness" variable. We defined all other permutations as *nondemocratic.*

The operationalization of the dimension regarding the authority for foreign policy decision making was based on variables 2.4 and 2.5 in Polity II, "monocratism" and "executive constraints," respectively. "Monocratism" consists of five categories, ranging from "pure individual executive" to "collective executive"; the "constraints" variable has seven categories, from "unlimited [executive] authority" to "executive parity." We used the categorization of these two variables to create our three types of institutional arrangements, dictatorships, divided democracies, and pure democracies. The table below presents the values on "monocratism" and "executive constraints," respectively, that we used to place a state in its category. The first number refers to the value on "monocratism," the second to the value on "executive constraints."

Values on Polity II Variables 2.4 and 2.5

Dictatorship	1,1; 1,2; 1,3; 1,4; 2,1; 2,2; 2,3; 2,4; 3,1; 3,2; 4,1; 4,2; 5,1
Pure democracy	3,3; 3,4; 3,5; 3,6; 3,7; 4,4; 4,5; 4,6; 4,7; 5,2; 5,3; 5,4; 5,5; 5,6; 5,7
Divided democracy	1,5; 1,6, 1,7; 2,5, 2,6,; 2,7

NOTES

We wish to thank Peter J. Partell for his invaluable assistance with the data analysis, Stuart Bremer for providing us with the MID data, Nicholas van de Walle for allowing us to use his updated data on leadership change, and the participants of the University of California, Davis, conference on Strategic Politicians, Institutions, and Foreign Policy for their comments and suggestions. Financial support from the National Science Foundation (grants SBR–9511289 and SBR–9507909) is gratefully acknowledged.

1. Morrow used the term *autonomy* to refer to the concept we refer to as proaction. Though the two terms are identical conceptually, we adopt the different name in order to avoid the confusion involved in using a word (i.e., *autonomy*) that for many has a distinct meaning different from that intended.

2. This variant of the model also enables us to generalize a number of traditional perspectives for analyzing international relations. For example, by assuming a unitary actor that values only security, we can capture the key assumptions of realism.

3. It is, of course, possible for the groups to be of different size. If group 1 or 3 was sufficiently large (i.e., it contained over half the population), the median voter could be a member of one of these groups.

4. Note that, while the foreign policy portfolio would always be determined by the median voter's indifference contours, it is possible for the identity of the median voter to change. This occurs under quite specific circumstances, which depend on the precise shape of the production possibility frontier, how this shape changes with changes in the environment, and the actor's indifference contours.

5. Note that it would be fairly easy to show that in a situation in which a state's production possibility frontier moves significantly outward (e.g., if it increased its relative power substantially) the leader could propose a foreign policy portfolio that is quite distant from that favored by the median voter, and everybody (or nearly so) would support this over the old status quo. This could provide an explanation for the "bipartisan consensus" over foreign policy in the post–World War II United States. When relative capabilities have increased so dramatically, the president can propose about any foreign policy and have it supported by nearly everyone. Conversely, when relative capabilities are waning (as happened in the United States in the 1960s) we would expect substantial disagreement over foreign policy as the proaction seekers and the security seekers maneuver to preserve their interests.

6. Our decision to use dispute initiation as an act directed toward increasing a state's proaction is viable and theoretically sound if the first act in a MID can be taken as the true initiation of the conflict. Often some diplomatic demands precede MIDs, but we take the decision to escalate matters into the military realm as reflecting a strong preference for an alteration in the status quo ante instead of representing a preemptive act motivated by a desire to maintain that status quo. If some dispute initiations are, in fact, security seeking, we are subjecting our hypotheses to more difficult tests than if we are correct: the behavioral distinctions that result from the different types of states will be clouded operationally. If we are right, but the MID coding rules make it more difficult to determine who the "real" initiator is, our results will be weaker than a "true" test would reveal.

7. Dispute reciprocation is addressed in Morgan and Palmer 1997; the domestic variant of our model will be applied to reciprocation in future work.

8. Dictatorships are the least powerful of the three types of states, and divided democracies are the most powerful. It would be ideal if power were statistically independent of regime type, and we will discuss the implications of the existence of the relationship between power and regime type for the analysis as we continue.

9. In the five periods, the bottom two-thirds were those states with CINC values of less than 1.94, 1.12, .71, .49, and .30, respectively.

REFERENCES

Abrams, R. 1980. *Foundations of Political Analysis.* New York: Columbia University Press.

Bienen, H., and N. van de Walle. 1991. *Of Time and Power: Leadership Duration in the Modern World.* Stanford: Stanford University Press.

Bremer, S. 1980. National Capabilities and War Proneness. In *The Correlates of War II: Testing Some Realpolitik Models,* edited by J. D. Singer. New York: Free Press.

Bremer, S. 1993. Democracies and Militarized Interstate Conflict. *International Interactions* 18:231–49.

Bueno de Mesquita, B., and D. Lalman. 1992. *War and Reason.* New Haven: Yale University Press.

Bueno de Mesquita, B., and R. Siverson. 1994. Political Survival and International Crises. Paper delivered at the annual meeting of the Peace Science Society.

Bueno de Mesquita, B., R. Siverson, and G. Woller. 1992. War and the Fate of Regimes: A Comparative Analysis. *American Political Science Review* 86:638–46.

Dixon, W. 1993. Democracy and the Management of International Conflict. *Journal of Conflict Resolution* 28:42–68.

Dixon, W. 1994. Democracy and the Peaceful Settlement of International Conflict. *American Political Science Review* 88:14–32.

Downs, A. 1957. *An Economic Theory of Democracy.* New York: Harper and Row.

Doyle, M. W. 1986. Liberalism and World Politics. *American Political Science Review* 80:1151–79.

Enelow, J. M., and M. J. Hinich. 1984. *The Spatial Theory of Voting.* Cambridge: Cambridge University Press.

Gochman, C. S., and Z. Maoz. 1984. Serious Interstate Disputes, 1816–1976. *Journal of Conflict Resolution* 28:585–616.

Gurr, T. R., K. Jaggers, and W. H. Moore. 1989. Polity II: Political Structures and Regime Change, 1800–1986. University of Colorado. Mimeo.

James, P., and J. R. Oneal. 1991. The Influence of Domestic and International Politics on the President's Use of Force. *Journal of Conflict Resolution* 35:307–22.

Levy, J. S., and L. I. Vakili. 1992. Diversionary Action by Authoritarian Regimes. In *The Internationalization of Communal Strife,* edited by Manus I. Midlarsky. London: Routledge.

Maoz, Z., and N. Abdolali. 1989. Regime Types and Interstate Conflict, 1816–1976. *Journal of Conflict Resolution* 33:3–36.

Morgan, T. C., and C. Anderson. 1995. Domestic Support and External Conflict: Great Britain, 1950–1992. Rice University. Mimeo.

Morgan, T. C., and K. N. Bickers. 1992. Domestic Discontent and the External Use of Force. *Journal of Conflict Resolution* 36:25–52.

Morgan, T. C., and S. H. Campbell. 1991. Domestic Structure, Decisional Constraints, and War. *Journal of Conflict Resolution* 35:187–211.

Morgan, T. C., and G. Palmer. 1997. A Two-Good Theory of Foreign Policy: An Application to Dispute Initiation and Reciprocation. *International Interactions* 22:225–44.

Morgan, T. C., and V. L. Schwebach. 1992. Take Two Democracies and Call Me in the Morning: A Prescription for Peace? *International Interactions* 17:305–20.

Morrow, J. D. 1991. Alliances and Asymmetry: An Alternative to the Capability Aggregation Model of Alliances. *American Journal of Political Science* 35:904–33.

Most, B., and H. Starr. 1984. International Relations Theory, Foreign Policy Substitutability, and "Nice" Laws. *World Politics* 36:383–406.

Ostrom, C. W., and B. Job. 1986. The President and the Political Use of Force. *American Political Science Review* 80:541–66.

Ray, J. L. 1993. Wars between Democracies: Rare or Nonexistent? *International Interactions* 18:251–76.

Richards, D., T. C. Morgan, R. K. Wilson, V. L. Schwebach, and G. Young. 1993. Good Times, Bad Times, and the Diversionary Use of Force. *Journal of Conflict Resolution* 37:504–35.

Rummel, R. J. 1975–81. *Understanding Conflict and War.* Vols. 1–5. Beverly Hills, CA: Sage.

Rummel, R. J. 1985. Libertarian Propositions on Violence between and within Nations. *Journal of Conflict Resolution* 29:419–55.

Russett, B. 1993. *Grasping the Democratic Peace.* Princeton: Princeton University Press.

Siverson, R. M., and J. Emmons. 1991. Birds of a Feather: Democratic Political Systems and Alliance Choices in the Twentieth Century. *Journal of Conflict Resolution* 35:285–306.

The Effect of Foreign Policy Statements on Foreign Nations and Domestic Electorates

Alastair Smith

Domestic politics affects a leader's choice of foreign policy. A leader's success internationally affects her survival at home. This essay considers the relationship between domestic and international politics. In particular, I explore how domestic political factors affect a leader's choice of foreign policy, how the stated policy goals in one country affect behavior in other states, and how international events affect the reelection of leaders.

The format of this essay is perhaps a little unorthodox. In the next several pages, I informally outline the intuition and logic of the model. These simple arguments serve two purposes. First, they help provide the substantive motivation for the essay, highlighting the interaction between domestic and international politics. Second, these arguments introduce the logic of the formal model without the mathematical baggage required to rigorously prove the results. Having provided the direction of the essay, I refer to several relevant areas of the literature. The assumptions of the model are introduced informally, and I discuss the applicability of the model to a range of international events. The formal model is then described in detail. Rather than simply presenting the equilibria, I build up the results one stage at a time. I start by considering how the electorates' evaluation of a government's domestic and international performance affects reelection. I then work backward through the decisions made in international crises. The final stage is to examine which foreign policy goals governments announce that they will pursue. The results of the model explain how domestic and international politics interact. I discuss the substantive implications of these results.

In order to illustrate the substantive goals of this essay, I will outline some of the intuition and modeling assumptions. I explore the case of a conflictual situation between two nations, F and D. Suppose that nation F is contemplating some action X that nation D does not want it to undertake. This action could be anything in the international arena. Recent illustrative examples might include Serbian shelling of civilians in Bosnia, the Iraqis invasion of Kuwait, the refusal of military leaders in Haiti to step down, or repeated Chinese violations of U.S. intellectual property rights. The leader in nation D, whom I call R, declares a foreign policy statement. For example, a possible statement might be: "If nation F does X, then we will intervene with action Y." To keep the illustration simple yet interesting, suppose that F wants to do X only if D does not do Y. The threat of D doing Y might deter F from doing X. With respect to these examples, appropriate threats might be to bomb Serbian artillery, liberate Kuwait, invade Haiti, or impose trade sanctions on Chinese exports. There are several questions that interest me. When is this policy statement credible? How do domestic and international circumstances affect the choice of statements? How does the foreign policy statement affect the behavior of nation F and the behavior of the electorate in nation D?

Suppose that some types of leaders are prepared to undertake action Y in response to action X but other types of leaders are not. It is not always credible that nation D will intervene. We could define the leader's type (R) in a variety of ways. In this essay, I define R's type in terms of competence. Competence is defined more rigorously later. For the current illustration, competent leaders fight better than incompetent ones do.

Suppose that the foreign policy statement m_1, "If nation F does X, then we will retaliate with action Y," sometimes deters nation F from action X.[1] Since nation D does not want F to carry out action X, all leaders in nation D should make the policy statement m_1. However because all types of nation D send the same message, whether or not their leaders are competent, it is not credible that all types of nation D will carry out their threats (action Y). If all types pool on the message m_1, then nation F should always ignore the message. If this is the case, then foreign nations and domestic electorates should always ignore everything that politicians say. Empirically this is not the case: few histories ignore the role of prewar posturing, while the domestic rally effects associated with aggressive foreign policies are well documented (Mueller 1973). Deterrence does occur, and public opinion is affected by foreign policy statements.

Although the actual physical cost of making a policy statement is low, such statements have political costs. In this paragraph, I want to illustrate the intuition about how these political costs are generated. For brevity, the arguments are less than rigorous. Suppose, for example, that the government makes statement m_1. This statement may deter nation F; however, suppose it does not always succeed. If R, the leader of nation D, having made a commitment, fails to implement action Y, then she reveals something about her type to the electorate. In response, the electorate removes the leader. If leaders value officeholding, then having made statement m_1 they are more likely to undertake action Y since they do not want to be removed from office. If the electorate removes governments that do not honor their commitments, then governments can credibly commit. The policy statement m_1 deters nation F because of the domestic political consequences of not honoring a commitment. Governments have an incentive to make the statement m_1 because they can affect nation F's actions. However, the governments also face a risk from doing so because if nation F calls their bluff then they are faced with either carrying out action Y, which they may not want to do, or being removed from office.

A leader's propensity to take these risks depends upon domestic political circumstances. Domestically popular leaders might prefer not to risk being removed from office because they fail to live up to their foreign policy commitments. Alternatively, leaders who expect to be removed from office face little risk from not fulfilling their foreign policy commitments. Therefore, domestic political circumstances affect a leader's choice of foreign policy. As a consequence, domestic politics also affects whether foreign nations believe the foreign policy messages that leaders announce.

Domestic politics affects a leader's foreign policy choice. The choice of foreign policy and domestic politics interact to affect the beliefs of foreign nations. From these beliefs, foreign nations calculate the likelihood that the domestic nation will intervene if they act. Therefore, foreign nations consider the foreign policy message and the domestic context in which it was sent before deciding whether to act. If the foreign nation does act, then the leaders in the domestic nation consider the domestic consequences of not intervening given the policy statement they made. Domestic politics affects international politics through R's choice of foreign policy and F's choice about whether to act. International politics affects domestic politics because voters care about their leaders' international performance. The model attempts to unravel this endogeneity between international and domestic politics.

Literature Review

In this section, I consider three aspects of the international relations literature. This review is not intended to be comprehensive. Instead, it highlights the endogeneity between the strategic interactions between nations, the choice of foreign policy, and domestic consequences of international events. I use the literature review to show that theoretical and empirical relationships exist between various factors in international and domestic politics. The purpose of this essay is to show that all of these relationships must be simultaneously considered.

Strategic Interactions between Nations

Nations consider the response of other nations before acting. A clear example of this is Bueno de Mesquita and Lalman's *War and Reason* (1992). In this book, they present empirical tests to support their claims that nations choose actions conditional on how they expect other nations to respond. Deterrence theory provides another stunning example of strategic behavior between nations (Huth and Russett 1990; Jervis 1990; Zagare 1990; Achen and Snidal 1990; Nalebuff 1991; Langlois 1991). Since much of this essay deals with deterrence, I will explain the standard deterrence arguments using the notation that I use in the rest of the essay. Some nation F wants to carry out some act X. Typical examples might be to invade another country or discriminate against the goods of another country. However, nation F only wants to do X if nation D does not retaliate. F would rather live with the status quo than become involved in a fight with D. Deterrence occurs if nation D can convince nation F that it will retaliate.

The Choice of Foreign Policy in Response to Domestic Pressures

Ostrom and Job (1986) find that domestic political factors are more important in explaining foreign policy choice than international factors are. Although James and Oneal (1991) subsequently claim that international factors have a larger impact than Ostrom and Job initially estimated, they also conclude that domestic factors have the largest impact on foreign policy decision making. Page and Shapiro (1983) have also found that Congress tends to alter foreign policy to bring it more in line with public opinion. This phenomena is not restricted to the United States. For example, Snyder (1987) found that domestic political coalitions drove foreign policy in Germany prior to World War I. These articles conclude that international politics are, at least in part, driven by domestic factors.

The domestic popularity of leaders affects their incentives to pursue aggressive foreign policies (Smith 1996b). Political leaders who face domestic unrest may engage in diversionary international actions. Levy (1989) provides a comprehensive summary of diversionary war theories. The basic idea behind these theories is that if the leader does nothing then he will be removed from office. If the leader gambles on an adventurous foreign policy and succeeds, then the leader might retain office. Since the leader anticipates being removed from office anyway, he faces little downside if his foreign policies turn sour.

Foreign Policy Outcomes Affect a Leader's Ability to Survive

Ninic and Hinckley (1991) and Hurwitz and Peffley (1987) find evidence that the electorate's evaluation of a president's foreign policy performance is an important determinant of their voting decisions. For example, Ninic and Hinckley find that voters evaluate the government's issue by issue handling of international events to form an assessment of the government's abilities. The voters use this assessment to decide whether or not to retain the government. They find empirical support for this process at both the aggregate and individual levels.

The impact of international events on the survival of political leaders is not restricted to democratic systems. Bueno de Mesquita et al. (1992, 1995) find that, for all regime types, international outcomes affect the survival of political leaders. Leaders that lose wars are more likely to be removed than are successful leaders.

This brief literature review provides evidence that international and domestic politics are related. However, there are problems in dealing with these relationships separately. We cannot assess the effect of international events on domestic politics without simultaneously assessing the effect of domestic politics on international events. The following example illustrates why. Suppose that a leader loses a war and is subsequently removed from office. The literature review suggests two possible explanations for this series of events. First, as Bueno de Mesquita et al. (1992, 1995) claim, a leader who loses a war reveals himself or herself to be incompetent. The voters replace this incompetent leader with an alternative leader.[2] Second, diversionary war theory provides an alternative explanation. If a leader anticipates being thrown out of office, then the leader starts a war in the hope of surviving. In this explanation, the war is not the cause of the leader's removal; it is simply a by-product of the leader attempting to retain office.

In the first scenario, international events drive domestic politics. In the second scenario, domestic politics drives international events. Which explanation is correct? Obviously, from this single, unidentified event it is impossible to know. It is likely that both explanations are partially correct. To overcome this problem, I simultaneously model the effect of domestic politics on international events and the effect of international events on domestic politics. In the next section, I informally introduce the modeling assumptions.

An Informal Introduction to the Game

The game combines aspects of both international and domestic competition. There are two nations: a foreign nation, F, and a domestic nation, D. The foreign nation is a unitary actor. However, the domestic nation, D, contains three actors: an incumbent party R, an opposition party L, and a median voter E. The game takes place in two phases. There is an international phase during which F and D interact on some international issue. In the domestic phase that follows, the electorate, E, decides whether to retain the incumbent, R, or elect the alternative, L.

The structure of this game can be applied to many different international situations. For convenience, I will characterize the problem in deterrence terms. However, the implications of the results are applicable to other aspects of international relations. The foreign and domestic nations are in competition over some issue. For example, nation F might want to act against a third party. The members of the domestic nation do not want to see the third party attacked. If F attacks, then D could intervene in the conflict. Internationally, there are three possible outcomes to this situation. First, F might decide not to act against the third party. I refer to this outcome as the status quo (SQ). Second, F acts against the third party and D does not intervene. This outcome is called acquiesce (ACQ). Finally, F could decide to act and D could decide to intervene. When D counters F's act, a war occurs (WAR).

Political leaders frequently make policy statements. These policy statements range from formal commitments, such as forming alliances or joining international organizations, to simple statements of policy goals. This essay asks, how do these policy statements affect the behavior of foreign nations? For example, if D threatens F, does this make F more or less likely to act?

These descriptions of both international events and policy statements are somewhat abstract. To provide some substantive motivation, consider the following range of international events in which the United States has participated. At the highest extreme, President Kennedy, in 1962, demanded that the Soviet Union withdraw nuclear missiles stationed in Cuba. Fortunately, whether the United States was prepared to intervene was never directly tested, as the Soviets did not act against U.S. wishes. At a lower level, within the past year U.S. declarations of foreign policy have affected the behavior of states. The countries that constitute the former Yugoslavia have sometimes obeyed U.S. and UN calls for a cease-fire; at other times, these states have continued to shell civilians. U.S. threats to invade Haiti have been sufficient for its military government to resign. In other circumstances, the United States has intervened militarily against states that act against it. For example, Libya's refusal to stop state-sponsored terrorism led to U.S. military intervention in 1986 in the form of an air raid. The form of events that I consider is not restricted to military confrontations. The events could just as well be economic in nature. Recently, the U.S. policy of threatening China with trade sanctions convinced the Chinese government to no longer act against the intellectual property rights of U.S. companies.

This list of examples is in no way intended to be comprehensive. The list merely provides some illustrations of the phenomena that this essay attempts to explain. For clarity, during the rest of the essay I confine my discussion to cases of potential war and leave the extension of the model into other substantive areas for the reader.

A government's foreign policy performance affects the electorate's evaluation of the government (Nincic and Hinckley 1991). At election time, the voters decide whether to keep the current incumbent, R, or select a new government, L. Both domestic and international performance affects whether a government will be retained or removed at the election. A leader that is successful internationally is more likely to survive than an unsuccessful leader is (Bueno de Mesquita et al. 1992; Bueno de Mesquita and Siverson 1995). However, a leader's prospects of reelection can also affect her choice of foreign policy. The best known manifestation of this is diversionary war theory (see Levy 1989 for a recent survey). Diversionary war theory suggests that leaders with domestic problems adopt aggressive foreign policies. In the model, the electorate evaluates the government on both domestic and international issues. The results show that a government's domestic performance affects its foreign policy decisions.

Throughout the essay, I refer to the process by which governments are selected as elections. Rather than model the whole electorate, I consider E to be the median voter. In two-party competitions, the vote of the median voter determines the election (Downs 1957). Many countries are nondemocratic. In these countries, E should be thought of, not as the median voter in the population as a whole, but as the median member of the group that chooses the political leader. If, for example, a regime relies on the military for support, then E is the head of the military.

The Game

Formally, there are four players: F, E, R, and L. F is a foreign nation. R is the incumbent leader in a domestic nation. L is an alternative political leader. E is the median voter in the domestic nation. There is incomplete information in the game. The competence of political leaders specifies their type (Harsanyi 1967–68).

Leaders have differing abilities in conducting foreign policy and running the domestic economy. Voters care about both international and domestic outcomes. A leader's ability to organize domestic policy is defined as domestic competence, d. A leader's domestic competence, $d \in D$, affects economic performance. Highly competent leaders produce good domestic outcomes, while incompetent leaders produce poor outcomes. The voters learn about R's ability, d_R, during R's time in office by observing domestic performance. At election time, the voters also learn something about the opposition's domestic competence by its ability to campaign. All else being equal, the voters select the most competent leader.

Voters also care about leaders' ability to run foreign policy. This is referred to as international or foreign policy competence. Competent leaders perform much better than incompetent leaders do when conflict occurs. Because of their superior abilities, competent leaders are more likely to win wars or other confrontational situations. A leader's international competence is represented by $c \in C$.

The Structure of the Game

The game is composed of two phases: an international game and a domestic game. The international game is shown in figure 1.

0. The domestic competence, d_R, of the incumbent party R is revealed. The electorate, E, is able to observe R's performance. R's domestic competence affects R's electoral prospects.
1. The incumbent, R, announces a foreign policy message, $m \in M$. Both the electorate, E, and the foreign nation, F, observe R's signal.
2. Having observed R's message, m, the foreign nation, F, decides whether or not to act (A or $\sim A$). As discussed previously, this act could be an attack, a change in trade policy, support of terrorist organizations, or an increase in armaments. If F does not act, then the outcome is the status quo (SQ).
3. If F acts, then the incumbent, R, decides whether or not to counter F's act by intervening (I or $\sim I$). If R does not intervene, then the outcome is acquiescence (ACQ). If R intervenes, then the outcome is a war (WAR). The outcome of the war depends upon R's international competence. Therefore, the electorate learns about R's international competence, c_R, if a war occurs.[3]
4. Following the international game, an election occurs. The alternative leader, L, campaigns, and then the electorate, E, decides whether to retain R or elect L (R or L).

Payoffs

Political leaders receive payoffs from both international and domestic events. If R is reelected, then it receives a payoff of Ψ associated with the benefits of officeholding. All domestic actors, R, L, and E, receive payoffs from the international game. If the outcome is $z \in Z = \{SQ, ACQ, WAR\}$, then their payoffs from the international game are $V(z, c_R)$, where c_R is R's international competence. These international payoffs are given in table 1.

The function $q(c)$ is continuous and increasing in c_R. The more competent is the incumbent, R, the better is the expected outcome of war and hence the higher the domestic nation's payoff. There is a cost of fighting. I assume that $1 > q(c_R)$ − cost for all types. The foreign nation, F, also receives payoffs associated with international outcomes. F's most preferred outcome is ACQ. There is incomplete information about how much F values succeeding international. F's type is defined as a. If a war occurs, then F's payoff is $\theta(c_R, a)$, where θ is a continuous increasing function in a, a continuous weakly decreasing function in c_R, and $\theta(c_R, a) < a$ for all c_R, These assumptions mean that F prefers

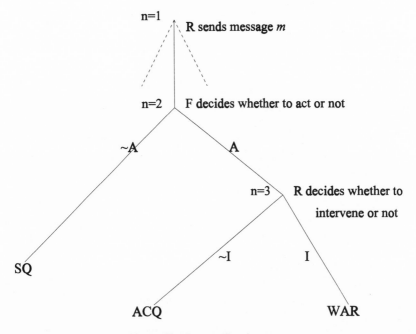

n=1   R sends message *m*

n=2   F decides whether to act or not

~A   A

n=3   R decides whether to
intervene or not

SQ

~I   I

ACQ   WAR

Fig. 1. The international game

to obtain its goals without having to fight and that if F does fight it prefers to fight an incompetent opponent.

The electorate cares about the domestic and international competence of its political leaders. E cares about how its leaders perform after the election. If the international outcome is z and E reelects the incumbent R, then its payoff, $U_E(z, \text{R elected})$, depends upon z, the domestic competence of R both before and after the election and the international competence of R in the period after the election.[4]

$$U_E(z, \text{R elected}) = V(z, c_R) + 2d_R + c_R.$$

TABLE 1. International Payoffs

Outcome	SQ	ACQ	WAR
Payoff for R and E	1	0	$q(c_R) - \text{cost}$
Payoff for F	0	$a > 0$	$\theta(c_R, a)$

Alternatively, if the voters elect L, then their payoff is

$$U_E(z, \text{L elected}) = V(z,c_R) + d_R + d_L + c_L.$$

Beliefs

This is a game of incomplete information. Neither E nor F knows the incumbent's type. In this model, R actually has two types: domestic competence and international competence. E and F have common beliefs about the government's type and the opposition's type. In most of what follows, I refer mainly to the incumbent, R. Given this, I frequently drop the subscript denoting R and L when there is no ambiguity.

   Domestic Competence: $d_R, d_L \in D \subset \Re$. E and F's beliefs about d_i is distributed $g_i(d_i)$. The cumulative probability is $G_i(d_i)$. Thus, $G_R(\delta)$ is E and F's prior beliefs that $d_R \leq \delta$. For all the numerical examples, I assume that $g_i(\ )$ is the standard normal density.

   International Competence: $c_R, c_L \in C = [0,1]$. This is distributed uniformly over the unit interval $c_R \sim U[0,1]$. Let $\lambda(c_R)$ be E and F's beliefs about c_R. $\Lambda(c_R)$ is the cumulative probability of c_R. Given the uniform prior, $\lambda(c_R) = 1$, $\Lambda(c_R) = c_R$, and $E[c_L] = 1/2$.

   F's type: $a \in A \subset \Re$. R, L, and E's prior beliefs about a are given by $h(a)$, where $h(a)$ is a continuous function.

Actions and Strategies

The incumbent, R, chooses which foreign policy announcement to make and whether to intervene if F acts. The set of possible foreign policy statements is M. Thus, at $n = 1$, R chooses $m \in M$. If F acts, then R decides whether or not to intervene: I or $\sim I$. Having observed R's foreign policy message, F decides whether or not to act. Thus, at $n = 2$, F chooses A or $\sim A$. The electorate decides whether or not to reelect R. Thus, at $n = 4$, E chooses R or L.

   R's strategy is the pair (σ_R, s_R), where $\sigma_R: C \times D \to \Delta M$ and $s_R: C \times D \times M \to [0,1]$. $\sigma_R(m,c_R,d_R)$ is the probability that an incumbent of international competence c_R and domestic competence d_R sends message m. $s_R(c_R,d_R,m)$ is the probability that R of international competence c_R and domestic competence d_R intervenes, having sent the message m.

   The foreign nation's strategy is s_F, where $s_F: M \times D \times A \to [0,1]$. Thus, $s_F(m,d,a)$ is the probability that F acts given the message, m, R's domestic performance, d, and F's type, a.

   The electorate's strategy is s_E, where $s_E: M \times Z \times D \times D \to [0,1]$. $s_E(m,z,d_R,d_L)$ is the probability that E reelects R, given that R sent message m, the international outcome was z, and the domestic competence of R and L are d_R and d_L, respectively.

For convenience, I frequently drop the d_i terms from descriptions of strategies. Also, I typically use c rather than c_R. Unless otherwise explicitly stated, nonsubscripted terms refer to R.

Before moving on to the result, I define several terms. These terms represent some of the dependent variables of interest. I introduce them here to ensure that they do not become hidden within the subsequent math. They are defined more rigorously later. $\gamma(m) = \gamma(d_R,m)$ is the probability that R intervenes given that R sent the foreign policy message m. $\alpha(m) = \alpha(m,d_R)$ is the probability that F acts given that R sent message m. Finally, $P(m,z) = P(m,z,d_R)$ is the probability that E reelects R given message m and outcome z.

Results

The Reelection Decision

At the start of the game, the voters observe R's domestic competence. Subsequently, they observe R's foreign policy statements and the international events that follow. Just before the election, they observe L's campaign. The voters then decide whether to retain R or replace R with L.

If the voters reelect R, then their expected utility is

$$E[U_E(R \mid m,z,d_R,d_L)] = V(z,c) + 2d_R + E[c_R \mid m,z].$$

If the voters elect L, then their expected utility is

$$E[U_E(L \mid m,z,d_R,d_L)] = V(z,c) + d_R + d_L + E[c_L]$$

$$= V(z,c) + d_R + d_L + 1/2.$$

The electorate's beliefs about R's international competence are determined via Bayes's rule given R's strategy. Thus,

$$E[c \mid m,\text{SQ}] = \int_0^1 c\, \sigma_R(m,c)dc$$

$$E[c \mid m,\text{ACQ}] = \int_0^1 c\, [1 - s_R(c,m)]\, \lambda_R(c|m)dc,$$

where

$$\lambda_R(c|m) = \sigma_R(m,c) / \int_0^1 \sigma_R(m,c)dc$$

$$E[c \mid m,\text{WAR}] = c.$$

By assumption, R's competence is revealed when it actually fights.

R is reelected when E believes that it is more competent than the alternative leader, L.

$$s_E(m,z,d_R,d_L) = 1$$

if $E[c \mid m,z] + d_R \geq 1/2 + d_L$. Otherwise, it is

$$s_E(m,z,d_R,d_L) = 0.$$

Having observed the domestic competence of both R and L, the voters decide which leader they prefer. Prior to L's election campaign, E does not know L's domestic competence. However, given that the distribution of d_L, although not the realized value of d_L, is common knowledge, R can calculate the probability that it will be reelected for any given message and outcome: $P(m,z)$.

$$P(m,z) = P(E[c \mid m,z]) = \text{Prob.}(d_L \leq E[c \mid m,z] + d_R - 1/2)$$

$$= G(E[c \mid m,z] + d_R - 1/2).$$

The Decision to Intervene

If the foreign nation acts, then R must decide whether or not to intervene. As the previous section demonstrates, R can calculate the probability with which it is reelected. If R decides to retaliate, then its expected payoff depends upon its international competence.

$$E[U_R(I \mid c,m)] = q(c) - \text{cost} + \Psi P(E[c \mid m,\text{WAR}])$$

$$= q(c) - \text{cost} + \Psi P(c).$$

If R does not retaliate, then the voters do not know its type with certainty. Its expected payoff is

$$E[U_R(\sim I \mid c,m)] = \Psi P(E[c \mid m,\text{ACQ}]).$$

Whether R decides to intervene depends upon international factors, $[q(c) - \text{cost}]$, and the probability of reelection, $\Psi P(c) - \Psi P(E[c \mid m,\text{ACQ}])$. Therefore,

$$s_R(c_R,d_R,m) = 1,$$

if $q(c) - \text{cost} + \Psi P(c) \geq \Psi P(E[c \mid m, \text{ACQ}])$. Otherwise,

$$s_R(c_R, d_R, m) = 0.$$

Since $q(c)$ and $P(c)$ are increasing in c, the value of intervening increases as R becomes more competent. Given the message m, define $c^{\ddagger}w(m)$ as the type that is indifferent about whether or not to intervene;[5]

$$q[c^{\ddagger}(m)] - \text{cost} + \Psi P[c^{\ddagger}(m)] = \Psi P(E[c \mid m, \text{ACQ}]).$$

Thus, if $c \geq c^{\ddagger}(m)$, then R intervenes; otherwise, R acquiesces if F acts.

Given R's intervention strategy, the probability that R intervenes is the probability that $c \geq c^{\ddagger}(m)$ given the message m. Define the probability that R intervenes, given message m, as $\gamma(m)$:

$$\gamma(m) = \int_{c^{\ddagger}(m)}^{1} \lambda_R(c \mid m) dc.$$

The Foreign Nation's Decision to Act

Having observed the foreign policy message m, F's beliefs about R's type are $\lambda_R(c \mid m)$. F's expected payoff for acting depends upon these beliefs and its type.

$$E[U_F(A \mid m, a)] = \int_0^1 \{a[1 - s_R(c, m)] + \theta(c, a) s_R(c, m)\} \lambda_R(c \mid m) dc.$$

If F decides not to act, then its payoff is zero.

$$E[U_R(\sim A \mid m, a)] = 0.$$

F only acts when the expected payoff of doing so is greater than zero. Therefore,

$$s_F(m, a) = 1$$

if

$$[1 - \gamma(m)] a + \int_{c^{\ddagger}(m)}^{1} \theta(c, a) \lambda_R(c \mid m) dc \geq 0,$$

Otherwise,

$$s_F(m, a) = 0.$$

Since $\theta(c,a)$ is increasing in a, F is more likely to act as its type increases. Define $a^+(m)$ as the type indifferent between whether or not to act.

Therefore, $a^+(m)$ such that

$$1 - \gamma(m)a^+(m) + \int_{c^+(m)}^{1} \theta[c,a^+(m)] \lambda_R(c|m)dc = 0.$$

Knowing that a is distributed with a cumulative probability function $H(a)$, the probability that F acts given the message m is $\alpha(m)$.

$$\alpha(m) = \int_{a^+(m)}^{\infty} h(a)da = 1 - H[a^+(m)].$$

The Interaction of International and Domestic Politics

The previous sections characterize the electorate's decision to retain R, R's decision to intervene, and F's decision to act. These decisions all depend upon the foreign policy signal that R sends. The message that R sends affects whether F acts, whether R intervenes, and whether the voters retain R. The question I address next is which signal R sends in equilibrium.

When R makes a foreign policy statement, it conveys information about its type to the other players. However, although the message has costly international and domestic consequences, the message itself is costless to send. As such, these forms of signaling games are often referred to as "cheap talk." Banks (1991, 23–26) provides a summary of the general properties of equilibria in these games. In the main text, I intend to describe the sequential equilibria to the game and illustrate their properties with several examples. The appendix contains proofs of the equilibrium properties that I just assert in the text.

I start by considering the simple case where the foreign policy messages are uninformative. Having characterized these equilibria, I examine their substantive implications. Following this, I examine the more complicated, but substantively more interesting, informative equilibria.

Uninformative Equilibria

There are always pooling and babbling equilibria in cheap talk games. In these equilibria, all types send the same messages with the same probability. Since everyone makes the same statements, there is no information in the messages. Thus, all pooling and babbling equilibria are uninformative, as the following babbling equilibria demonstrate.

An Uninformative Babbling Equilibrium

$\sigma_R(m,c) = \sigma_R(m,c')$ for all $m \in M$ and for all c and c'.

$s_F(m,a) = 1$ if $a \geq a^{\ddagger}$ for all m,

$s_F(m,a) = 0$ otherwise.

$s_R(m,c) = 1$ if $c \geq c^{\ddagger}$ for all m,

$s_R(m,c) = 0$ otherwise.

$s_E(m,z) = 1$ if $E[c \mid m,z] + d_R \geq 1/2 + d_L$,

$s_E(m,z) = 0$ otherwise,

where $c^{\ddagger}, a^{\ddagger}$ and $E[c \mid m,z]$ are as defined earlier.

Since all messages are sent in equilibrium, R cannot convey information about its type to either E or F. R is indifferent between all possible messages. The equilibrium is characterized in terms of finding those types that intervene given the prior beliefs held by E and F. Thus, whatever message R sends, $c^{\ddagger}$ is the type that is indifferent about whether to intervene or not:

$$q(c^{\ddagger}) - \text{cost} + \Psi P(c^{\ddagger}) = \Psi P(E[c \mid \text{ACQ}]) = \Psi P(c^{\ddagger}/2).$$

Implications of the Babbling Equilibrium

In the babbling equilibrium, as shown in figure 2, neither the electorate nor the foreign nation learns about the incumbent's type from the foreign policy statement. When F decides whether to act, it ignores the policy statement. However, domestic politics still affects international behavior. The identity $q(c^{\ddagger}) - \text{cost} + \Psi P(c^{\ddagger}) = \Psi P(E[c \mid \text{ACQ}]) = \Psi P(c^{\ddagger}/2)$ determines whether R intervenes should F act. R's decision is affected by both international and domestic factors. I consider the international factors first.

As the cost of fighting increases, R receives a lower payoff if it intervenes. This means that fewer types intervene. As the cost of fighting increases, then fewer types intervene (as cost increases, $c^{\ddagger}$ increases and γ decreases). Similarly, if F is powerful relative to the domestic nation, then R's expected payoff is small. As F increases in power relative to R, then $q(c)$ is smaller, and hence $c^{\ddagger}$ is larger. This implies that R is less likely to intervene.

Domestic factors also affect the probability that R intervenes. R's decision

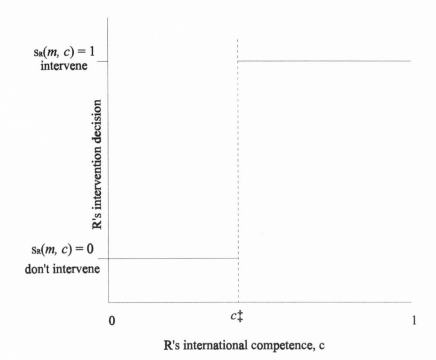

Fig. 2. Babbling equilibrium

to intervene contains information about R's type. Specifically, if R intervenes, then its type is fully revealed. If R does not intervene, then E knows that R's type is less than $c^{\ddagger}$. Therefore, in equilibrium the electorate is more likely to re-elect R if R intervenes: $P(c \geq c^{\ddagger}) > P(c^{\ddagger}/2)$. As the value of officeholding increases, R is more likely to intervene: as Ψ increases, $c^{\ddagger}$ decreases, and hence γ increases.

As diversionary war theories predict, domestic popularity affects whether nations engage in aggressive foreign policies. Suppose that R performs extremely poorly domestically: $d_R << E(d_L) = 0$. The electorate is extremely unlikely to reelect R whatever its international competence: $G(d_R + E[c] - .5)$ is close to zero if d_R is very low. Therefore, R's international performance is unlikely to have any affect on the outcome of the election. R bases its decision to intervene on international factors. Similarly, if R is extremely competent domestically, then its international performance is unlikely to affect the outcome of the election. Under both these extremes, international factors drive the decision to intervene: $q(c^{\ddagger}) \approx \text{cost}$. Between these extremes, R is more likely to intervene than international factors alone predict.

The equilibrium predicts that R intervenes if $c \geq c^{\ddagger}$, where $c^{\ddagger}$ is such that $q(c^{\ddagger}) - \text{cost} + \Psi P(c^{\ddagger}) = \Psi P(c^{\ddagger}/2)$. If R's domestic performance is around the average domestic performance, then the difference between $P(c^{\ddagger})$ and $P(c^{\ddagger}/2)$ is large.[6] When elections are competitive, by which I mean that R and L are equally likely to win, the impact of international competence on the outcome of elections is large. Since $P(c^{\ddagger}) > P(c^{\ddagger}/2)$, competitive elections make leaders hawkish. Indeed, it has been observed that second-term presidents, who can't run for reelection, are dovish compared with first termers.

Suppose that an internationally competent leader is unpopular at home, that is, the leader has below average domestic competence. This leader is unlikely to be reelected. However, if this leader demonstrates her international competence to the electorate she is far more likely to gain reelection. Thus, competent leaders have domestic incentives to intervene even if internationally they should remain neutral [$q(c) < \text{cost}$]. Now consider the incentives facing moderately competent types. On an international basis, they should not intervene. However, because all competent types intervene, nonintervention leads the voter to believe that the government is not particularly competent. Therefore, to avoid being identified with the incompetent governments, moderately competent governments also intervene. This iterative cycle drives lower and lower types to intervene to avoid being labeled as incompetent. When the probability of reelection is just below 50 percent, a small change in beliefs can have a big effect on the probability of reelection (Smith 1996a; Hess and Orphanides 1995).

Domestic politics affects whether R intervenes. Domestic politics also affects whether the foreign nation acts. The probability that F acts is inversely related to the probability that R intervenes. Competitive political processes make leaders more likely to intervene. This, in turn, makes foreign nations less likely to act in the first place. Domestic politics in one country affects foreign policy decisions in another.

To clarify these arguments, consider the following stylized comparison. Consider case 1. The leader of the domestic nation is an absolute dictator. This dictator cannot be removed from office. Therefore, the dictator only intervenes when $q(c) \geq \text{cost}$. Foreign nations know that the dictator is unlikely to intervene. Therefore, foreign nations are likely to act. Thus, if the domestic nation is dictatorial, then γ is low and α is high. Now consider case 2: a democratic domestic nation in which the political leader is facing a close election. This leader knows that her international performance will be critical in determining her fate at the ballot box. As argued earlier, this makes the democratic state intervene even when international factors suggest that it should not. Knowing that the domestic nation is likely to intervene, the foreign nation is unlikely to act. For democracies, γ is high and α is low. These stylized cases suggest that if the domestic nation is dictatorial then the outcome is likely to be ACQ. However, for a democratic domestic nation the outcome is likely to be either SQ or WAR.

The analysis of the babbling equilibrium implies that domestic and international politics are interrelated. In the next section, I consider informative equilibria. I show that statements of foreign policy can affect the behavior of both foreign nations and domestic electorates. In analyzing informative equilibria, I concentrate on the effects of different messages on E and F. The above implications remain true; however, for clarity I will not emphasize these results.

Informative Equilibria

In the babbling equilibrium, all types send foreign policy messages with the same probability. Consequently, there is no information in the message. Upon hearing these messages, neither E nor F change their behavior. However, empirically we often observe that foreign policy statements alter public opinion. In this section, I seek to explain why.

There are many informative equilibria. I characterize several of these to demonstrate their properties. All informative equilibria have certain properties. I characterize them in the appendix rather than the main text.

Informative Equilibrium 1

In this equilibrium, internationally competent types send the message $m1 \in M1$ and intervene if F acts. The internationally incompetent types send message $m2 \in M2$ and never intervene. This equilibrium is demonstrated graphically in figure 3. Since the electorate's strategy and the foreign nation's strategy were characterized earlier, I will not explicitly state these strategies again.

If $c \geq c1$, then R sends message $m1 \in M1$.
If $c < c1$, then R sends message $m2 \in M2$, where $M1 \cap M2 = \varnothing$ and $M1 \cup M2 = M$.
R intervenes if message $m1$ is sent; otherwise, R acquiesces: $s_R(c,m1) = 1$ and $s_R(c,m2) = 0$.

The electorates' beliefs given the message sent and outcome are as follows.

$E[c \mid m, \text{WAR}] = c$ for any m,

$E[c \mid m2, \text{SQ}] = c1/2, E[c \mid m2, \text{ACQ}] = c1/2, E[c \mid m1, \text{SQ}] =$

$(1 + c1)/2$

$E[c \mid m1, \text{ACQ}] = 0.$[7]

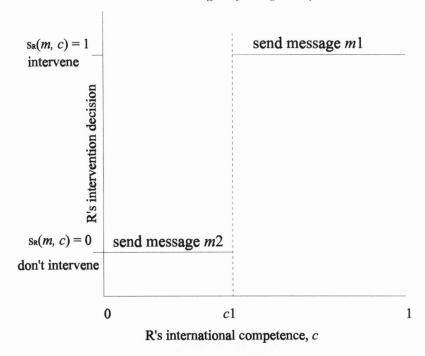

Fig. 3. Informative equilibrium 1

In equilibrium, high types send $m1$ and thereby threaten F that they will intervene if F acts. If F does act, then they intervene as they threaten to do so. Lower types send $m2$. This signal tells both the voters and F that R is not a high type. However, it does not completely reveal R's type.

If this is an equilibrium, then those types that send message $m1$ must actually want to intervene, while those types that send $m2$ must not want to intervene if F acts. Therefore,

$$q(c) - \text{cost} + \Psi P(c) \geq \Psi P(0)$$

for $c \geq c1$, and

$$q(c) - \text{cost} + \Psi P(c) \leq \Psi P(c1/2)$$

for $c < c1$.

Next, we must ensure that high types want to threaten F by sending message $m1$. The expected utility of sending $m1$ conditional on intervening is

$$E[U_R(m1 \mid c \geq c1)] = \alpha(m1)[q(c) - \text{cost} + \Psi P(c)]$$

$$+ [1 - \alpha(m1)]\{1 + \Psi P[(1 + c1)/2]\},$$

where $\alpha(m1)$ is the probability that F acts given message $m1$.

The expected utility of sending message $m2$ conditional on acquiescing if F acts is

$$E[U_R(m2 \mid c < c1)] = \alpha(m2)[P(c1/2)] + [1 - \alpha(m2)][1 + \Psi P(c1/2)].$$

As I prove in the appendix, in equilibrium, R's expected utility is a continuous, weakly increasing, monotonic function of c. Therefore, at $c = c1$,

$$E[U_R(m1 \mid c1)] = E[U_R(m2 \mid c1)].$$

Given $q(.)$, $g(.)$, $h(.)$, cost, and d_R, $c1$ is determined by solving this identity. Figure 4 shows how $c1$ varies as a function of cost for some numerical examples.

By sending message $m1$, R threatens F that it will intervene. This reduces the incentive for F to act. Sending message $m1$ sometimes deters foreign nations. In addition, the message also tells the voters that R is competent. Despite these incentives, not all types send message $m1$.

Given that $m1$ deters F and tells the voters that R is competent, why do any types want to send $m2$? Although $m1$ can deter F, it does not always do so. Sometimes F will act even when it hears the message $m1$. If R intervenes, then the voters learn about its type. If R does not intervene, having sent $m1$, then the voters believe that R is of the lowest type. There is a problem for low types of R sending the message $m1$; sometimes their bluff will be called. They are then faced with two unpleasant alternatives: (1) intervene when they expect to do badly or (2) acquiesce to F's actions, which convinces the voters that they are completely incompetent. Low types can avoid these unpleasant alternatives by sending message $m2$.

Sending the message $m1$ is a lottery. Sometimes R wins: nation F is deterred and the voters think R is competent. Unfortunately, sometimes R loses: nation F acts, which means that R must either intervene under unfavorable conditions or tell the electorate that it is really incompetent. High types find losing the lottery less costly than low types do because they perform better when they intervene. Therefore, it is only high types that enter the lottery.

By sending message $m1$, R mortgages its political future. If R sends the message $m1$ but does not intervene, then the electorate think that R is incompetent. There is an electoral cost to sending $m1$ and not intervening. This cost enables R to credibly commit to intervene. R can affect international events when international factors alone predict that R should never intervene. By ty-

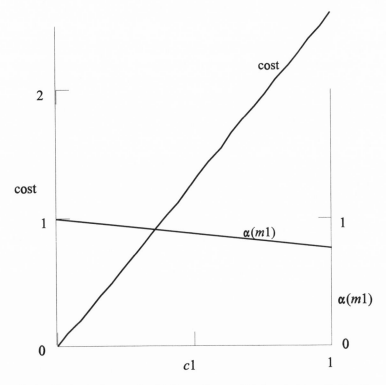

Fig. 4. Numerical example of informative equilibrium 1. ($d_R = 0$, $\Psi = 5$, $P(c) = \Phi(c - .5 + d_R)$, $q(c) = c$, $\gamma_r(m1) = 1$, $\gamma_r(m2) = 0$, $\alpha(m1) = 1 - c1/4$, and $\alpha(m2) = 1$.)

ing their political futures to intervening, leaders can credibly commit to intervening. Fearon's (1994) model of the effect of domestic audience costs on the escalation of international events shows how domestic politics affects international events. In this model, the domestic audience costs that Fearon discusses are endogenously generated by the domestic electoral system.

The message $m1$ partially deters F from acting. However, the message $m1$ never completely deters F. The knowledge that R will intervene deters some types of F, but others act even though they know that R will intervene. In this equilibrium, R can never completely deter F. Suppose that this were not true. Then, simply by sending the message $m1$, R could deter F and simultaneously convince the voters that it is competent. If F were completely deterred, then R would never have to prove its competence because the situation in which it is forced to intervene would never occur. However, in this situation all types would want to send $m1$; doing so, they gain both internationally and domestically. However, if all types want to send message $m1$, then F is not deterred by $m1$ and E learns nothing from the message $m1$. In this situation, $m1$ can only convey information if it does not completely deter F. In the appendix, I consider conditions under which a foreign policy statement can completely deter foreign nations.

In this equilibrium, as cost increases the proportion of nations that send message $m1$ declines. Eventually, as the cost becomes too large, no types threaten F and only pooling equilibria exist. Leaders can signal their intent to E and F because they can tie their political futures to carrying out their stated policy goals. Therefore, in order to credibly commit to a foreign policy and to convey information leaders need competitive electoral processes. The statements of lame ducks and absolute rulers should be ignored. However, a competitive electoral process can make a leader's foreign policy statements informative.

In the equilibrium above, high types threaten F with message $m1$, while the lower types pool on message $m2$. In this equilibrium, the probability that F acts is lower if R sends the message $m1$: $\alpha(m1) < \alpha(m2)$. Next, I characterize an equilibrium in which the highest types do not threaten F; instead, the moderate types send a threatening message.

Informative Equilibrium 2

In this equilibrium, the highest and lowest types send the same message, $m1$. However, only the high types intervene if F acts. The moderate types send message $m2$ and always intervene if F acts. This equilibrium is demonstrated graphically in figure 5. Since the electorate's strategy and the foreign nation's strategy were characterized earlier, I will not explicitly state them again.

If $c1 \geq c < c2$, then R sends message $m2 \in M2$.
If $c \geq c2$ or $c < c1$, then R sends message $m1 \in M1$, where $M1 \cap M2 = \varnothing$ and $M1 \cup M2 = M$.
R intervenes if $c \geq c1$; otherwise, R acquiesces: $s_R(c \geq c1,.) = 1$ and $s_R(c < c1,.) = 0$.

The electorates' beliefs given the message sent and the outcome are as follows.

$E[c \mid m, \text{WAR}] = c$ for any m,
$E[c \mid m2, \text{SQ}] = (c1 + c2)/2$,
$E[c \mid m2, \text{ACQ}] = 0$,
$E[c \mid m1, \text{SQ}] = (1 + c1^2 - c2^2)/2$,
$E[c \mid m1, \text{ACQ}] = c1/2$.

In equilibrium, types greater than $c1$ intervene if F acts. However, these high types do not send the same message. The highest types, $c \geq c2$, send

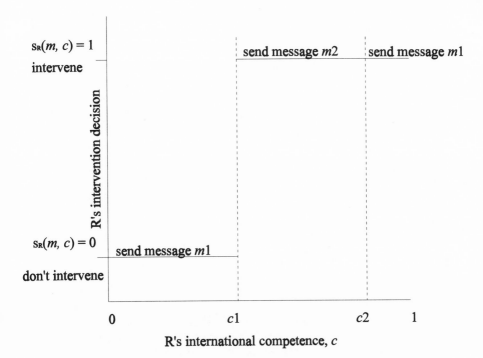

Fig. 5. Informative equilibrium 2

message $m1$. The lowest types, $c < c1$, those that do not intervene, also send message $m1$. Those types between $c1$ and $c2$ send message $m2$ and intervene if F acts. If this is an equilibrium, then those types above $c1$ must actually want to intervene given the message they sent. Therefore, if message $m1$ is sent, then

$$q(c) - \text{cost} + \Psi P(c) \geq \Psi P(c1/2)$$

for $c \geq c2$ and

$$q(c) - \text{cost} + \Psi P(c) \leq \Psi P(c1/2)$$

for $c < c1$. If R sends message $m2$, then in equilibrium

$$q(c) - \text{cost} + \Psi P(c) \geq \Psi P(0)$$

for $c1 \geq c > c2$.

Next, we must ensure that types $c > c2$ want to send message $m1$. The expected utility of sending $m1$, conditional on intervening, is

$$E[U_R(m1 \mid c \geq c2)] = \alpha(m1)[q(c) - \text{cost} + \Psi P(c)]$$

$$+ [1 - \alpha(m1)]\{1 + \Psi P[(1 + c1^2 - c2^2)/2]\}.$$

In equilibrium, types $c \in [c1, c2]$ receive expected utility

$$E[U_R(m2 \mid c1 \geq c \geq c2)] = \alpha(m2)[q(c) - \text{cost} + \Psi P(c)]$$

$$+ [1 - \alpha(m2)]\{1 + \Psi P[(c1 + c2)/2]\}.$$

In equilibrium, types $c < c1$ receive expected utility

$$E[U_R(m1 \mid c < c1)] = \alpha(m1)[\Psi P(c1/2)]$$

$$+ [1 - \alpha(m1)]\{1 + \Psi P[(1 + c1^2 - c2^2)/2]\}.$$

The probability that F acts given message $m1$ is $\alpha(m1)$, and the probability that F acts given message $m2$ is $\alpha(m2)$. Since R's expected utility is a continuous increasing function of c, at $c2$, $E[U_R(m1 \mid c \geq c2)] = E[U_R(m2 \mid c1 \geq c \geq c2)]$ and, at $c1$, $E[U_R(m2 \mid c1 \geq c \geq c2)] = E[U_R(m1 \mid c < c1)]$. These conditions imply that

$$[\alpha(m1) - \alpha(m2)]\{q(c2) - \text{cost} + \Psi P(c2) - 1 - \Psi P[(1 + c1^2$$

$$- c2^2)/2]\} = [1 - \alpha(m2)]\{P[(c1 + c2)/2] - P[(1 + c1^2 - c2^2)/2]\}$$

and that

$$\alpha(m1)\{\Psi P(c1/2) - 1 - \Psi P[(1 + c1^2 - c2^2)/2]\}$$

$$- \alpha(m2)\{q(c1) - \text{cost} + \Psi P(c1) - 1 - \Psi P[(c1 + c2)/2]\}$$

$$= \Psi P[(c1 + c2)/2] - \Psi P[(1 + c1^2 - c2^2)/2].$$

Solving these identities, reveals $c1$ and $c2$. Figure 6 contains numerical examples of these equilibria.

Message $m2$ deters the foreign nation from acting. By sending the message $m2$, R reduces the probability that F acts because R commits itself to intervening. As in the previous equilibrium, leaders can stake their political fu-

Example	c1	c2	$\gamma(m1)$	$\gamma(m2)$	$\alpha(m1)$	$\alpha(m2)$	φ	cost	d_R	$E[c|m1]$	$E[c|m2]$
1	0.216	0.900	0.316	1	1	0.93	5	0.561	0	0.118	0.558
2	0.237	0.900	0.297	1	1	0.93	5	0.535	−0.5	0.123	0.569
3	0.169	0.800	0.542	1	1	0.95	5	0.420	0	0.194	0.485

Fig. 6. Numerical examples of informative equilibrium 2

tures on intervening. Those types between $c1$ and $c2$ send message $m2$. If the message $m2$ fails to deter F, then R intervenes. R intervenes because failure to do so convinces the voters that R is incompetent.

The least competent leaders do not commit themselves. Although they could deter F by sending message $m2$, the political cost of having their bluff called is too great. These types send message $m1$ and do not intervene. Incompetent leaders avoid making commitments they cannot honor. Why do the highest types, $c \geq c2$, also avoid commitment? These types intervene even without the political commitment of the message $m2$. Why? If these high types send message $m2$, they may deter F. However, highly competent governments want the opportunity to intervene because they can demonstrate their competence to the electorate. These types could credibly commit to deterring F, but they actually want a war. To encourage F to act, these high types mimic incompetent leaders by sending $m1$. Morrow (1994) and Smith (1998) characterize this form of behavior in alliance formation.

In the first informative equilibrium, F is never completely deterred. However, in this second informative equilibrium it is possible for the message $m2$ to completely deter F. This can happen if the beliefs of the voters are such that expected competence given $m1$ is higher than expected competence given $m2$. In this situation, all types $c < c2$ are indifferent between sending $m1$ and sending $m2$. The advantage of sending $m2$ is that it deters F. The advantage of sending $m1$ is that, although it does not completely deter F, the voters believe that R is extremely competent. This scenario is discussed in the appendix.

Before discussing the implications of these results, I want to comment generally on informative equilibria. I have considered only two examples of the many equilibria. However, these examples capture many of the general characteristics. First, types can never completely separate (Crawford and Sobel 1982). The most information that can ever be transmitted is that different groups of types send different messages. The messages associated with each group convey information about the distribution of types. In general, the more a message convinces E and F that R is a competent type, the harsher the political cost of failing to intervene should F act.

In equilibria, R's expected utility is a continuous, weakly increasing function of c. It strictly increases for those types that intervene because as their type increases they perform better. However, those types that do not intervene all receive the same expected utility because the voters cannot tell one type from another. All equilibria are bifurcating in this way. Whatever messages R sends, lower types do not intervene and higher types do intervene. In equilibrium, there is some type $c^{\ddagger}$ such that all types above $c^{\ddagger}$ are seen to intervene when F acts and all types below $c^{\ddagger}$ are seen to acquiesce when F acts. This property is formally characterized in the appendix.

General Implications

By way of conclusion, I want to address two issues: (1) the implications of the results for empirical investigations of the domestic/international relationship and (2) the theoretic benefits of endogenizing domestic audience costs. I start by summarizing the modeling strategy.

International interactions are modeled as deterrence situations: a foreign nation wants to exploit a domestic nation. However, the foreign nation prefers to do so when the domestic nation will not resist. Whether or not the domestic nation is prepared to resist, it prefers not to be attacked. Hence, the domestic nation has an incentive to discourage the foreign nation from attempting to exploit it in the first place. As demonstrated earlier, in deterrence situations cheap talk is ineffective. However, the introduction of domestic politics allows for the possibility of informative communication.

The international crisis model is supplemented with a model of domestic politics. I assume that political leaders have different characteristic that affect the foreign policies they choose and their ability to carry out these policies. I assume that voters care about these characteristics. Given this, the voters' beliefs about their leader will affect their voting decisions. Political leaders want to stay in office. Their actions and foreign policies reveal something about their characteristics to the voters. In order to stay in office, leaders choose actions that are likely to convince the voters that they are a type that should be reelected. These actions might not correspond to the best interests of the state. In this particular model, I assume that leaders differ in their ability to care about foreign policy. This particular assumption results in political leaders choosing hawkish foreign policies. Obviously, different assumptions about the characteristics of leaders lead to different results. Although alternative assumptions produce slightly different predictions, the key result is that domestic politics creates biases in the formation of foreign policy (see, e.g., Hess and Orphanides 1995; Downs and Rocke 1995; and Smith 1996a).

Leaders have an incentive to appear like a type that the voters will reelect. The desire to appear reelectable enables leaders to make credible commitments internationally. The voters believe that leaders who fail to honor their commitments are not the type of leader they wish to retain. Therefore, having made a commitment, leaders have a incentive to honor it.

Although this essay is theoretical in nature, it has implications for the empirical study of international relations. In particular, the modeling of strategic behavior alerts us to nonrandom selection problems that make statistical inference difficult. The basis behind most common statistical procedures is to assume that there is a process that generates events or data. Some of these events are randomly collected and called a sample. By examining the properties of this sample, we make statistical inferences about the process responsible for generating the data. Unfortunately, if the selection of events in the sample is not random then our statistical inferences about the data-generating process will be wrong (Achen 1986). As I shall outline with two specific cases, the strategic decision making of political leaders creates nonrandom selection problems.

The basic argument in this essay is that international outcomes affect domestic survival. As such, leaders choose those policies that help them survive. It is this second statement that makes the first so hard to study. Suppose, empirically, that we wish to estimate the impact of international outcomes on domestic survival. An obvious research design might be to look at the outcome of all international crises and see whether or not the leaders survived. Unfortunately, such a research design would not produce reliable results. As the model predicts, political leaders choose foreign policies that help them survive. Specifically, leaders choose foreign policies that are likely to result in outcomes that will help them get reelected. With respect to studying the role of outcomes on domestic survival, this implies that the set of international outcomes is selected, in part, on the basis of their domestic consequences. The value of the dependent variable, domestic survival, affects whether or not an event is selected in the sample. Selecting the sample on the basis of the dependent variable makes statistical inference unreliable.

As a second example of the statistical problems created by nonrandom selection, I examine how domestic conditions affect a leader's choice of foreign policy. Theoretically, we anticipate that different domestic conditions lead to different foreign policy choices. Specifically, the model predicts that hawkish policies are adopted when foreign policy evaluation will be important. To test this hypothesis, a sensible starting point is to examine all crises and observe how leaders responded as a function of their domestic circumstances. The model predicts that as elections approach leaders become more hawkish. Empirically, Gaubatz (1991) finds the contrary: democratic leaders are more likely to become involved in wars early in their terms. This would appear to falsify the hypothesis. Unfortunately, such an inference is invalid because of selection effects.

The deterrent nature of international relations means that as a nation becomes more likely to resist it is less likely to be challenged: the probability that the foreign nation attacks is inversely related to the probability that the domestic nation will intervene. If the hypothesis is correct, as an election approaches the domestic leader is more hawkish. If challenged, then she is likely to resist. However, precisely because she will resist, she is unlikely to be challenged. As discussed earlier, for any given crisis upcoming elections mean that the event is likely to end in either SQ or War; without an election, ACQ is more likely. This produces a selection effect. Prior to an election, foreign nations know that leaders have a domestic incentive to resist. Therefore, foreign nations only challenge when they anticipate victory. Thus, the sets of crises that occur early and late in the electoral term are different. It is impossible to make statistical inferences about the hawkishness of policies unless we control for the strategic behavior of other states.

Stoll's (1984) investigation of the electoral cycle and the use of force produces results that are consistent with this selection effect. The theory suggests that as U.S. elections approach the president's visible use of force should increase. The sampling argument suggests that nations avoid challenging the United States at this time. Stoll finds that, empirically, whether the use of force increases depends upon whether the United States is at war. When the United States is involved in a war, upcoming elections increase the use of force; this is consistent with the hawkish behavior predicted. Since a foreign nation is already involved in a fight, we have the opportunity to observe the president's hawkish behavior. However, during peacetime, upcoming elections are associated with a reduction in the use of force. There are two interpretations of this result: either the hypothesis is wrong or foreign nations are choosing not to challenge the United States during these hawkish periods. Unfortunately, without further testing it is impossible to determine which explanation is correct.

The model implies that it is difficult to empirically study the relationships between international and domestic politics. However, deductive modeling sharpens our focus with regard to empirical testing. Models, by capturing strategic behavior, alert us to nonrandom sample selection. Although modeling cannot provide all the answers, a theoretical understanding of how data are generated allows us to recognize problems with statistical inference and allows us to interpret our results correctly.

A major theoretical contribution of this model is to endogenize domestic audience costs. Fearon's (1994) crisis bargaining model assumes the existence of these costs. This essay provides a microfoundation for the use of such costs. On the whole, the predictions between this model and Fearon's are closely related. However, there are additional benefits from modeling domestic audience costs rather than assuming them. The explicit domestic model allows the credibility of commitments and the probability that leaders will make commitments to be related to domestic political conditions. These comparative statics generate additional empirically falsifiable hypotheses, which can be used to test the validity of the model. For example, the model shows that domestic audience costs only exist when the electorate's evaluation of a leader's foreign policy skill will be important in the next election. Thus, lame duck, second-term U.S. presidents are less able to communicate effectively with foreign adversaries. They also behave less aggressively and hence are exploited more often. In contrast, first-term U.S. presidents facing a close election are hawkish. Leaders in this position have the ability to deter adversaries with simple cheap talk statements. However, although they have the ability to use these credible threats, they should do so with care. If their bluff is called and they fail to respond, then they are likely to suffer electorally.

In general, the model predicts that leaders that take aggressive policy stances will be the most popular. However, leaders who adopt these hawkish policies but fail to follow through are the least popular. Despite these general trends, the specific implications of a foreign policy message depend upon the domestic context in which it was sent. Thus, the domestic implications, the international implications, and the probability that the message is sent all depend upon the domestic incentive to send it.

This essay models the interaction between international and domestic politics. International outcomes affect the survival of domestic political leaders. In turn, domestic circumstances affect the foreign policies that leaders pursue and the credibility of these policies. There is an endogeneity between domestic politics and international events. This essay is a first attempt to unravel these relationships.

APPENDIX

The examples in the main test utilized several equilibrium characteristics. This appendix formally characterizes these properties.

PROPERTY 1. *In equilibrium, R's expected utility is a continuous, weakly increasing, monotone in R's international competence, c_R.*

Proof. I start by showing that $E[U_R(c)]$ is weakly increasing in c.

Consider the payoff that some type, c, receives if it sends the equilibrium message $m(c)$:

$$E\{U_R[c,m(c)]\} = \alpha[m(c)]\zeta[c,m(c)]$$

$$+ \{1 - \alpha[m(c)]\} - \{1 + \Psi P(E[c \mid m(c)]\},$$

where $\zeta[c, mc(c)] = \text{MAX}\{q(c) - \text{cost} + \Psi P(c), \Psi P(E[c \mid$

$m(c), \text{ACQ}])\}$.

Now consider type $c' > c$. Whatever strategy c' pursues, it must at least as good as mimicking c; $E\{U_R[c',m(c')]\} \geq E\{U_R(c,m(c)]\}$. This is because $q(c)$ is increasing in c and $P(c)$ is weakly increasing in c. Thus, $\zeta[c,m(c)]$ is weakly increasing in c. Therefore, high types get weakly better payoffs than low types do.

Next, I show that $E\{U_R[c,m(c)]\}$ is a continuous function in c. Consider the types c and c', where $c' = c + \varepsilon$.

In equilibrium, $E\{U_R[c',m(c')]\} \geq E\{U_R[c',m(c)]\}$ and $E\{U_R[c,m(c)]\} \geq E\{U_R[c,m(c')]\}$. As $\varepsilon \to 0$, then $\zeta[c,m(c)] \to \zeta[c'[m(c)]$ and $\zeta[c',m(c)] \to \zeta[c',m(c')]$. Therefore, as $\varepsilon \to 0$, $E\{U_R[c,m(c)]\} \to E\{U_R[c',m(c')]\}$. Therefore, $E\{U_R[c,m(c)]\}$ is continuous.   QED

PROPERTY 2. *Observationally, if a type* c' *does not intervene given its equilibrium message then all types less than* c' *do not intervene whatever their equilibrium message: if* $s_R[c',m(c')] = 0$, *then for all* $c < c'$ *if* $am(c)] > 0$ *then* $s_R[c,m(c)] = 0$, *where* $m(c)$ *is a message that type* c *sends in equilibrium.*

Remark. Formally, property 2 does not ensure that all types $c < c'$ do not intervene if F acts. However, if F acts in equilibrium, then this property holds. Only in cases of complete deterrence can $c < c'$ intervene. However, since F never acts in these cases, this behavior is unobservable. Complete deterrence is discussed in property 3 and in the discussion following informative equilibrium 2.

Proof. Consider the type c', which does not intervene given its equilibrium message, $m(c')$: $s_R[c',m(c')] = 0$. This implies that $q(c') - \text{cost} + \Psi P(c') \leq \Psi P\{E[c \mid m(c'),\text{ACQ}]\}$. Now consider another type, $c'' < c'$, which sends the equilibrium $m(c'')$ with positive probability. Suppose that F's best response given the message $m(c'')$ is to sometimes act: $\alpha[m(c'')] > 0$. If type c'' mimics type c' then $E\{U_R[c',m(c')]\} = E\{U_R[c'',m(c')]\}$.

Having sent its equilibrium message $m(c'')$, suppose that type c'' intervenes if F acts. The expected payoff of c'' is

$$E\{U_R[c'',m(c'')]\} = \alpha[m(c'')][q(c'') - \text{cost} + \Psi P(c'')]$$

$$+ \{1 - \alpha[m(c'')]\}(1 + \Psi P\{E[c \mid m(c'')]\}).$$

Since type c'' can obtain the same payoff as c' obtains by mimicking c' and since expected payoffs are increasing in type, $E\{U_R[c'',m(c'')]\} =$

$E\{U_R[c',m(c')]\}$. However, $\zeta[c,m(c'')]$ is strictly increasing in type. Therefore, if $\alpha[m(c'')] > 0$, then $E\{U_R[c',m(c'')]\} > E\{U_R[c'',m(c'')]\}$. This implies that c' would prefer to send message $m(c'')$ rather than $m(c')$, which is a contradiction. Therefore, for all types $c < c'$, either $S_R[c,m(c)] = 0$ or $\alpha[m(c)] = 0$. QED

PROPERTY 3. *If there exists a message* m' *that completely deters F,* $\alpha(m') = 0$, *then either the message is uninformative,* $\sigma_R(m',c) = \sigma_R(m',c')$ *for all c and c', or there is an alternative message* m'' *that does not completely deter F such that the voters believe that R's expected competence is higher given the message* m'' *than the message* m' *(there exists* m'' *such that* $\alpha[m''] > 0$ *and* $E[c \mid m''] > E[c \mid m']$).

Proof. Suppose that there exists some message m' such that $\alpha(m') = 0$. First, I show that if all alternative messages also deter F then the message must be uninformative. Second, I show that if m' is informative then there exists an alternative message m'' that does not complete deter F such that $E[c \mid m''] > E[c \mid m']$. In addition, I indicate the form of this equilibrium.

Suppose that the equilibrium message m' completely deters F: $\alpha(m') = 0$. Suppose that there exists an alternative message that also completely deters F, but $E[c \mid m''] > E[c \mid m']$. Since F is completely deterred by both messages, $E[U_R(c,m'')] = 1 + \Psi P(E[c \mid m'']) > E[U_R(c,m')] = 1 + \Psi P(E[c \mid m'])$. Therefore, all types prefer to send message m''. This contradicts message m' being sent in equilibrium. If there are multiple message sent in equilibrium and all these messages completely deter F, then $E[c \mid m'] = E[c \mid m'']$. Therefore, if F is completely deterred by a set of messages, then E and F's beliefs are identical for all of these messages: these messages are uninformative.

I now consider informative messages. Suppose that $\alpha(m') = 0$ but $\alpha(m'') > 0$. First suppose that if m'' is sent then no types intervene. Under these circumstances, $\alpha(m') = 0$ implies that $\alpha(m'') = 0$. Therefore, some types must intervene, having sent m'.

Second, suppose that m'' is sent and some types intervene.

$$E[U_R(m'',D \mid c)] = \alpha(m'')[q(c) - \text{cost} + \Psi P(c)]$$

$$+ [1 - \alpha(m'')]\{1 + \Psi P[E(c \mid m'')]\}.$$

The first term of this expression is increasing in c. Since $E[U_R(c)]$ is a continuous weakly increasing function of c and both m' and m'' are sent, there exists at least one type $c^\ddagger$ such that $E[U_R(c^\ddagger,m')] = E[U_R(c^\ddagger,m'')]$. Choose one of these $c^\ddagger$s. Call this type $c^\ddagger 1$. Suppose that this $c^\ddagger 1$ sends m'' and intervenes. For all $c > c^\ddagger 1$, $E[U_R(c,m'')] > E[U_R(c,m')]$, and, for all $c < c^\ddagger 1$, $E[U_R(c,m'')] > E[U_R(c,m')]$. However, this implies that $\gamma(m'') \geq \gamma(m')$ and $E[c \mid m''] > E[c \mid$

m'], which contradicts $\alpha(m') = 0$ and $\alpha(m'') > 0$. Therefore, there must exist another $c^{\ddagger}$, call this type $c^{\ddagger}2$, such that type $c^{\ddagger}2$ does not intervene having sent message m''. For type $c^{\ddagger}2$, $E[U_R(c^{\ddagger},m')] = 1 + \Psi P(E[c \mid m']) = E[U_R(c^{\ddagger},m'')]$ $= \alpha(m'')\{\Psi P[E(c \mid m'',\text{ACQ})]\} + [1 - \alpha(m'')]\{1 + \Psi P[E(c \mid m'')]\}$. Suppose that $E[c \mid m''] \leq E[c \mid m']$. Since $\zeta[c,m(c)]$ is increasing in c, $E[c \mid m''] > E[c \mid m'',\text{ACQ}]$. This contradicts $c^{\ddagger}2$ being indifferent between m' and m''.

Therefore, if there is an informative message, m', that completely deters F, then there is an alternative message, m'', such that $E[c \mid m''] > E[c \mid m']$. In particular, there exist at least two regions of types that send message m''. Some high types, which will intervene, must send m'' to ensure that $E[c \mid m''] > E[c \mid m']$. In addition, some lower types, which will not intervene, must send m'' to ensure that F is not completely deterred: $\alpha(m'') > 0$. This type of situation is represented in informative equilibrium 2. However, I have been unable to find any numerical examples that satisfy these conditions.   QED

NOTES

1. A more realistic way that nations might say m_1 is by forming an alliance.

2. Bueno de Mesquita et al. are explicitly aware of this endogeniety problem.

3. For simplicity, I assume that R's competence, c_R, is completely revealed during a war. This is not a critical assumption. R's type could be revealed probabilistically.

4. In the period before the election, E receives a payoff associated with R's actual handling of a situation. After the election, E does not know what situations the nation will face. However, whatever the circumstances, E prefers to have a competent leader. c_R reflects E's expected payoff from international events following the election.

5. If there is no type that is indifferent, then set $c^{\ddagger}(m)$ to either 0 or 1. If no type wants to intervene, then $c^{\ddagger}(m) = 1$. If all types want to intervene, then $c^{\ddagger}(m) = 0$.

6. In probit analysis, the marginal impact of independent variables is greatest when the probability of an event is 1/2. The intuition behind this result is identical.

7. The expected competence of R given message $m1$ and outcome ACQ is not defined by Bayes's rule. Given the equilibrium strategy, this outcome never occurs; therefore, Bayes rule is undefined. I follow standard equilibrium refinements and place all the probability weight on the type with the greatest incentive to defect. In this particular case, the type with the least incentive to intervene is $c = 0$. Therefore, $E[c \mid m1,\text{ACQ}]$ $= 0$. See Banks 1991 14–17, for a discussion of equilibrium refinements.

REFERENCES

Achen, Christopher H. 1986. *The Statistical Analysis of Quasi-Experiments*. Berkeley: University of California Press.
Achen, Christopher H., and Duncan Snidal. 1990. Rational Deterrence Theory and Comparative Case Studies. *World Politics* 41:143–70.

Banks, Jeffrey S. 1991. *Signaling Games in Political Science.* New York: Harwood Academic.

Bueno de Mesquita, Bruce, and David Lalman. 1992. *War and Reason.* New Haven, CT: Yale University Press.

Bueno de Mesquita, Bruce, and Randolph M. Siverson. 1995. War and the Survival of Political Leaders: A Comparative Analysis of Regime Type and Accountability. *American Political Science Review* 89:841–55.

Bueno de Mesquita, Bruce, Randolph M. Siverson, and Gary Woller. 1992. War and the Fate of Regimes: A Comparative Analysis. *American Political Science Review* 86, no. 3: 638–46.

Crawford, Vincent, and Joel Sobel. 1982. Strategic Information Transmission. *Econometrica* 50:1431–51.

Downs, Anthony. 1957. *An Economic Theory of Democracy.* New York: Harper and Row.

Downs, George W., and David M. Rocke. 1995. *Optimal Imperfection?* Princeton: Princeton University Press.

Fearon, James D. 1994. Domestic Political Audiences and the Escalation of International Disputes. *American Political Science Review* 88:577–92.

Gaubatz, Kurt Taylor. 1991. Election Cycles and War. *Journal of Conflict Resolution* 35:211–44.

Harsanyi, John. 1967–8. Games with Incomplete Information Played by Bayesian Players. *Management Science* 14:159–82, 320–34, 486–502.

Hess, Gregory D., and Athanasios Orphanides. 1995. War Politics: An Economic, Rational-Voter Framework. *American Economic Review* 85:828–46.

Hurwitz, John, and Mark Peffley. 1987. The Means and Ends of Foreign Policy as Determinants of Presidential Support. *American Journal of Political Science* 31:236–58.

Huth, Paul K., and Bruce Russett. 1990. Testing Deterrence Theory: Rigor Makes a Difference. *World Politics* 41:466–501.

James, Patrick, and John R. Oneal. 1991. The Influence of Domestic and International Politics on the President's Use of Force. *Journal of Conflict Resolution* 35:307–32.

Jervis, Robert. 1990. Rational Deterrence: Theory and Evidence. *World Politics* 41:183–207.

Langlois, Jean-Pierre P. 1991. Rational Deterrence and Crisis Stability. *American Journal of Political Science* 35:801–32.

Levy, Jack S. 1989. The Diversionary Theory of War: A Critique. In *Handbook of War Studies,* edited by Manus I. Midlarsky. Ann Arbor: University of Michigan Press.

Morrow, James D. 1994. Alliances, Credibility, and Peacetime Costs. *Journal of Conflict Resolution* 38:270–97.

Mueller, John D. 1973. *War, Presidents, and Public Opinion.* New York: Wiley.

Nalebuff, Barry. 1991. Rational Deterrence in an Imperfect World. *World Politics* 43:313–35.

Nincic, Miroslav, and Barbara Hinckley. 1991. Foreign Policy and Evaluation of Presidential Candidates. *Journal of Conflict Resolution* 35:333–55.

Ostrom, Charles W., Jr., and Brian L. Job. 1986. The President and the Political Use of Force. *American Political Science Review* 80:541–66.

Page, Benjamin I., and Robert Y. Shapiro. 1983. The Effects of Public Opinion on Policy. *American Political Science Review* 77:175–90.

Smith, Alastair. 1996a. Diversionary Foreign Policy in Democratic Systems. *International Studies Quarterly* 40:133–53.

Smith, Alastair. 1996b. Rational Choice Rallys around the Flag. Washington University. Manuscript.

Smith, Alastair. 1998. Deterring Enemies and Reassuring Friends: Extended Deterrence and Alliance Formation. *International Interactions* (Forthcoming).

Snyder, J. 1987. *Myths of Empire: Domestic Structure and Strategic Ideology.* Columbia University. Mimeo.

Stoll, Richard J. 1984. The Guns of November. *Journal of Conflict Resolution* 28:231–46.

Zagare, Frank C. 1990. Rationality and Deterrence. *World Politics* 41:238–59.

War and the Survival of Political Leaders: A Comparative Study of Regime Types and Political Accountability

Bruce Bueno de Mesquita and Randolph M. Siverson

On April 6, 1982, six days after the Argentine invasion of the Falkland Islands, the *New York Times* correspondent in Buenos Aires gave this evaluation of the position of Argentine president Leopoldo Galtieri: "Political leaders here . . . agree he has greatly enhanced his political power and stature" by invading the Falkland Islands. At the same time Galtieri's political fortunes were in ascent, British prime minister Margaret Thatcher was being attacked by the British press for what was perceived as a tardy reaction to the situation. In those few days, her political fortunes fell almost as much as those of Galtieri had risen. However, less than four months after Galtieri's stature had been ascendant he was out of office, while slightly more than a year after successfully repelling the Argentine forces, Thatcher and her party were returned to parliamentary power by a large majority.[1]

Of course, the Falklands War was not a major conflict on the scale of, say, World War II or the Crimean War, and its value as a case from which we may generalize about the effects of war is limited. Nonetheless, it does serve as a striking example of the relationship investigated here—the effects of war on the tenure of political leaders and their regimes among nations involved in war.

We first discuss the relationship between war performance and the subsequent fate of national political leaders. We then offer a model and seven related hypotheses accounting for what happens to leaders because of their war policies and describe our data and research design before reporting the results of our tests of four of the hypotheses. Because of presently existing data limitations, tests of three of the hypotheses must be postponed.

The research presented here represents an extension of our previous work on the political consequences of war in which we examined the effects of a state's initial position in a war (i.e., initiator or target), its outcome, and the costs of the war on the probability of the nonconstitutional overthrow of the state's political regime (Bueno de Mesquita, Siverson, and Woller 1992). Although the research reported here shares a broad set of interests in linkage politics with the earlier work (Rosenau 1969), it differs significantly in that the model is both more rigorous and more extensively specified than that used in the previous work. Moreover, because our present focus is on the survival *time* of the individual political leaders who were responsible for government policy at the point the state entered the war, our empirical tests are both more sensitive than those in the previous article and speak more clearly to neorealist explanations of international politics and war. As we shall show, our results obtain even when we control for the dependent variable in the previous study, nonconstitutional regime overthrow. Consequently, the results here capture the strong additional effects on leadership survival that follow from our model, above and beyond the effects shown in our earlier analysis.[2]

War Performance and the Fate of Leaders

Norpoth has observed that "War and economics have few rivals when it comes to making or breaking governments" (1987, 949). Our attention is directed at the "war" part of this assertion. Although many probably agree with the idea, the evidentiary base on which this assertion rests is fairly narrow in terms of the range of time periods and governmental types studied and also, in some respects, ambiguous.[3] Data for the United States and the United Kingdom indicate that international crises and war can have an effect on the public's evaluation of political leaders. In the context of the United States, various studies (but most notably Brody 1992; Brody and Page 1975; Kernell 1978; and Mueller 1973) have attempted to connect variations in presidential popularity to foreign policy events and participation in international crises. Although Mueller and Kernell portray presidents as generally benefiting from the short-run "rally" effects of foreign policy events, Brody's analysis draws out a more complex process in which a president may or may not enjoy a gain in popularity, depending upon a variety of factors, the most notable being the articulation of criticism by opinion leaders from either the media or the political opposition. However, there is little direct evidence bearing on the effect of war itself, although it is obviously worth pointing out that neither Truman nor Johnson was willing to hazard a try at reelection while engaged in wars that had divided the American public.

More broadly, with respect to the United Kingdom, Norpoth, using time-series methods, examined the impact of economic performance and the course of the Falklands War on the citizen ratings of Thatcher and the Conservative Party between June 1979 and July 1985. He concluded that the independent effect of the Falklands victory was worth between five and six additional percentage points to the vote for the Conservatives in the 1983 general election victory.[4]

All of these results are intriguing, but their domain is limited to the United States and Great Britain in the second half of the twentieth century. Absent is any broadly based theory or research on the general question of the effects of war involvement and outcome on the political fortunes of the leaders who were responsible for them, even when those leaders presided over nondemocratic governments. This lacuna represents a major gap in our understanding of political accountability and the implications of such accountability for the selection of foreign policies.

Are political leaders and their regimes at greater hazard if they involve their nations in war than if they do not? Are their political fortunes affected by the outcome of these wars? Does the effect, if any, fall equally across different types of political systems? Is the anticipation of domestic political punishment for failed policies an important element in shaping how nations relate to each other or, as suggested by neorealists, are these domestic factors minor features in the arena of international politics?

We contend that there are strong reasons to believe that a close connection exists between war and the domestic fate of governments and that the consequences of that connection can be and are anticipated by political leaders. Defeat in war almost always alters the loser's freedom of action in some measure, reducing the nation's autonomy over its own foreign policy or depriving the vanquished state of sovereignty over some portion of its citizens, territory, or national product (Morrow 1987). Compared with the often ambiguous outcomes of international conflicts and crises (see, e.g., Kernell 1978; Mueller 1973; and Brody 1992), or even economic policy, evidence of loss from a war is much clearer to populations. Moreover, in nations without functional electoral systems, such evidence is far clearer to members of the elite, who themselves may have both the opportunity and motive for replacing leaders.

How can we assess the effects of war involvement and outcome on political leaders? One straightforward factor that would seem to be intimately tied to the welfare of any national leader is whether, given war participation, that leader's tenure in office is shortened or lengthened as a consequence of the state's performance in the war. Continuation in office may reasonably be seen as a reward, while removal from office (as opposed to natural death) in one way or another may be seen as punishment. We propose that leaders care about maintaining themselves in power—that they seek to maximize their reselection and, through the opportunities offered by continuing in power, to promote their own policy objectives. To achieve their objectives, they must anticipate the effects their policies will have on the politically relevant domestic audience (Fearon 1994). Consequently, we expect that they will ex ante try to avoid policies that they believe will ex post foreshorten their hold over the perquisites of political leadership.

The Problem of Political Survival

We begin with several assumptions. First, all politics is competitive. The issues over which—like the rules in which—the competition takes place differ across political units, and both the issues and the rules are subject to change. This portrait of politics is, of course, not remarkable.

Second, we assume that political leaders are intent on maintaining themselves in power and use the available tools of power and rules to accomplish this end. In like manner, we assume that all political leaders have opponents, most of whom are members of the leader's own political system, with their own ambitions for office. At the same time, leaders will often pursue policies that place them in opposition to those outside their own political systems. Broadly speaking (and leaving natural causes aside), leaders are subject to removal by their internal and external opposition or quite possibly some combination of the two. To be sure, we cannot dismiss instances in which a leader is removed by his or her "friends," who fear the costs to themselves of the leader remaining in power, but in this case, the friends have become opponents. Finally, given the opportunity, each opponent will be willing to pay a certain price to remove a leader.

Leaders, of course, recognize the existence of opposition and the designs of others on the offices they hold. They consequently select policies intended to minimize the opportunities available to those seeking to remove them from power.

The ambition to remain in power, then, encourages political leaders to behave more responsibly than if they viewed the holding of office as a burden rather than a prize (Bueno de Mesquita and Organski, forthcoming; Fearon 1994; Morgan and Bickers 1992). Enhancing the welfare of relevant constituents (to the extent that it is successful) removes from the opposition the most salient issues that can be used against a leader.

Several studies have tried to express a generic theory of the domestic politics relevant to foreign policy decision making (G. Allison 1971; Bueno de Mesquita, Newman, and Rabushka 1985; Bueno de Mesquita and Stokman 1994; Putnam 1988; Richards et al. 1993; Tsebelis 1990). We share with several of these approaches an interest in building on Black's (1958) median voter theorem and incorporating the notion that leaders want to be reselected. We also share the notion that voting is just a special case of the articulation of power or political influence and control, so that Black's theorem, suitably adapted, is relevant to policy formation in authoritarian as well as democratic regimes (Bueno de Mesquita, Newman, and Rabushka 1985; Bueno de Mesquita and Stokman 1994). It is just that in authoritarian regimes the median voter or pivotal power is drawn from a much smaller set of constituents than is true in democracies. In authoritarian regimes, then, as in democratic governments, the clique of leaders who can count on support from a majority of the relevant resources—whether they be guns, dollars, or votes—can expect to win office and retain it. With this in mind, we suggest the following model of governmental accountability for decisions about war.

Suppose that each nation consists of a set of stakeholders interested in influencing foreign policy decisions. In a democracy, this set may include everyone or nearly everyone in the society. In more authoritarian regimes, the set probably includes a more limited array of organized or unorganized interests. The military, politically active religious groups, business interests, government bureaucrats, and the population at large are a small sampling of such possible stakeholders. Each of these various groups engages in strategic maneuvers to promote its particular foreign policy agenda at the expense of alternative approaches to international politics.

At the end of the process of bargaining and possible logrolling, competing and allied internal interests come to a decision. We assume that the decision is equivalent to the policy stance of the median "voter," in other words, the policy preference of the median power holder at the end of the bargaining process. Of course, since voting per se often does not take place or is not meaningful (especially in authoritarian societies) this median position is that policy supported by the individual or group that can count on the ability to mobilize more than half of the sum of all stakeholders' utilized power on behalf of its agenda against any possible challenge. The median stakeholder is the pivot around whom a winning coalition forms.

For the purposes of the present analysis, we do not elaborate a complete theory of domestic political decision making and its relationship to foreign policy. Instead, we describe a simplified model of implications that follow from such theories of domestic interest group competition. By keeping the model simple, we naturally raise the prospects of having fairly robust results, and we focus on broad generalizations, as opposed to detailed nuances, about the role of foreign policy in the retention of the leader in power. Additionally, because our model is rather general it cannot rule out some alternative explanations of the phenomena we discuss. That said, it is important to consider these caveats in the context of a model that is an integrated whole and generates a number of significant, testable hypotheses.

In describing these implications, we begin by assuming that preferences across policy issues are single peaked. This means that for each stakeholder the utility for any given resolution of an issue declines monotonically with the Euclidean distance from that decision maker's most preferred choice (i.e., the stakeholder's ideal point). We further assume that all utility functions are quadratic, reflecting the notion of declining marginal utility. This latter assumption is for ease of computation and does not materially affect our results.

Although many problems in international affairs and foreign policy are

quite complex, involving the possibility of trade-offs and linkages across policy issues, we assume that this is not true of the most fundamental questions.
For problems that involve the risk of war, we assume that issues collapse to a
single policy dimension having to do with the overall contribution of the puta-
tive policy to the welfare of the leadership's backers and opponents. This is
broadly consistent with the realist notion that treats the state as a unitary actor.

Our view, however, differs from the realist approach in that the selection of
policy options and the accompanying demands and actions taken in the international arena are not dictated by external, structural considerations. Rather, the
choice of goals and actions is given shape by the domestic agenda of the leadership as well as by the feasibility constraints of the external environment. Prudent
leaders make choices that they think will help them retain power: they choose in
such a way that they do not precipitate an internal overthrow of their authority.
Consequently, their foreign policy goals may be seen as endogenous to their domestic political concerns rather than just to the international system's structure.

Because we have assumed single-peaked preferences and unidimensional
issues on questions related to the threats of warfare, and because we propose
that the coalition controlling a majority of political influence within a nation is
expected to get its way, Black's (1958) median voter theorem can be applied.
This means that the policy objective of the interested party located at the median of the distribution of power on the policy in question is the objective expected to prevail internally. The median power occupies the position that can,
in head-to-head competition with any other proposed policy, muster a majority
coalition. As such, it is the policy stance that maximizes internal political security, the position least susceptible to internal defeat.

With the median voter theorem in mind, we assume that on questions that
involve the risk of war all nations can be summarized by examining the characteristics of three critical stakeholders:

1. The stakeholders or interested parties, denoted as V, who control the median power position
2. The incumbent leader, called I
3. A challenger, called C, who wishes to gain control over the government's foreign policy.

So, with the state denoted as S we can say $\{V, I, C\} \in S$. V, of course, is itself
an element in the preference distribution of all the stakeholders or interested
parties in S. We assume further that policy objectives over which war is waged
fall along a single policy continuum, denoted as R, with $\{X_C^*, X_C, X_V^*, X_I, X_I^*\}$
$\in R$ (Terms with a superscript asterisk are ideal points and belong to the actor
named by the subscript. Terms without superscripts are the publicly taken policy positions of the subscripted actor.) The term X_C^* represents the ideal point,

or most preferred foreign policy, of the challenger for power, and X_C expresses the actual policy position openly supported by the challenger in its attempt to woo median stakeholder V away from supporting I. The other terms have analogous interpretations.

Incumbents can have an advantage over challengers in our model because they can earn political credit for their past performances or demonstrations of reliability if they pursue foreign policies that satisfy V. This means that V can gain utility from the past performance of the incumbent, which is broadly consistent with the idea of retrospective voting (Fiorina 1981). Incumbents with bad records are more likely to be turned out; incumbents with good records from V's perspective have an edge in the ongoing campaign to remain in power. But incumbents also have a disadvantage because V bears the costs associated with the foreign policies pursued by the incumbent and V is not reluctant to pass judgment on I in response to these costs. I can accumulate negative credits as well as positive ones. Costs occur as a result of actions in wartime, whether the war ultimately proves to be successful or not, and potentially arise as a consequence of policies by I that alienate V.

Let R denote the accumulated costs or benefits associated with the past performance of political leaders. We assume that the more constituents who have to be satisfied by a political leader, the smaller R is—and, indeed, as the number of constituents rises, so does the likelihood that $R < 0$. This is consistent with the notion of the coalition of minorities effect identified by Mueller (1973). The longer a leader has been in power, the greater the opportunity the leader has to alienate part of his or her coalition of supporters, gradually eroding the chances of holding onto support from the median voter (Powell and Whitten 1993; Rose and Mackie 1983). In authoritarian regimes, where fewer constituencies have to be satisfied, leaders are better able to fulfill the wants of their crucial backers. Consequently, $R > 0$ is probably true for authoritarian leaders, while $R < 0$ is more likely to be true for leaders in democratic states. In any event, whether positive or negative, it is likely that R for democratic leaders is smaller than R for authoritarian leaders. R_t is the benefits or costs from the leader's performance on the job at a specific time in the past (denoted by the index t) with $t = 0$ being the present.

If a current wartime policy is implemented and succeeds (i.e., the nation in question wins the war), we assume that the reliability benefits R are increased by $R_0 > 0$, but if the policy fails then $R_0 \leq 0$. R_0 is, then, one of the critical elements at stake for an incumbent engaged in a war. R_t decays over time so that recent demonstrations of reliability are more valuable to V (and, therefore, to I) than are demonstrations in the more remote past. Similarly, recent policy failures are more costly than old ones that have been survived. We denote this decay effect by discounting earlier demonstrations of competence or incompetence by d_t, with $0 < d < 1$, so that

$$R = R_0 + \sum_{t=n}^{1} d^t R_t.$$

The benefits of competence ($R > 0$) or the costs of incompetence ($R < 0$) are realized by I only as long as he or she remains in power. Consequently, when an incumbent is replaced, R returns to zero for the former incumbent. Since the challenger has not yet had an opportunity to demonstrate competence or incompetence, V expects $R = 0$ when the challenger first comes to power.

Incumbents, of course, serve only for a finite (though usually indeterminate) time. We denote this by specifying that R accumulates over the interval from the time when the leader first comes to power, $t = n$, to the present moment, $t = 0$. The leader's tenure in office, then, at the time a war starts, is the interval from $t = n$ to $t = 0$ (i.e., the moment the war starts). Assuming that R_t is a constant that decays in value at the rate d^t, then R is a logarithmic function of tenure in office that reflects the marginally declining impact of past successes or failures on the current evaluation of I's job performance.

In addition to the costs or benefits associated with the leader's overall performance, we assume that there are direct transaction costs associated specifically with waging war. Let L denote the transaction costs or losses borne by the society (i.e., summarized by V) as a result of the implementation of wartime actions by I. These costs represent a burden of war that leaders must overcome if they are to be kept in office.

The fundamental dynamic in our conceptualization of domestic politics revolves around the expectation that incumbents wish to retain power and challengers wish to replace incumbents. This means that actor I wishes to remain more appealing to V than is C. However, I and C not only want power, but they also have policy objectives of their own. That is why we have defined their ideal points as well as their public stances on the policy questions of the day. Thus, our candidates for leadership may be pulled in two directions: to do what V wants and to do what they themselves want on foreign policy questions. They are not merely motivated by a desire for power and may be quite principled in terms of their policy interests. But, when torn between personal preferences and constituent expectations, the successful political leader is likely to be someone who recognizes that politics is the art of the possible.

The political costs and benefits of alternative choices that are reflected by these assumptions are summarized as a set of utility values. Table 1 displays the utilities for I, C, and V under the four scenarios of interest to us:

1. I is expected to win the war it wages and I is retained in power.
2. I is expected to win but is removed from power anyway, being replaced by C.
3. I is expected to lose the war and is retained nevertheless.
4. I is expected to lose and is replaced.

TABLE 1.   Utilities

	Incumbent	Challenger	Median "Voter"
Wins and is retained	$-(X_I - X_I^*)^2 + R$	$-(X_C^* - X_I)^2$	$-(X_V^* - X_I)^2 + R - L$
Wins and is replaced	$-(X_C - X_I^*)^2$	$-(X_C^* - X_C)^2$	$-(X_V^* - X_C)^2$
Loses and is retained	$-(X_I - X_I^*)^2$	$-(X_C^* - X_I)^2$	$-(X_V^* - X_I)^2 + \sum_{t=n}^{1} d^t R_t - L$
Loses and is replaced	$-(X_C - X_I^*)^2$	$-(X_C^* - X_C)^2$	$-(X_V^* - X_C)^2$

The incumbent, I, can be sure of retaining power only as long as V believes it is better off with I than with C. I remains the incumbent if V's utility for retaining I is greater than V's utility for replacing I with C. With P defined as V's subjective probability estimate that I will win the war in which it is involved, V will retain I in power if

$$P[-(X_V^* - X_I)^2 + R - L] + (1 - P)[-(X_V^* - X_I)^2$$

$$+ \sum_{t=n}^{1} d^t R_t - L] > -(X_V^* - X_C).^2 \tag{1}$$

Several inferences can be drawn from expression 1. Solving for PR_0, which reflects the expected political takes for both I and V from the war, we see that retention in office requires that

$$PR_0 > (X_I + X_C - 2X_V^*)(X_I - X_C) - \sum_{t=n}^{1} d^t R_t + L. \tag{2}$$

The incumbent has control over several factors in expression 2. These include selecting events for which the probability of success is believed to be high and picking policies that are not so objectionable to V that the policies become an encumbrance to I's retention of power. I naturally tries to pick X_I to ensure that the inequality in expression 2 is satisfied, while C, of course, picks its policy position to try to thwart I. Yet C and I are also constrained in selecting a policy because neither I nor C will wander so far from their respective ideal points that gaining or holding power is a pyrrhic victory.

It is evident from expression 2 that C has little incentive to locate itself at the same policy position as I. Being Tweedledum to I's Tweedledee (Downs 1957) simply means that I will be retained if

$$PR_0 > L - \sum_{t=n}^{1} d^t R_t. \tag{3}$$

It is evident from expression 3 that if $R > 0$, then, barring costs expected to be large enough to offset all of I's reliability credits, C has no chance of removing I no matter how poor I's chances of bringing the country to a victorious outcome in the war. Even if $P = 0$ (i.e., defeat is expected to be a sure thing), the expected costs must outweigh the credit for past performance accumulated by V in order for C to be chosen over I. Of course, if R_t is negative, C has an easier time removing I. Even in that case, however, rather than be Tweedledum, C's best hope of gaining power is to support a position sufficiently close to X_V^*. Even in the worst case for I, when C adopts X_V^*, I can retain power provided that

$$PR_0 + \sum_{t=n}^{1} d^t R_t - L > (X_I - X_V^*)^2. \tag{4}$$

Clearly, we see in expression 4 that I is constrained to stay relatively close to V's ideal point if C adopts that position. I can drift away only to the extent that its past reliability and the expected reliability gains from the present war are large enough to offset its policy difference *and* the expected transaction costs from the war. If its past performance has accumulated costs rather than benefits, then, of course, I will have a more difficult time holding on to power, having to rely exclusively on the benefits derived from the current war.

Is it possible for I to prefer that C gain power rather than choosing a policy stance, X_I, that is more distasteful to I than losing power to C? In order for I to prefer a government led by C over a government led by I, it must be true that

$$-(X_I - X_I^*)^2 + R < -(X_C - X_I^*)^2 \tag{5}$$

if I expects to win the war, or

$$-(X_I - X_I^*)^2 < -(X_C - X_I^*)^2 \tag{6}$$

if I expects to lose the war.

Expressions 5 and 6 suggest some consequential differences between democracies and authoritarian states, given our assumption that R for democracies is smaller than R for authoritarian states (including the prospect that $R < 0$ is more likely for democratic than for authoritarian leaders). Expression 5 implies that democratic leaders are more likely to leave office voluntarily than are authoritarian rulers. If $R > 0$, then it should be obvious that I would never pick X_I such that X_C is preferred by I to its own position. Consequently, I cannot prefer a government led by C to a government led by itself as long as $R > 0$ in our model, which presumably includes all authoritarian and some democratic leaders. Authoritarian leaders can be expected to seek to hold office for life, never stepping aside on principled grounds. Some democratic leaders can be expected to behave quite differently, even choosing to lose office rather than pursue objectionable policies.

I can, of course, choose a different policy position than *C*, but the choice will be in favor of a policy closer to *I*'s ideal point and never farther away. Then the range of policy choices that *I* can make is constrained. *C* will do best, in terms of maximizing its chances of being selected to replace *I*, by picking *V*'s ideal point as its own policy position (even though that is not *C*'s ideal point), as we have already mentioned. *I*, then, can drift away from the median stakeholder's policy preference up to the limit of the value of the reliability benefits that *I* generates for *V*, less whatever costs are associated with *I*'s war policy. If *I*'s accumulated *R* values are negative, then *I* cannot drift away from *V*'s ideal point, presuming that it is known to *I*. Avoiding war must thus be inherently better than waging war for *I* unless $R_0 > L$.[5]

It is evident, then, that X_I is endogenous, being chosen strategically (as is X_C) to facilitate *I*'s retention of power and to maximize *I*'s expected utility. X_C, naturally, is chosen by *C* to try to reverse the above inequalities in an attempt to induce *V* to prefer *C* to *I*. The threat of being replaced by *C* constrains *I* not to wander too far from X_V^*, while *I*'s own policy concerns constrain the incumbent not to drift too far from its own ideal point. Leaders who want to retain power can rarely afford to hold an uncompromising commitment to the pursuit of the policies represented by their ideal points. Such "true believers" are unlikely to survive politically unless they happen to have the good fortune that their ideal point is the same as X_V^*.

In the scheme we have proposed, *I* can have a distinct advantage over *C* and can also suffer a distinct disadvantage from its actions. The advantage stems from its reputation for reliability if that is positive. In expression 2, the authoritarian incumbent's past record of performance decreases the size of the right-hand side of the inequality, making it easier to stay in power even if the war is lost. The opposite is true for democratic leaders for whom $R < 0$. And the bigger the prospective stakes in the war (R_0) for *I*, the more likely it is that the incumbent will fight even with a small chance of success. These implications of our simple model give us the following initial hypotheses:

Hypothesis 1: The odds in favor of political survival increase as a function of the logarithm of the time the leader has already been in office for authoritarian leaders, while the odds of survival increase less—or even decrease—for democratic leaders.

Hypothesis 2: The greater the prospective benefits of the war (PR_0), the more likely it is that the incumbent will wage the war rather than resolve its differences through other means. Conversely, the smaller those prospective benefits, the less likely it is that the retention threshold will be passed and therefore the less likely that the incumbent will risk its position by fighting and the more likely that the incumbent will be deposed if it does take the risk of fighting.

Both of these hypotheses are testable. However, only the first one is central to the concerns addressed here. Consequently, we test hypothesis 1 and defer a test of hypothesis 2 to a future study focused on war behavior rather than leadership retention.

The incumbent must bear the burden for the failure of diplomacy and for the lost lives and property that are bound to result from war (L). This term, of course, makes it harder to keep power. The gains of reputation, if any, may be offset by the expected losses in the war. This suggests that the selection of wars to fight is itself endogenous. We have already seen that PR_0 influences the likelihood that a leader will be retained in office. The size of this term is within the control of political leaders to the extent that leaders can choose to resolve disputes short of war if the value of PR_0 is expected to be too small to lead to retention. Thus, we have already seen one way in which war selection is endogenous to domestic political circumstances. Now we see that the endogeneity also extends to the impact that war costs are expected to have on domestic politics.

A leader can reduce the size of L by offering concessions to a foreign adversary in the hope of precluding a war so costly that it threatens to drive one from power. Likewise, one can eschew initiating a war expected to culminate in such high costs. Consequently, the wars we observe in nature are presumably a biased sample of the prospective wars that were considered and rejected. It follows then that the observed wars are those expected to have low enough costs that they would not jeopardize the leader's retention of power. This suggests two additional hypotheses:

Hypothesis 3: All else being equal, the greater the expected costs in war (L), the more likely it is that the incumbent will be replaced through the domestic political process.

Hypothesis 4: All else being equal, the greater the expected costs from a prospective war, the higher the probability is that the leader will not engage in war but will resolve international differences through other means such as negotiation.

Hypotheses 3 and 4, like 1 and 2, are testable. Hypothesis 3, like hypothesis 1, is focused on our central concern with the accountability of political leaders. Consequently, it will be tested here. Hypothesis 4, like hypothesis 2, is more oriented toward an investigation of dispute escalation than it is to an evaluation of the survival of political leaders. We defer to a later study any tests of hypothesis 4.

The reliability variable in our model reveals several important features of incumbency. The longer a leader has been in power prior to the onset of a war, the greater the opportunity the leader has had to amass credit for reliability or to lose supporters as part of the coalition of minorities effect. The latter effect is more likely to arise the more dependent the leader is on multiple constituencies, while the former effect is more likely to be realized by authoritarian leaders who must satisfy more limited constituencies. Thus, all else being equal, the longer an authoritarian incumbent has been in power, the more likely it should be that the incumbent will be retained in office once a war begins, even if the war is lost. The beneficial effects of a long prewar incumbency should be significantly muted (and can even be reversed) in democracies relative to authoritarian states. This can be seen more clearly from expressions 7 and 8:

$$R - L > (X_I - X_C)(X_I + X_C - 2X_V) \tag{7}$$

$$\sum_{t=n}^{1} d^t R_t - L > (X_I - X_C)(X_I + X_C - 2X_V) \tag{8}$$

Expression 7 denotes the conditions under which V prefers to retain I if I wins the war, while expression 8 denotes the conditions for retaining I when I loses the war. Of course, the left side of 7 is strictly larger than the left side of expression 8, because $R_0 > 0$ in a victorious war, so that the incumbency advantage is, not surprisingly, greater if one is victorious. This suggests a fifth hypothesis:

> Hypothesis 5: Tenure in office has a greater beneficial impact on the political survival of incumbents expected to win their wars than on incumbents expected to lose.

From expression 2, it is evident that the longer an authoritarian I (or a democratic I not suffering from the coalition of minorities effect) has been in power (and therefore the greater the accumulated reliability benefits), the smaller P can be and still satisfy the requirements for retention in office. In a comparative static sense, this means that the longer the tenure of an authoritarian leader is, the easier it is for that leader to believe that he or she can survive the political consequences of losing a war. Consequently, authoritarian "old-timers" in office can more readily afford to pursue foreign policies that represent a gamble, with a high risk of failure. Newcomers to power, conversely, cannot afford such boldness and are thus more likely to avoid high-risk gambles in foreign policy. All else being equal, then, long-surviving nondemocratic leaders should be more likely to wage losing wars (or wars in general) than are incumbents who are newer to their positions. We state this as our sixth hypothesis:

> Hypothesis 6: The longer an authoritarian leader has been in power, the higher the probability is that the leader will risk waging a war, including a war that ultimately is lost.

Hypothesis 6 suggests that long-standing authoritarian leaders engage in riskier wars not because of any inherent flaws in their characters but because of an inherent feature of the political conditions that keep them in power. Their country's political institutions facilitate their dangerous behavior. It is also evident that as the authoritarian incumbent's tenure in office grows longer I can afford to drift away from policies preferred by V because of the cushion provided by its reputation for reliability among its limited constituency. Paradoxically, those who have been reliable to their key followers in the past can afford to be less reliable to them in the future. Recall that in our model V is prepared to retain I in power even if C's policies are closer to those desired by V than are I's, provided $R > 0$. V selects its leaders in terms of an evaluation of overall welfare not just on the basis of current policy stances. This provides I with the opportunity to shift its policies closer to its own ideal point and away from V's preferences as I's reputation for reliability grows with its tenure in office. This suggests our final hypothesis:

> Hypothesis 7: The longer an authoritarian leader has been in power, the more likely he or she is to pursue personal policy preferences rather than the policies of V.

This final hypothesis, though interesting and a clear implication of our model, is, like hypotheses 2 and 4, reserved for a future study because it is not central to our concern with leadership survival.

Hypotheses 1, 3, 5, and 6 form the core of our present investigation. Each of these four hypotheses refers to a feature of leadership retention that links war behavior and regime type to domestic political considerations rather than the high politics of a realist or structuralist view of international affairs. These hypotheses represent summary statements of more detailed implications of the basic model of war choices we have delineated. Some are intuitive, but some are surprising.

In particular, we believe it is surprising that longevity in office makes leaders, particularly authoritarian leaders, more prone to wage wars, especially wars they can expect to lose. We also think it is surprising that longevity facilitates political survival for authoritarian leaders more than for democratic elites, especially in light of the proposition that it also facilitates the waging of losing wars. But even the intuitively more apparent hypotheses are important to test. We should always bear in mind that intuition can be fickle or wrong. Simply because something *seems* to make sense does not mean that it reflects how the world actually works. Also, we should feel greater confidence in counterintuitive propositions if they are part of a theoretical structure that yields many intuitively anticipated results. Finally, even when ideas seem intuitive, it is useful to pin them down within a logical structure so that we can see more clearly how they relate to other concepts and exactly how they relate to each other.

The Data

Hypotheses 1, 3, and 5 link the survival of political leaders after the onset of war to their prior tenure in office, expected costs, regime type, and the expected outcome, respectively. To test these hypotheses, we require data that permit us to relate the length of time a policymaker is able to remain in power after the onset of war, the outcome of the war, the costs of the war, the prewar tenure of the leader, the openness of the political regime, and the expectations that those around the leader had with respect to that leader's continued ability to rule. Most of the data are fairly straightforward, and some of them are widely available.

The states participating in war between 1816 and 1980 are given in the well-known collection of the Correlates of War project reported in Small and Singer's (1982) *Resort to Arms*. The data set not only reports on national involvement in all international wars between 1816 and 1980 with at least 1,000 battle-related fatalities but also identifies the states that were the eventual winners and losers. From this list we exclude several groups of states. First, we exclude states that participated in wars beginning after 1975 because of uncertainty with respect to the casualty data (the need for which we shall explain). Second, because we are interested in the domestic political aspects of war involvement, we also exclude those cases in which the relevant political leader is deposed by the direct use of force by an external party.[6] For example, the cases of the Netherlands and Belgium in 1940 are excluded from the data, as is the case of Germany in 1945. However, the case of Premier Tojo, who led Japan into war in 1941, is included in the data set since he was driven from office well before the end of the war and the U.S. occupation. Finally, although we originally intended to include cases in which the outcome was sufficiently unclear that it could be called a tie, all of these were associated with the Korean War. Rather than rest our analysis of this effect on only one war, we do not consider these cases. Our final data set consists of 191 cases of state war participation between 1823 and 1974.

Data measuring the duration in office of the political leaders who were the heads of the governments at the time the war began were derived from several sources. Our basic source of data was Spuler, Allen, and Saunder's (1977) *Leaders and Governments of the World.* These data were checked against the historical chronology given in Langer's (1972) *Encyclopedia of World History,* Bienen and van de Walle's (1991) *Of Time and Power,* and *The Cambridge Encyclopedia* (Crystal 1990, RR 42–67). Post-1965 data were also checked against *Facts on File.*

In selecting the relevant leader whose longevity in office is of interest, we identify the individual who was the *head of government* (as distinguished from the head of state, if relevant) at the time the war began. In the large majority of cases, the head of government was the individual most responsible for formulating and implementing policy regarding war decisions. In democratic countries, the identification was straightforward, with the prime minister, chancellor, or president (as appropriate) being the designated head of government. For nondemocratic governments, more judgment was required. We tried to ascertain whether there existed a cabinet or council of ministers or a comparable entity serving under the head of state or whether there existed a legislative body concurrent with the head of state. In either case, we identified the leader of this cabinet or council of ministers or the leader of the legislative body as the relevant decision maker. If such a council, cabinet, or legislative body existed concurrent with a head of state, Spuler and his colleagues identified the relevant ministers and generally provided enough information to determine which individual was the chief minister or leader and thus, by assumption, was responsible for policy. Of course, in some instances there is nothing to substitute for historical knowledge because the apparent constitutional form of the government had little to do with the actual exercise of political power. For example, we consider Stalin to have been the political leader responsible for the Soviet Union between 1928 and 1953, and Mao for China between 1949 and 1976, rather than anyone listed as being the leader of a council of ministers. Beyond this, in some instances the histories of the individual states were examined, and in a few cases these histories were particularly useful in determining who actually held political power.

From these data, the central items of information we ascertained were four: (1) the date the leader entered office, (2) the date the war began, (3) the date the leader left office, and (4) if the leader left before the end of the war, whether that exit was the result of death or a political removal.[7]

We are interested in ascertaining the effect of several variables on the survival of the political leader who takes a state into war. One of these is the outcome of the war. Here we focus our attention on wars in which there is a fairly clear winner and loser. We have taken the win/lose designations from the Correlates of War data set.

We are also concerned with the costs and benefits to a leader's political fortunes that result from longevity in office. We share with others the claim that democratic institutions impose political constraints (e.g., the coalition of minorities effect) on leaders to a greater degree than is true in authoritarian settings. Therefore, we assume that democratic leaders are constrained in their foreign policy choices by the acquisition either of reliability costs or smaller reliability benefits than is true for authoritarians over time, while authoritarian leaders are liberated in their actions by reliability credits that redound to them from the actions they take to satisfy their much more limited constituencies (Bueno de Mesquita and Lalman 1992; Maoz and Russett 1993; Morgan and Campbell 1991). Consequently, we are interested in the interactive effect of regime type with tenure in office as factors influencing political survival. The interaction of regime type and tenure is taken as our general indicator of R, the reliability cost or benefit in our model.

To calculate the impact of R from our model, we must specify whether each leader operated in a democratic or authoritarian setting. Gurr (1990) has undertaken an extensive survey of political systems in the nineteenth and twentieth centuries, reporting, among other things, a relatively rigorous measure of the extent to which various states were democratic. The scale runs from 0 (no democracy) to 10 (high democracy). All the states we cover are surveyed at the time of interest, so we have an estimate of the extent to which any state is democratic at, as nearly as possible, the time of the war onset. We measure the democraticness or authoritarianism of the institutions in each state by treating all cases that Gurr coded as 6 or above as democratic and those below 6 as authoritarian, coded as 1 and 0, respectively.[8] With this dummy variable, Demo, in place, we create TenureL*Demo. TenureL is the logarithm of a leader's total time in office prior to the war (plus 1), while TenureL*Demo is simply the product of Demo and TenureL.

In accordance with our hypotheses, we anticipate that TenureL*Demo increases the hazard of being removed from office relative to that experienced by authoritarian leaders while TenureL alone decreases the risk of removal. In other words, democratic leaders of states at war are expected to survive for a shorter time than their nondemocratic counterparts.

The transaction costs of war include losses in life and property and the attendant foregone opportunities that the destruction of lives and property entails. Although Organski and Kugler (1980) have been able to estimate some important dimensions of war cost for a few nations, we know of no data set that provides a usable measure of these costs for the number of nations with which we will deal. However, one reasonable alternative measure is available in the war lethality data contained in the Small and Singer data (1982, table 4.2). Small and Singer list for each nation's war participation the number of battle deaths per 10,000 population. This measure is particularly attractive because it is consistent across time and controls for population size. We expect this transaction cost measure to decrease the likelihood that a political leader will be retained in office.

At this point, it may be useful to lay out briefly the relationship between the hypotheses and the data. Hypothesis 1 indicates that the odds of political survival increase as a function of the logarithm of the time the leader has already been in office for authoritarian leaders (TenureL), while the odds of survival increase less or even decrease for democratic leaders TenureL*Demo. The sources used to provide estimates of the post-onset survival of leaders also provide the necessary data on the prewar tenure in office of each leader. Hypothesis 3 is testable against the reported battle deaths per 10,000 population, the form of which used here is the log because (1) the data are highly skewed and (2) increasing battle deaths probably have a decreasing marginal impact that would otherwise be exaggerated (Jackman 1993). In accordance with hypothesis 5, we expect that winning the war increases survival rates. The measure of war outcome is, of course, post hoc for leaders removed from office before the end of the war. It contains information that might not have been known to V at the time that the relevant constituents had to decide whether to retain or remove I. Here we treat the actual outcome as a post hoc indicator of probable expectations while the war was going on in those cases in which the leader was not retained to the end of the conflict.

Hypothesis 6 addresses expected changes in the conditions under which a leader would choose to wage a war. In particular, it indicates that the longer an authoritarian leader has been in power, the more likely it is that the leader will choose to wage war, including high-risk wars that are lost. The likelihood of choosing high-risk wars (i.e., wars lost more often on average) is expected to be negatively associated with tenure in office for democratic leaders. To test this proposition, we examine the relationship between the logarithm of tenure in office (as suggested by the time discounting of past performance) and the outcome of the wars fought, taking into account whether the leader headed a democratic or authoritarian regime. If the hypothesis is correct, then the logarithm of tenure in office will be negatively associated with the likelihood of winning the war for authoritarian leaders and will be positive for democratic leaders. A second test examines the prewar tenure of authoritarian leaders whose nations engaged in war, comparing that tenure with the average total seniority of leaders in states that did not engage in warfare. If our hypothesis is correct, leaders of warring states should, on average, have already been in office before the war started for a longer time than is true for the total tenure in office of their counterparts in states that did not wage war. Authoritarian old-timers, it should be recalled, are hypothesized to pursue riskier foreign policies than are their less senior counterparts.

To summarize, from hypotheses 1, 3, and 5 we have the following empirical expectations:

Leader's post-onset political survival $= a + b_1$ TenureL $- b_2$

TenureL*Demo $- b_3$ (battle deaths/10K)$L + b_4$ Win $+ \varepsilon$;

and from hypothesis 6 we expect

Win $= c - b_5$ TenureL $+ b_6$ TenureL*Demo $+ \varepsilon$;

and average prewar tenure in warring states $>$ average total tenure for authoritarian leaders of nonwarrring states.[9]

We add one additional test in which we control for nonconstitutional changes in the regime. In an earlier study (Bueno de Mesquita, Siverson, and Woller 1992), we reported a strong association between war performance and the survival of political regimes. Naturally, if a regime falls to domestic opposition, this may increase the likelihood that the individual key leader also falls from power. We are interested, therefore, in ascertaining the impact of our hypotheses on the survivability of leaders when we control for the effects of a nonconstitutional turnover in regime. The test adds the variable Noncon as follows:

Leader's postwar-onset political survival $= a + b_1$ TenureL $- b_2$

Tenure*Demo $- b_3$ (battle deaths/10K)$L + b_4$ Win $- b_5$ Noncon $+ \varepsilon$.

Event History and Survival Analysis

Our approach to testing the specification of the model involves the application of survival analysis, often referred to as event history (by sociologists) or duration analysis (by economists). The dependent variable in the present case, the length of time a leader remains in power after the onset of the war, is exactly the kind of problem for which survival analysis was designed. The fundamental element of survival analysis is the estimation of the hazard rate, which may be thought of as the natural rate for the ending of some event or process. Here we are interested in the hazard rate faced by political leaders from the time their states enter into wars.

The hazard rate has two elements. The first is the underlying baseline rate of termination, as if the event whose duration we are measuring is unaffected by anything. The second is the effect of the various covariates—specified as independent variables—that are seen as affecting the survival, in log-linear form, of the units of interest. In this case, those units are the leaders.

There are two key advantages to event history methods over others. The first of these is that they allow us to include within the analysis cases that otherwise would be excluded or treated improperly. In the present instance, some of the leaders in our data set died in office of natural causes. The use of regression methods makes these cases problematic because their inclusion would inappropriately treat them as the political "deaths" that are of interest, while their exclusion removes from the estimate the information that they survived in office at least until their deaths. Event history analysis, however, allows us to include such information because these cases are treated as "censored"—that is, they are identified as lasting at least as long as the time until biological death. The contribution of such censored cases to the likelihood is then produced through the survivor function rather than the density function that is used on the noncensored cases.[10]

Second, it permits the hazard rate to change with the passage of time. The exact nature of this variation is, in fact, a critical element in distinguishing among survival models. While there are several such models, a graph of the hazard for our data shows it to be monotonically decreasing. Many survival models do not apply to a monotonically increasing or decreasing hazard, but the Weibull model accommodates such a pattern (P. Allison 1984). A plausible alternative to the Weibull is the exponential model in which the hazard is constant. A graphic method of distinguishing between the appropriateness of these models is to plot $\log[-\log(S(t)]$ against $\log(t)$, where $S(t)$ is the survivor function defined by the Kaplan-Meier product limit estimate and (t) is survival time (Kalbflisch and Prentice 1980, 24). If the result is a straight line, the data may be judged to come from a Weibull distribution, but if the line has a slope of 1 the distribution is exponential. In the present case, the scatter is on a straight line, but with a slope of less than 1, supporting the judgment of a Weibull with a decreasing hazard.[11]

Data Analysis

We turn now to an examination of the effects of the variables that compose our model.[12] The main question is whether prior tenure in office (in combination with the authoritarianism or democraticness of the political system), battle deaths per 10,000 population, and war outcome have the anticipated effect on the length of time that a political leader survives in office after the onset of the war. Table 2 reports the results of the maximum likelihood estimates based on censored Weibull regression for both the initial model and the one incorporating nonconstitutional overthrow of the regime. The coefficients are the estimated effect of the variable on the *hazard* rate of leaders; thus, negative values indicate a decreased hazard, or longer survival. The results reported in table 2, column 1, reveal that all of the variables in the model have the predicted effect on political survival. Longer prewar tenure for authoritarian leaders and victory for all leaders extend time in office, while high overall battle deaths reduce subsequent time in office.[13] Our theory predicts that prewar tenure in office will be less advantageous to democratic leaders relative to their nondemocratic counterparts. Since the coefficient for the effect of the length of prewar tenure for democratic leaders is estimated through the interaction TenureL*Demo, we obtain the estimate of the coefficient for just the democratic leaders by summing the coefficients for the interaction and the prewar tenure of all leaders (i.e., .33 − .48 = .15). The coefficient of −.15 is greater than −.48, demonstrating that prewar tenure contributes less to the survival of the democratic leaders than of the authoritarian leaders, but is it, as we predict in the model, a significantly different effect? This can be shown by means of two *F*-tests. First, a test of the difference between this coefficient and the Tenure coefficient (−.48) yields an *F*

TABLE 2.   The Effect of War on the Political Survival Time of Leaders: Censored Weibull Regression Test of Hypotheses 1, 3, and 5

Independent Variables	(1) Coefficient	(2) Hazard Rate[a]	(3) Coefficient	(4) Hazard Rate[a]
TenureL	−.48**	.62	−.47**	.62
	(.09)		(.08)	
TenureL*Democracy	.33*	1.38	.36*	1.44
	(.16)		(.16)	
Log (battle-deaths/10K)	.08*	1.08	.07*	1.07
	(.04)		(.04)	
Win	−.28*	.75	−.26*	.77
	(.16)		(.15)	
Nonconstitutional overthrow			.51*	1.67
			(.19)	
Constant	−.53**		−.62**	
	(.19)		(.20)	
Sigma[b]	1.44		1.43	
	(.08)		(.08)	
χ^2	34.2		39.8	
Probability	<.01		<.01	

Note: Entries in columns 1 and 3 are unstandardized regression coefficients with standard errors in parentheses. $N = 191$.

[a]On the hazard rate, see note 15.

[b]On sigma, see note 16.

p < .05, one-tailed   **p* < .01, one-tailed

of 13.17 ($p < .001$). Second, we test the difference between $-.15$ and 0 and obtain an F of .76 ($p = .38$). As our model predicts, the leaders of democratic states derive less advantage from prewar officeholding than the authoritarians do; in fact, it is indistinguishable from no advantage whatsoever.[14]

The results are perhaps best understood as relative risks (or risk ratios), which are shown in Table 2, column 2.[15] In these expressions, values above 1.00 (the baseline) indicate an increased risk that the leader would not survive in office, while hazards below 1.00 indicate that the survival rate has risen as the hazard has fallen. More precisely, the hazard's deviation from 1.00 is interpreted as the percentage increase or decrease in the likelihood of political survival resulting from the marginal impact of the independent variable, so that the relative effects of the variables can be discerned by the magnitudes of the hazards.[16]

Exponentiating the coefficient given for authoritarian leaders ($-.48$) produces a hazard of .62, which means that a one-unit increase in the length of their prewar tenure (an order of magnitude, since we are using the log of tenure) reduces the postwar risk of removal by 38 percent. In contrast, similar tenure for democratic leaders produces no significant benefit in survival (exp. [$-.48 + .33$] = .86, which, as we have seen, is statistically indistinguishable from zero). Thus, regime type evidently makes an appreciable difference in the prospects of surviving a war politically, with democratic leaders placed at considerably higher risk than their authoritarian counterparts. Even victory does not enhance survivability as much as prewar tenure for authoritarians; nor does victory fully offset the increased hazard for democratic leaders. Victory reduces the overall risk of removal by 25 percent. Finally, all else being equal, it is easier for political leaders to survive low-cost wars than higher cost ones. The risk of being turned out of office increases by 8 percent with each order of magnitude increase in the log of battle deaths per 10,000 population.[17]

Hypotheses 1, 3, and 5 are well supported by the evidence. What about hypothesis 6, which contains one of our more surprising expectations? Recall that this hypothesis indicates that authoritarian leaders who have been around a long time are better able to engage in risky foreign policies, even gambling on wars that have a relatively high probability of ending in defeat. Newer leaders and democratic leaders, by contrast, are not expected to take such large risks and so pick and choose their fights more carefully, engaging in wars with a higher probability of victory. The results of the logit analysis bear out the hypothesis. The actual result is

Win = .49 − .35 TenureL + .77 TenureL*Demo,

with $N = 191$ and one-tailed probability = .002. The individual variables are also highly significant. The probability that the effect of TenureL arose by chance is only .017. For TenureL*Demo, the probability that its effect is due to chance is only .007.

Hypothesis 6 implies a second, equally surprising result. Relatively short-term authoritarian leaders have not had the opportunity to build up the reservoir of goodwill (R) among their few essential constituents that facilitates taking the risks of war. Democratic leaders are less likely than authoritarian leaders to have built up such a reservoir of goodwill after they have been in power for a long time. If democratic leaders are going to wage war, they are better off doing it early, before they have lost support as a result of the cumulative impact of the coalition of minorities effect. Consequently, on average we expect authoritarian leaders who engaged in war to have a longer prewar period in office than (1) the total tenure of all leaders who do not wage war and (2) democratic leaders who do wage war.

By moving slightly outside our data set, we can test these two expectations. Of our 191 cases, 106 are also to be found in the Bienen and van de Walle data set describing the political survival of 2,258 leaders around the world in the period since 1820. In this data set, the average total tenure of the nonwarring leaders is 3.32 years ($N = 2,152$), while the average total tenure of those leaders who ultimately engaged in war is 8.52 years ($N = 106$). The difference is highly significant, with $t = 6.9$. The average prewar tenure of all the authoritarian leaders in our data set is 5.66 years, which is significantly longer than the total tenure of all the nonwarring leaders in the Bienen and van de Walle data set. The average prewar tenure of democratic leaders is only 2.57 years, which is significantly shorter than the prewar longevity or leadership experience of authoritarian leaders. The result is surprising but consistent with our expectations. Long-serving authoritarian leaders are more likely to wage war than are relative newcomer democratic leaders. Democratic leaders are more likely to wage war early in their years in office, while their support is still high (Gaubatz 1991).

Hypothesis 6—like hypotheses 1, 3, and 5—seems to run directly counter to neorealist expectations and also to our general intuition. As such, it provides an additional basis from which to question the fundamental basis of neorealism and to suggest that greater attention be paid to the interplay between domestic politics and international affairs.

Before concluding, we examine the robustness of our results regarding hypotheses 1, 3 and 5 by controlling for the impact of nonconstitutional regime change produced by internal opposition. This test will help clarify the extent to which our model accounts for variations in leadership survival after controlling for regime change, a factor for which we have previously suggested an explanation (Bueno de Mesquita, Siverson, and Woller 1992). Table 2, column 3, contains the results of adding to our original model a dummy variable coded 1 for all the regimes that were overthrown by internal opposition either during the war or within three years of the war's end. As can be seen, even after controlling for nonconstitutional regime changes, the evidence in support of our hypotheses is quite robust. Nonconstitutional regime changes increase the risk of political removal by 67 percent, a very hefty effect. Still, the effects shown in the original model continue to obtain. The hazards, reported in column 4, show that authoritarian leaders continue to derive the same political benefits from their apparent ability to avoid problems such as the coalition of minorities. Similarly, winning- and battle-related costs both continue to have significant effects of about the same magnitude as those reported in the test that did not control for nonconstitutional regime change. In sum, our model's predicted effects are independent of our own earlier reported results for nonconstitutional regime change.

Conclusion

Our investigation has found that those leaders who engage their nations in war subject themselves to a domestic political hazard that threatens the very essence of the officeholding *homo politicus*—the retention of political power. The hazard is mitigated by long-standing experience for authoritarian elites, an effect that is muted for democratic leaders, while the hazard is militated by defeat and the high costs of war for all types of leaders. Additionally, we find that authoritarian leaders are inclined to fight wars longer after they come to power than democratic leaders are. Further, democratic leaders select wars that have a lower risk of defeat than is true for their authoritarian counterparts. These results, which are implied directly by the specification of our model, obtain across a time span of over 150 years and encompass a broad spectrum of political systems and types of leadership removal. The evidence is consistent with the claim that decisions to go to war are endogenous to the domestic political setting of the leaders.

Such a result runs counter to expectations derived from neorealist theory. In that theory, war policies are endogenous to the international system and not to the domestic political situation. This is seen most clearly in Waltz's proposition that

> the elements of *Realpolitik,* exhaustively listed, are these: the ruler's, and later the state's, interest provides the spring of action; *the necessities of policy arise from the unregulated competition of states; calculation based on these necessities can discover the policies that will best serve a state's interests;* success is the ultimate test of policy, and success is defined as preserving and strengthening the state. (1979, 117; emphasis added)

We agree that policymakers care about the security of their state (though perhaps this is not their paramount concern), and it is almost impossible to believe that the problem of maintaining or enhancing security does not enter into the calculations they make with respect to the policies that should be pursued. How does one square those facts with our assertion that internal political considerations are fundamental to external policy selection? The answer to this question depends upon what one takes to be the central assumption of neorealist theory.

If one proceeds from the basic neorealist assumption that *states* maximize their power to maximize their security and does not go further, then the theory is almost certainly false. However, if one extends the theory (in a way not previously done) by (1) assuming that *policymakers* want to stay in power both for the rents and the policy opportunities thus afforded (Lake 1992) and (2) observing that declining security (as indicated here by war loss and costs) shortens time in power, then the linkage between internal politics and external policies is established. Thus, the leader—whether president, prime minister, or president for life—who adopts policies that reduce the security of the state does so at the risk of affording his or her political opponents the opportunity to weaken the leader's grasp on power. Put differently, a leader's search for the security of the state intertwines with the search for policies that will maintain the leader in power against domestic opposition. The desire to remain in power thus provides the linchpin between the threats and uncertainties of the international system and the inevitable imperatives of fending off the domestic opposition.

Writing almost 25 years ago, James Rosenau lamented the fact that students of international relations did not have a well-developed framework—much less a well-developed theory—for linking political processes internal to the state with those that were external. In particular, he called attention to the absence of any theory that could account for the effect of foreign policy events on the tenure of political leaders:

> Consider the processes whereby the top political leadership of a society acquires the maintains its position of authority. To what extent are these processes dependent on events that unfold abroad? Under what conditions will the stability of cabinets and the tenure of presidents be reduced or otherwise affected by trends in the external environment? Are certain leadership structures more vulnerable to developments in the international system than others? Political theory presently offers no guidance as to how questions such as these might be researched and answered. (1969, 5)

More recently, Putnam (1988) called attention to the linkages between international and domestic politics. Putnam's conceptualization of the logic of two-level games is certainly an advance over much of the past work on linkage politics, but, although its concluding sentence is an admonition for empirical research, it fails to specify a model. The present research both specifies a model and offers data that are highly consistent with that model. With this knowledge in hand, we can no longer afford to treat domestic politics as ending at the water's edge, as neorealism is inclined to do. Foreign policy, instead, is better seen as intimately connected with the desire of leaders to maintain themselves in power.

NOTES

The authors acknowledge with gratitude the helpful advice of Timothy Amato, Colin Cameron, Kurt Taylor Gaubatz, Robert Hanneman, Dale Heien, Robert W. Jackman, David Rocke, Alastair Smith, Richard Tucker, Paul Warwick, and the anonymous referees. We also benefited from the able research assistance of Monica Barczak, Letitia Lawson, Ross Miller, Stephen P. Nicholson, and Eric Siegal. We thank the Berkeley YWCA and Raymond Wolfinger, both of whose assistance facilitated the completion of this work. Siverson's work was supported by the University of California's Institute on Global Conflict and Cooperation; additional support was received from the National Science Foundation under grant SBR–9409225. An earlier version of this essay was presented at the annual meeting of the American Political Science Association, Washington, DC, September 1–4, 1993.

1. We are indebted to Gary Woller for calling this particular example to our attention.

2. There is a different way of putting this: all the political leaders used in this study left office, but only 36 of the regimes were overthrown by nonconstitutional means, and in 20 of these the responsible leader at the time of the entry into war had been removed from office *before* the overthrow of the regime.

3. The literature on the effects of economic performance on regimes and political leaders is quite large. Good summaries of the research are to be found in Lewis-Beck and Eulau 1985 and Norpoth, Lewis-Beck, and Lafay 1991. Although almost all of this work is within the domain of democratic political systems, research by Londregan and Poole (1990) demonstrates that military coups are more likely when economic performance has been poor.

4. However, Sanders, Ward, and Marsh (1991) argue that the Falklands effect is exaggerated and Thatcher's rise in the polls can be traced more clearly to economic policies and conditions.

5. It should be noted that we assume a game of complete and perfect information here. In later investigations, we intend to examine the implications of uncertainty on the general effects suggested here.

6. To be sure, from a risk assessment point of view, policymakers cannot be indifferent to the possibility that a failed conflict policy may result in their removal by a foreign power. Indeed, it happens. In the present instance, however, we note that in the cases that would otherwise constitute our data base, removal by a foreign power took place only 19 times. However, our data probably understate the extent to which removal by this means occurs because in many such cases the initiator is so "successful" that the casualties are not sufficiently numerous to qualify the event for inclusion in the war data set (e.g., the U.S. intervention in Grenada).

7. Not all deaths are neatly managed because some are not natural. While Franklin Roosevelt died a nonpolitical death, Anwar Sadat did not. However, Sadat's assassins did not succeed in capturing power and replacing him with someone who would bring Egypt's policies closer to their own. All political leaders are potentially subject to assassination, but the success of such attempts in the absence of a group able to seize power may be random. Consequently, in cases in which assassins were not able to seize the state, we coded their departure as a "natural death." However, if a leader died as the direct result of a successful coup or revolution, the death was treated as a political removal.

8. One potential difficulty with this is that warfare sometimes changes governments. Few of such changes, however, are large enough to alter the state's score on the democracy index. For example, while the United Kingdom suspended elections during most of World War II, the democracy score remained unchanged at 10.

9. The two equations specified here are not intended to suggest a system of simultaneous equations but, rather, tests of hypotheses that follow directly from our model. Still, the dependent variable of one is an independent variable in the other, so it might be possible to conceptualize the argument as implying simultaneity. However, it should be noted that the factors hypothesized to explain the variable Win are also independent variables in the first equation and so cannot be used as instruments for Win. Having said that, we did test the argument as if there were a set of simultaneous equations. To do so, we calculated the predicted values of Win from a logit analysis and substituted those predicted values into the first equation. Not surprisingly, the predicted values of Win did not have a significant effect on the dependent variable, given that the predicted values were necessarily collinear with the effects of the remaining independent variables in the first equation. This had to be so since the remaining variables were exactly the same as the ones used to generate predicted values of Win. As our results show, however, Win itself is significantly related to the survival of political leaders even when the other independent variables are taken into account. This is the expectation derived from our model, and it suggests that additional factors explain war outcomes beyond those hypothesized here.

10. For a general introduction to survival methods, see P. Allison 1984. Applications in political analysis are growing. Some noteworthy examples of its use are to be found in the various papers of Warwick (1992a, 1992b, 1993). Also see King et al. 1990 and Hanneman and Steinback 1990.

11. Copies of the graph of the hazard and the plot of the integrated hazard against the log of survival time are available from Siverson.

12. The means, standard deviations, and ranges on the four main independent variables are

Variable	Mean	Standard Deviation	Min.	Max.
TenureL	1.34	.91	0[a]	3.45
Log (battle deaths/10K)	1.93	1.65	0[a]	6.32
Democracy	.24	.43	0	1
Win	.54	.49	0	1

[a]These values simply report numbers too small to register. For example, in the 1956 Suez War, the United Kingdom suffered 40 battle deaths, which, as a proportion of that state's population, is recorded in the data set at the value given above, zero.

13. In keeping with the fact that our model leads to expectations about the direction of each relationship, one-tailed tests of significance are reported in the table.

14. The model we have tested does not include the main effect of democracy even though the interaction of democracy and tenure is present. We do this because we have no theoretical reason for including democracy. Nonetheless, we now report the same model including democracy as a main effect, and from the very small changes in the co-efficients that attend this and the absence of a fit for democracy itself we conclude that there is no empirical reason for including it either.

Variable	Coefficient (standard error)
TenureL	−.51
	(.10)
TenureL*Democracy	.44
	(.25)
(Battle deaths/10K)L	.08
	(.04)
Win	−.26
	(.15)
Democracy	−.17
	(.31)
Constant	−.48
	(.21)
Sigma	1.44
	(.08)

15. Hazards are found by exponentiating the coefficients from the regression (P. Allison 1984, 28).

16. In Weibull regression, a shape parameter, sigma, describes whether the hazard is increasing or decreasing with time. When the hazard is decreasing, sigma has a value greater than 1.00. The value of sigma for our model is 1.44 (with a standard error of .08), so the hazard is decreasing, a result that is similar in character to that reported by Bienen and van de Walle (1991). In some statistics programs and in Greene 1993, the shape parameter is 1/sigma, in which case the effect of the shape parameter as increasing or decreasing the hazard relative to the baseline of 1.00 is the opposite of that given here.

17. Selecting the appropriate model for the overall hazard (in this case the Weibull) does not mean that other problems of misspecification are avoided. In ordinary least squares, diagnostics would be approached with the analysis of residuals. However, as Greene explains: "There is no direct counterpart to the set of regression residuals with which to assess the validity of the specification of the duration [i.e., survival] model" (1993, 722). Greene, nonetheless, does offer a test for specification, based on the use of "generalized residuals" (ε^2), to test the second moment restriction that $E(\varepsilon^2) = 2$ (1993, 722–23; Lancaster and Chesher 1985b, 37). Since some of our observations are censored, the residuals are appropriately adjusted as:

$$\hat{e}(t) = \begin{cases} \epsilon(t) \text{ if uncensored.} \\ \epsilon(t) + 1 \text{ if censored.} \end{cases}$$

With the adjusted residuals, the second-moment restriction is $s_e^2 = \Sigma(C_i/N)$, where s_e^2 is the sample variance of $\hat{e}(t)$ and $\Sigma(C_i/N)$ is the proportion of censored cases in the sample. The test statistic for the second-moment restriction is implemented by running an ordinary least squares in which unity is regressed on $(\hat{e}_i - 1)^2 - C_i$ and all $\partial\mathcal{L}_i/\partial\theta_j$ where θ_j ($j = 1, \ldots, k$) represent parameters of the model. The test statistic is computed as N, the sample size, multiplied by the uncentered R^2, and under the null hypothesis it has an asymptotic $\chi^2(1)$ distribution (Lancaster and Chesher 1985b). In the present instance, the value of the test statistic is .974, which is well below the 3.84 level necessary to reject the hypothesis at the 5 percent level. Additionally, we plotted the integrated hazard against the generalized residuals, the result of which was a 45-degree line characteristic of the Weibull (Lancaster and Chesher 1985a).

REFERENCES

Allison, Graham. 1971. *The Essence of Decision: Explaining the Cuban Missile Crisis.* Boston: Little, Brown.

Allison, Paul. 1984. *Event History Analysis: Regression for Longitudinal Event Data.* Quantitative Applications in the Social Sciences, no. 07-046. Beverly Hills, CA: Sage.

Bienen, Henry, and Nicholas van de Walle. 1991. *Of Time and Power.* Stanford: Stanford University Press.

Black, Duncan. 1958. *The Theory of Committees and Elections.* Cambridge: Cambridge University Press.

Brody, Richard A. 1992. *Assessing the President: The Media, Elite Opinion, and Public Support.* Stanford: Stanford University Press.

Brody, Richard A., and Benjamin Page. 1975. The Impact of Events on Presidential Popularity. In *Perspectives on the Presidency,* edited by Aaron Wildavsky. Boston: Little, Brown.

Bueno de Mesquita, Bruce. 1981. *The War Trap.* New Haven: Yale University Press.

Bueno de Mesquita, Bruce, and David Lalman. 1992. *War and Reason.* New Haven: Yale University Press.

Bueno de Mesquita, Bruce, David Newman, and Alvin Rabushka. 1985. *Forecasting Political Events.* New Haven: Yale University Press.

Bueno de Mesquita, Bruce, and A. F. K. Organski. Forthcoming. *Principles of International Politics.*

Bueno de Mesquita, Bruce, Randolph M. Siverson, and Gary Woller. 1992. War and the Fate of Regimes: A Comparative Analysis. *American Political Science Review* 86:638–46.

Bueno de Mesquita, Bruce, and Frans Stokman. 1994. *European Community Decision Making.* New Haven: Yale University Press.

Crystal, David. 1990. *The Cambridge Encyclopedia.* Cambridge: Cambridge University Press.

Downs, Anthony. 1957. *An Economic Theory of Democracy.* New York: Harper and Row.

Eulau, Heinz, and Michael Lewis-Beck. 1985. *Economic Conditions and Electoral Outcomes: The United States and Western Europe.* New York: Agathon.

Fearon, James D. 1994. Domestic Political Audiences and the Escalation of International Disputes. *American Political Science Review* 88:577–92.

Fiorina, Morris. 1981. *Retrospective Voting in American National Elections.* New Haven: Yale University Press.

Greene, William H. 1993. *Econometric Analysis.* 2d ed. New York: Macmillan.

Gurr, Ted Robert. 1990. Polity II: Political Structures and Regime Change, 1800–1986. Interuniversity Consortium for Political and Social Research, University of Michigan.

Hanneman, Robert A., and Robin L. Steinback. 1990. Military Involvement and Political Instability: An Event History Analysis, 1940–1980. *Journal of Military and Political Sociology* 18:1–23.

Jackman, Robert W. 1993. *Power without Force.* Ann Arbor: University of Michigan Press.

Kalbfleisch, John D., and Ross Prentice. 1980. *The Statistical Analysis of Failure Time Data.* New York: Wiley.

Kernell, S. H. 1978. Explaining Presidential Popularity. *American Political Science Review* 72:506–22.

King, Gary, James Alt, Nancy Burns, and Michael Laver. 1990. A Unified Model of Cabinet Dissolution in Parliamentary Democracies. *American Journal of Political Science* 34:846–71.

Lake, David A. 1992. Powerful Pacifists: Democratic States and War. *American Political Science Review* 86:24–37.

Lancaster, Tony, and Andrew Chesher. 1985a. Residual Analysis for Censored Duration Data. *Economics Letters* 18:35–38.

Lancaster, Tony, and Andrew Chesher. 1985b. Residuals, Tests, and Plots with a Job Matching Illustration. *Annales de L'Insee* 59–60:47–70.

Langer, William L. 1952. *Encyclopedia of World History.* Boston: Houghton Mifflin.

Lewis-Beck, Michael, and Heinz Eulau. 1985. Economic Conditions and Electoral Outcomes in Trans-National Perspective. In *Economic Conditions and Electoral Outcomes: The United States and Western Europe,* edited by Heinz Eulau and Michael Lewis-Beck. New York: Agathon.

Londregan, John B., and Keith Poole. 1990. Poverty, the Coup Trap, and the Seizure of Executive Power. *World Politics* 27:151–83.

Maoz, Zeev, and Bruce Russett. 1993. Normative and Structural Causes of Democratic Peace, 1946–1986. *American Political Science Review* 87:624–38.

Morgan, T. Clifton, and Kenneth Bickers. 1992. Domestic Discontent and the External Use of Force. *Journal of Conflict Resolution* 36:25–52.

Morgan, T. Clifton, and Sally Howard Campbell. 1991. Domestic Structure, Decisional Constraints, and War. *Journal of Conflict Resolution* 35:187–211.

Morrow, James D. 1987. On the Theoretical Basis of Risk Attitudes. *International Studies Quarterly* 31:423–38.

Mueller, John. 1973. *War, Presidents, and Public Opinion.* New York: Wiley.

Norpoth, Helmut. 1987. Guns and Butter and Governmental Popularity in Britain. *American Political Science Review* 81:949–59.

Norpoth, Helmut, Michael Lewis-Beck, and Jean-Dominique Lafay. 1991. *Economics and Politics: The Calculus of Support.* Ann Arbor: University of Michigan Press.

Organski, A. F. K., and Jacek Kugler. 1980. *The War Ledger.* Chicago: University of Chicago Press.

Powell, G. Bingham, and Guy D. Whitten. 1993. A Cross-National Analysis of Economic Voting: Taking Account of the Political Context. *American Journal of Political Science* 37:391–414.

Putnam, Robert. 1988. Diplomacy and Domestic Politics: The Logic of Two-level Games. *International Organization* 42:427–60.

Richards, Diana, T. Clifton Morgan, Rick K. Wilson, Valerie Schwebach, and Garry D. Young. 1993. Good Times, Bad Times, and the Diversionary Use of Force. *Journal of Conflict Resolution* 37:504–35.

Rose, Richard, and T. T. Mackie. 1983. Incumbency in Government: Asset or Liability? In *Western European Party Systems,* edited by Hans Daalder and Peter Mair. Beverly Hills, CA: Sage.

Rosenau, James N., ed. 1969. *Linkage Politics.* New York: Free Press.

Sanders, David, Hugh Ward, and David Marsh. 1991. Macroeconomics, the Falklands War, and the Popularity of the Thatcher Government: A Contrary View. In *Economics and Politics: The Calculus of Support,* edited by Helmut Norpoth, Michael Lewis-Beck, and Jean-Dominique Lafay. Ann Arbor: University of Michigan Press.

Small, Melvin, and J. David Singer. 1982. *Resort to Arms.* Beverly Hills, CA: Sage.

Spuler, Bertold, C. G. Allen, and Neil Saunders. 1977. *Rulers and Governments of the World.* Vol. 3. London: Bowker.

Tsebelis, George. 1990. *Nested Games.* Berkeley: University of California Press.

Waltz, Kenneth. 1979. *Theory of International Politics.* Reading, MA: Addison-Wesley.

Warwick, Paul. 1992a. Ideological Diversity and Government Survival in Western European Parliamentary Democracies. *Comparative Political Studies* 25:332–61.

Warwick, Paul. 1992b. Rising Hazards: An Underlying Dynamic of Parliamentary Government. *American Journal of Political Science* 36:857–76.

Warwick, Paul. 1993. Economic Trends and Government Survival in Western European Parliamentary Democracies. *American Political Science Review* 86:875–87.

Contributors

Bruce Bueno de Mesquita is a Senior Fellow at the Hoover Institution, Stanford University. He is the author of *The War Trap* and coauthor of *War and Reason.* He has also written books on the politics of India and forecasting the future of Hong Kong's political status. He is the author of numerous articles on international conflict, policy analysis, and comparative politics.

Kurt Taylor Gaubatz is Assistant Professor of Political Science at Stanford University. His papers have appeared in the *Journal of Conflict Resolution, World Politics, Journal of Democracy,* and *International Organization.* In 1996–97 he was a National Fellow at the Hoover Institution, Stanford University.

Michael J. Gilligan is Assistant Professor of Politics at New York University. He is author of *Empowering Exporters: Reciprocity, Delegation, and Collection Action in American Trade Policy.*

W. Ben Hunt is Associate Professor of Political Science and Associate Director of the John Tower Center for Political Studies at Southern Methodist University. He is the author of *Getting to War* and coauthor, with Michael Laver, of *Policy and Party Competition.*

Keisuke Iida is Assistant Professor of Politics at Princeton University. His research interests include international cooperation theory and game theory. He has recently finished a book manuscript on international monetary cooperation among the United States, Japan, and Germany.

Atsushi Ishida received his Ph.D. from the University of Chicago in 1995. He is currently Assistant Professor of International Politics at the Faculty of Law, Tokyo Metropolitan University. He was Visiting Assistant Professor of Political Science at Emory University when completing his essay for this volume.

Lisa L. Martin is Professor of Government at Harvard University. Her publications include *Coercive Cooperation: Explaining Multilateral Economic Sanctions.* Her current research projects include empirical analysis of the effects of international institutions on state behavior and a study of the role of national legislatures in international cooperation.

287

Fiona McGillivray is Assistant Professor of Political Science at Washington University. Her research interests are international trade, comparative political institutions, and political economy. In 1997–98 she was a National Fellow at the Hoover Institution, Stanford University.

T. Clifton Morgan is Professor of Political Science at Rice University. He has published *Untying the Knot of War: A Bargaining Theory of International Crises* and a number of articles in professional journals. His current research interests involve the study of economic sanctions and the development of a formal model of comparative foreign policy.

Glenn Palmer is Associate Professor of Political Science at Texas A&M University. His research has centered on collective-goods analyses of alliances, and has appeared in *International Studies Quarterly,* the *American Journal of Political Science,* and the *American Political Science Review.* His current work investigates the effect of alliance membership on foreign policy (particularly conflict) behavior.

Kenneth A. Schultz is Assistant Professor of Politics and International Affairs at Princeton University. At the time his essay in this book was written he was a Dwight D. Eisenhower/Clifford Roberts Graduate Fellow.

Randolph M. Siverson is Professor of Political Science at the University of California, Davis. He is the author (with Harvey Starr) of *The Diffusion of War.* His articles have appeared in numerous journals including the *American Political Science Review,* the *Journal of Conflict Resolution,* and the *American Journal of Political Science.*

Alastair Smith is Assistant Professor of Political Science at Washington University. He received his Ph.D. in political science from the University of Rochester in 1995. His work focuses on game theoretic models of politics, particularly with respect to international politics. In 1997–98 he was a National Fellow at the Hoover Institution, Stanford University.

Barry R. Weingast is a Senior Fellow, Hoover Institution, and the Ward C. Krebs Family Professor and Chair, Department of Political Science, Stanford University. His research focuses on the political foundation of markets, economic reform, and regulation. His papers have appeared in a number of journals, including the *Journal of Law, Economics, and Organization, World Politics, Journal of Political Economy,* and *Journal of Economic History.*

DATE DUE

GAYLORD			PRINTED IN U.S.A.